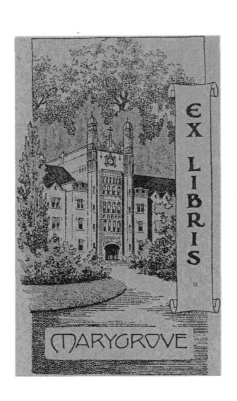

EX LIBRIS

MARYGROVE

HER MAJESTY
Elizabeth

EMPRESS ELIZABETH

HER MAJESTY
Elizabeth

*of Austria-Hungary,
the Beautiful, Tragic Empress of Europe's
Most Brilliant Court*

By

Marie Louise, Countess Larisch von
Wallersee-Wittelsbach

With Paul Maerker Branden and
Elsa Branden

DOUBLEDAY, DORAN & COMPANY, INC.
GARDEN CITY, NEW YORK
1934

Contents

CHAPTER ONE

My Royal Relatives *1*

CHAPTER TWO

An Empress in Love *36*

CHAPTER THREE

The Command to Marry *67*

CHAPTER FOUR

Strange Honeymoon *102*

CHAPTER FIVE

The Secret of an Empress *148*

CHAPTER SIX

Farewell to Love *188*

CHAPTER SEVEN

Silence Is Not Always Golden *218*

v

CONTENTS

CHAPTER EIGHT

Royalty Among the Reds   253

CHAPTER NINE

American Interlude   281

CHAPTER TEN

The Circle Closes   287

vi

Illustrations

Empress Elizabeth   *Frontispiece*

Facing Page

King Ludwig II of Bavaria and his then fiancée, Duchess Sophie of Bavaria   70

Duke Ludwig of Bavaria, father of Countess Larisch and brother of Empress Elizabeth   70

Countess Larisch at the time of her first marriage   110

Countess Larisch, as a "child bride"   110

Captain William "Bay" Middleton   118

Rudolf, at the time of his engagement   118

Empress Elizabeth in her forties   150

Count Hans (Johann Nepomuk) Wilczek   166

Countess Larisch and the young Archduchess Valerie   166

Courtsinger Otto Brucks in gala uniform   238

Countess Larisch at the time of her marriage to Otto Brucks, 1897   238

Countess Larisch and her mother, Baroness von Wallersee, 1872   238

Countess Larisch during her American years   286

Countess Larisch and her second husband, Otto Brucks   286

Introduction

My purpose in publishing these memoirs is not to reveal sensational secrets. Rather, I wish to recount faithfully the experiences of my life, tracing each and every link of that chain which irrevocably binds me to famous figures of history. Much will be comprehended now which in former years, out of consideration for the living, I felt compelled to evade or to omit.

It was the intention of *My Past*, published in 1913, to contradict false statements—over and anon repeated in the public print, either maliciously or erroneously—involving me, most unpleasantly, in the ominous Meyerling tragedy. In *My Past*, I have stated the full truth in connection with that tragedy as far as it was known to me; in the present volume, I have added details which I did not deem advisable to disclose in 1913.

In the course of years, the specters of Calumny and Scandal have stalked my path with ruthless persistence. It is a sad fact that up to this very day my name invariably is as-

sociated with the Meyerling tragedy of 1889. To become a
historical character in this manner naturally is distasteful
to me. I shall never cease to fight for my good name. It is
toward this end that I now relate the story of my life—a
life splashed with curious color and marked by great and
sudden'changes. My youth, my close association with my
imperial aunt, Empress Elizabeth, the marriage that was
forced upon me, the sorrows that visited me in later years
—all this is embodied in the present story, which I assembled
from my diaries and from documents left by my parents.
That celebrated personages, closely connected with my own
fate, should play a prominent rôle in my memoirs seems
only natural.

In my literary labors I have received valuable assistance
from Paul Maerker Branden and Elsa Branden. Their
generous aid is no less appreciated than their fine friendship
brought back from my sojourn in the United States.

MARIE LOUISE VON WALLERSEE-WITTELSBACH
ci-devant COUNTESS LARISCH

HER MAJESTY
Elizabeth

The Imperial House of Hapsburg | The Royal House of Wittelsbach

EMPEROR FRANCIS I OF AUSTRIA

ARCHDUKE FRANCIS CHARLES & SOPHIE

EMPEROR MAXIMILIAN OF MEXICO AND CHARLOTTE OF BELGIUM

KING MAXIMILIAN I OF BAVARIA

DUCHESS LUDOVICA & DUKE MAXIMILIAN OF BAVARIA

DUKE LUDWIG AND BARONESS WALLERSEE ④

COUNTESS LARISCH

HELEN

QUEEN OF NAPLES

MATHILDA

SOPHIE

①

②

③

EMPEROR FRANCIS JOSEPH I & ELIZABETH OF WITTELSBACH

CROWN PRINCE RUDOLF & STEPHANIE OF BELGIUM

FAMILY TREE OF *Countess Larisch von Wallersee-Wittelsbach*

① HELEN, PRINCESS OF THURN AND TAXIS
① MATHILDA, COUNTESS TRANI
③ SOPHIE, DUCHESS OF ALENÇON
④ NÉE HENRIETTA MENDEL.

Chapter One

MY ROYAL RELATIVES

ILENCE is golden. Always bear that in mind, Marie," my imperial aunt, Elizabeth of Austria, admonished me when she chose me for her confidante. The Empress-Queen was then a woman of forty and I a girl of just sixteen. Her solemn words impressed me, and I abided by her advice for many years—alas, too many! Because I "saw nothing, heard nothing, said nothing—especially in *affaires d'amour*," I now find myself described in the pages of history with annoying frequency as a half-mysterious, half-villainous actress in the dynastic drama of the imperial Hapsburgs to which only the end of the World War wrote *finis*. But today, at the biblical three-score-and-ten *plus,* I have decided to tell my story.

I propose to permit the reader a peep through the keyhole of the Hapsburg closet. Do not imagine, however, that it is my purpose to rattle the imperial skeletons. I merely intend to lift, here and there, dusty corners of the royal purple so that historical untruths may be rectified at last. I shall not only attempt to prove that the ghosts that clatter through the crumbling castles are kin of those that rumble in the cupboards of the commoner, but also that historical truth is frequently so strange as to put even the most fantastic fiction to shame.

My òwn life's story is a fair example, leading from the imperial palace in Vienna, where I was lady-in-waiting to my fascinating aunt, to my present humble home in one of the oldest cities of my native Bavaria. Now, a septuagenarian, I have returned to live in the shadow of the very convent where I was born. The circle seems complete.

Meanwhile I have roamed the world and, in the inverted order of the old saw, have traveled from riches to rags, at least figuratively speaking. Perhaps nothing presents more clearly the two great contrasts in my life than the day in New York City, back in 1926, when the Theatre Guild invited me, as the last surviving niece of the one-time Emperor of Mexico, to be present at the American *première* of Franz Werfel's *Juarez and Maximilian.* That night I came from my less than modest lodgings on the top floor, rear, of a third-rate sailors' boarding house in Hoboken, N. J., to see my uncle's sad fate enacted on the stage. My still abundant hair done up *à l'impératrice* in heavy braids around my head, as fashion decreed half a century ago, I bore a striking resemblance to my imperial Aunt Elizabeth. In the theater I noticed the wondering glances of those about me: they shook their heads as if seeing a ghost. I felt like shaking my own head, for there, on the stage, moved the wraiths of loved ones whom I once had known well. They were all dead and gone—only I was left to tell the story. . . .

If, in telling my story, I make no pretense at mincing words, it must be remembered that I was not only brought up to be a finished young lady, but also an accomplished horsewoman. Then, too, Empress Elizabeth—Aunt Sissy to me—inoculated me with her sarcasm.

I do not want people to draw the wrong conclusion that life has embittered me, because it hasn't! On the contrary, I look back over the long stretch of eventful years with a smile rather than a sneer. Of course, like many another, if I had my life to live over again, I would know what pitfalls to avoid. Certainly I should never again want to act a part in the tragi-comedy of history; but such things are not always of our own choosing. Undoubtedly, fate thrust a strange rôle upon me. Had I not been born a morganatic flower on the family tree of the royal Wittelsbachs, but first blinked at the light of day from under a letter carrier's lowly roof, my life would have been much happier.

Royalty, it seems, aside from other prerogatives, has the doubtful privilege of begetting two kinds of progeny: Offspring and Love Children. While the former primarily preserve the exalted family tree from dry rot, the latter perpetuate the parents' innate personality. I think the fact that I was a love child myself accounts for Aunt Sissy's great interest in me from the very moment I was ushered into this world. For the Empress of Austria deeply resented being a mere human incubator for the perpetuation of the Hapsburg dynasty. To her, I became for a time what modern psychology would call a vicarious fulfillment of her most cherished wish dream: a child all her own and not one that merely meant another link in the dynastic chain.

After that very human urge of hers had been gratified, her maternal love for me gradually gave way to less idealistic considerations. First, I had been her favorite niece; later, I became her most trusted amanuensis.

The Tragedy of Royal Love Children still remains to be written: Perhaps, in these pages, I shall make a small contribution to this mooted chapter on yesterday's morals. I certainly have seen enough of them to speak as an authority. There are the "natural children"—as they are often biologically rather than discreetly called—of my aunts, Elizabeth, the Empress of Austria, and Maria, erstwhile Queen of Naples and the Two Sicilies. Then there is the "American" love child of my cousin, Crown Prince Rudolf of Austria-Hungary; and last and least, there am I, myself, a love child.

My father, Duke Ludwig of Bavaria, was a young, dashing captain in a crack cavalry regiment, when he met my mother, plain Henrietta Mendel. For many years her father had served the Grand Duke of Hesse as personal valet, enjoying the confidence of his royal master. In gratitude for his services, the Grand Duke furnished the necessary funds to launch my mother and her older sister Elise on a stage career. Elise, in time, became a celebrated opera singer; my mother, however, did not feel any strong inclination for the stage, but the wish of the Grand Duke was a command. A first engagement was secured for her at Augsburg. It was there that His Royal Highness, Duke Ludwig of Bavaria, member of the reigning House of Wittelsbach, resplendent in his cavalry uniform, with high boots and clanking spurs, galloped right into the heart of the young actress. His proposal of marriage caused bitter quarrels in the exalted family. Nevertheless, he remained firm and, with the help of his imperial sister, Elizabeth, who happened to be visiting in Munich at that crucial moment, he finally succeeded in obtaining the consent of the family. However, upon the insistence of his father, Duke Maximilian, he had to renounce his first-born rights to succession.

From their very first meeting, Empress Elizabeth became greatly attached to her commoner sister-in-law. To assuage the ruffled feelings of the royal family, she was accorded the title of Baroness von Wallersee by King Maximilian of Bavaria, chief of the House of Wittelsbach. "Your mother Henrietta," the Empress would say to me in later years, "was the most beautiful girl I ever saw and touching in her shyness and modesty." It was primarily on the strength of the affection Aunt Sissy felt for her that my mother was never treated as an inferior. She was not only on excellent terms with Empress Elizabeth but also with Queen Maria of Naples, the Empress's younger sister. It seems that both Majesties found in my mother a woman whose inborn understanding of life and love had not been corrupted by the artificialities of court routine. More than once, the Empress as well as the Queen took their innermost secrets to Mother. Upon her death, a whole sheaf of notes of the most intimate character came into my possession, under the stipulations of her will.

Not only feminine royalty felt drawn to my mother; Emperor-King Francis Joseph I looked upon her with favor, too. Once, in my presence, he introduced her to his exalted relative, the Grand Duke Ferdinand of Tuscany—"Uncle

Nando"—as "my dear sister-in-law Henrietta." at Gödöllö, he frequently led my mother to the dinner table. And although she had been the daughter of a commoner, upon her death, my mother was entombed at the ducal mausoleum in Castle Tegernsee.

My parents brought me up with Spartan simplicity but, at the same time, surrounded me with devoted love. While my father saw to it that I spent twice as much time with his horses as with my dolls, and finally succeeded in making a tolerable circus rider of me, performing bareback and other stunts, my mother insisted that I receive a good general education. I recall as vividly as if it happened only yesterday how my maternal grandmother, Duchess Ludovica, flew into a not so royal rage when she heard that I was receiving instructions in Latin, shorthand, and music. None of her own children had had such a thorough education. As a matter of fact, none of them had learned more than seemed absolutely necessary for princes and princesses of royal blood. My father's sisters used to walk through the streets of Munich without any chaperons, and their general upbringing had not been exactly high-toned. Plain meals were served with no great show of ceremony. As one especially characteristic touch of my father's inbred simplicity, I remember his predilection for "dunking" at the breakfast table. Not even in an imperial castle would he forego his beloved custom of dipping his morning roll in the coffee cup.

Of my father's many sisters and brothers, the two to whom I not only became most attached but who also figured in my life conspicuously were my two *Majestäten Tanten*—"majesty aunts"—Empress Elizabeth and Queen Maria. Of course, I had other aunts, but they were mere Royal Highnesses and were not addressed as Majesties. There was Aunt Helen, Princess of Thurn and Taxis; Aunt Sophie Charlotte, Duchess of Alençon; and Mathilda Ludovica, Countess Trani.

It was between my Aunt Empress—*Tante Kaiserin*—and my Aunt Queen—*Tante Königin*—that I shuttled back and forth when a child. They were both extremely beautiful. While Empress Elizabeth sparkled with rare intelligence and was given to clever sarcasm and the quick coining of *bons mots,* Queen Maria was rather phlegmatic and melancholic. It was said of Aunt Maria that she was still lamenting her first and only love—something which could not exactly be said of Aunt Sissy.

The Empress was a curious mixture of formidable sphinx and good fairy. When I came to know her intimately, she was just rounding out her fortieth year. Perhaps the "dangerous age" accounted for her peccadillos which alternately fascinated and exasperated me, then a girl of sixteen. Despite her mature years, Aunt Sissy was not only of striking appearance, her girlish figure kept in trim by long walks and horseback riding, but still radiant with beauty. She was the fortunate possessor of that outstanding female asset which, during my American sojourn, I came to know as "that schoolgirl complexion." Incidentally, Aunt Sissy was the first woman I ever met who used a compact—only we did not call it that at the end of the last century. A tiny golden case, it contained a small quantity of *poudre de riz* of French make.

The first time I remember riding horseback in company with the Empress was as a little girl. My blonde hair flew wildly as I cantered with my adored aunt through the Pràter, Vienna's Central Park. People stopped, lifted their hats or bowed deeply. Their eyes followed me and my fluttering mane. When we returned to the *Hofburg*—the imperial palace—that day, Aunt Sissy issued the order that I was to wear my hair *à l'impératrice* in future. I have never changed my style of hairdress to this very day.

Aunt Sissy herself had the most wonderful hair I have ever seen. Healthy, luxurious hair has been a family characteristic of ours, but nobody could claim hair quite like Aunt Sissy's. It was chestnut in color with a reddish glint. The Empress was very proud of her hair and gave it the best of care. A Mrs. von Feyfalik wielded the imperial brush and comb for decades; it was she who taught my maid how to dress my hair.

In my eyes Aunt Sissy seemed to possess the beauty of a fairy queen, especially when she was in good humor. At times her lovely brown eyes flashed gay mischief and then, again, angry disapproval. She had an enchanting smile, and her voice was soft and melodious. I was completely fascinated by her, and my happiness knew no bounds whenever I was told that I would meet "Aunt Empress."

Naturally, I was delirious with joy when, during my visit to the Empress at Feldafing in Bavaria, in the summer of

1876, she suddenly remarked to my parents: "Why not leave Marie with me?"

I was not permitted to stay then and there but, two days later, I returned from Munich, not with bag and baggage, but bringing along horse and saddle, which seemed much more important to me and certainly to my imperial aunt. That day marked the beginning of a new period in my life. It was then that I became the steady companion of my exalted aunt.

At first I was shy, and more than once I wished myself at home. But the Kaiserin was extremely kind, and her little daughter, the Archduchess Valerie, at that time eight years old, seemed greatly attached to me. When I did not accompany the Empress on her morning canter, I spent my time with "the little woman"—*die kleine Frau*—the young archduchess's nickname at court.

I had to accustom myself to many new things, and it was the Empress herself who "trained" me, as my father referred to this part of my education. Aunt Sissy told me how to behave on different occasions, what I should and what I should not do. She made it especially clear to me when it was safe to speak and when it was wise to remain silent. It was during one of my sojourns at Feldafing that my imperial aunt impressed upon my unsophisticated sweet-sixteen consciousness the strict maxim, "Silence is golden."

In September, joined by my parents, I accompanied Aunt Sissy to Gödöllö near Budapest, fall residence of the imperial family. This castle, surrounded by beautiful woods abounding with game, was presented by the Hungarian

nation to Emperor Francis Joseph I when he was crowned
Apostolic King of Hungary in 1867, following the so-called
Ausgleich—Compromise—which concluded the Magyar
revolution of 1848.

In Vienna, during the colder months, opera and court
balls were the attractions while, in Gödöllö, during fall, the
chase was the main activity. Hunting became an official
function. Looking extremely well astride one of his blue-
ribbon thoroughbreds, the Emperor and his guests wore the
prescribed dress, consisting of crimson frock coat and high
silk hat. Only Count Nicholas Esterházy, as Master of the
Hunt, wore a green coat. He was the most important personage from meet to mort—the bugle call at the kill termi-
nating the hunt.

All these things I knew only from hearsay. Now I would
become part and parcel of this glittering life. I don't think
I slept a wink that first night at Gödöllö. I had ridden in a
paperchase, but here, in Gödöllö, I would experience my
initial fox hunt. I was trembling with suppressed excitement. In the morning, the Empress's waiting woman came
into my room with one of Auntie's riding habits over her
arm. I donned it eagerly, and we found that it fitted perfectly. "It is Her Majesty's command that if it fits, I should
leave it here for Your Grace," the waiting woman said and
disappeared.

I stood before a tall mirror, admiring myself in an almost new, extremely well-tailored riding habit with all the
necessary accessories. The most valuable piece of jewelry
could not have given me a greater thrill. I had, of course,
fine riding habits which had been given to me by Aunt

Maria, who used to send me clothes from Paris. This habit, however, was different. It had been tailored with the utmost smartness; in a word, it was fit for an empress.

When Aunt Sissy and I arrived at the meet, the Empress was greeted by the Master of the Hunt, Count Nicholas Esterházy. All the other gentlemen saluted solemnly by doffing their high silk hats. The Empress introduced me first to Count Esterházy, then to Count Elemér Batthyány. Although she merely said, "This is my niece Marie," something in her voice and in the way she looked at the Magyar nobleman puzzled me.

On this day, for the first time, I felt the heavy breath of history upon me. It was 1876, and only a little less than three decades after the Magyars had revolted against the Hapsburgs under the leadership of their aristocracy, headed by Count Ludwig Batthyány, father of Elemér. The latter, deeply devoted to the Empress, loyally recognized her as Queen of Hungary. However, he would have nothing to do with Francis Joseph as Apostolic King of Hungary. He could never forget that the Kaiser had signed his father's death warrant.

That day of the season's first fox hunt, Count Elemér, after greeting the Empress and being introduced to me, actually slighted the monarch in the most flagrant manner imaginable. He turned his horse and, without so much as a salute, rode off brusquely. The affront was so noticeable that I pondered over it until the chase got under way.

I did not notice any difference from the paperchase I had attended in Bavaria, until my horse suddenly refused to take a wide ditch. I had to sit tight to the saddle, otherwise I would have been thrown. Suddenly, while I was still struggling with my mount, trying to force it to take the obstacle, I heard a voice beside me: "Can I be of any assistance to you, Baroness?" The voice was well modulated and had an interesting Hungarian intonation. I did not reply or even turn around. I did not intend to give anybody the satisfaction of saying that I had encountered difficulties at my very first fox hunt. I turned my mount around, gave him the spurs, and, cracking the crop over him, I forced the stubborn animal to take the ditch with an elegant jump. Then I raced on.

The cavalier who had offered his assistance was Count Elemér Batthyány. He escorted me for the rest of the chase, and I felt gratified that I had proved myself a good horsewoman. When we returned to Castle Gödöllö, Aunt Sissy remarked rather slyly: "Count Nicky Esterházy expressed himself very favorably about you. You should feel very proud indeed, for, as a rule, young girls bore him terribly."

I was not at all flattered. Count Esterházy had struck me as a medium-sized, stoutish man with intelligent, penetrating eyes, rather blasé and super-sophisticated. That, at least, was the first impression I had of him. After a while, Aunt Sissy, apparently for no reason at all, added: "Did you notice how Elemér Batthyány acted to the Kaiser? His mother is behind it all. She's still preaching the gospel of hate against the Emperor, despite all I have done to reconcile the Magyars with the ruling house." She sighed.

I knew, and almost everybody else in the whole Dual Monarchy knew, how for years and years Aunt Sissy had schemed and worked to bring about the Compromise. However, there were still some intransigents keeping alive the old antagonism.

"By the way," the Empress continued, "how did you like Elemér? I noticed he was riding with you all the time, and he certainly tried to entertain you." Her voice sounded ironical, but she nevertheless appeared pleased.

I was still too much dazzled by my new life to ponder long over Aunt Sissy's enigmatic remarks.

While we were at Gödöllö, Crown Prince Rudolf came on one of his infrequent visits to his mother. Aunt Sissy did not seem very happy over her son's arrival. I had not seen my cousin for some years and still remembered him as a mere boy. He was a few years my senior. Despite international gossip, I never entertained the slightest intention of finding favor in his eyes. Certainly, I never planned to win him in order to become Empress-Queen, as has been stated. Rudolf was never very sympathetic toward me, and somehow, even today, when I think of him, I recall his annoying habit of pulling my long braids when we were children.

Of course, Rudolf did nothing of the sort any longer, for he was a young man now. Although just as sarcastic and fidgety as formerly, he conversed intelligently. He meanwhile had studied assiduously and was keenly interested in everything. Even the Empress, who felt somewhat estranged from her son, as a result of her mother-in-law's interference, had to admit that Rudolf carried a good head on his broad shoulders.

In an offhand way, Aunt Sissy warned me to be rather careful and restrained with Rudolf. He had a habit of "pumping" people and making arrogant, insinuating remarks. When he saw me at Gödöllö, he looked at me in his supercilious manner and drawled: "I see you are wearing your hair in a crown like Mother. You are still the same monkey you used to be."

"Of course," I snapped back. "We are relatives, aren't we?"

Rudolf laughed.

There were many more such verbal duels between us. Fortunately I did not see much of him, because he was off hunting most of the time. But whenever I ran across him, he felt called upon to tease me.

Once, when he had seen me exchange a few words with Count Elemér, he sneered: "Tell me, Marie, are they putting you on the marriage market? Well, if it's Elemér, you certainly have my blessings. On the other hand, it would be still funnier if they made you marry Nicky Esterházy." Rudolf broke into raucous laughter.

This conversation occurred after a Sunday dinner, while the Emperor was still in the room. Nevertheless, I made the curt rejoinder: "I don't have to do anything of the kind. Nobody can make me marry anybody. Besides, nobody has such ideas."

That evening I reported the conversation to Aunt Sissy. After a brief pause, she commented: "Thank heaven, Rudolf is going to leave us the day after tomorrow."

This wide gulf twixt mother and son struck me as distinctly queer, at that particular moment. Their strained relations could only be attributed to that meddling old woman, Archduchess Sophie, doting but self-willed mother of the Emperor.

No sooner had Cousin Rudolf left than an English couple arrived in Gödöllö whom Aunt Sissy had met in England the year before. As both of them were extremely good equestrians, the Empress had invited them, overlooking everything else; her impulsiveness became the more evident the farther she was removed from Vienna and its strict etiquette. The *naïveté* of the couple in matters of court life was simply overwhelming. The Englishman was a well-to-do squire from Cheshire, while his wife was an unassuming person, not too well educated and obviously ill-at-ease in imperial surroundings. When the Empress conversed with her, the Englishwoman, to the great consternation of the entire court, would "Yes, ma'am" and "No, ma'am" her instead of addressing her imperial hostess as "Your Majesty." What probably was accepted in her own home as wholesome struck us as singularly crude. The British lady was neither good-looking nor young; besides, she dressed in such atrocious taste that even my mother, who always thought up excuses for everybody, could not help shaking her head. The Squire was a genial soul, endowed with a stentorian voice. He never allowed himself to become the least bit flustered.

Since they had not yet met the Emperor, Aunt Sissy arranged to have the English couple dine at the same table with the Kaiser as soon as the monarch arrived for a few days' hunting. The Squire was apparently pleased but not at all awe-struck. As Uncle Emperor did not speak English and the Squire hardly knew any German, Aunt Sissy entrusted me with the task of acting as interpreter. During those strenuous talks, with the always slightly taciturn Emperor on one side and the everlastingly talkative Englishman on the other, I more than once deplored the fact that I was nearly as well versed in the Anglo-Saxon tongue as in my native German. Now and then the Squire, racking his brain for every German word he knew, but primarily relying on expressive gestures and the loudness of his voice, sought to converse with the Emperor directly, his long arms waving in front of me like the sails of a Dutch windmill. With a friendly if somewhat quizzical smile and a nod of his head, the Emperor would pretend to understand what his guest wished to say. But it was plain that he had not the slightest idea what the Englishman was talking about. Time and again, Uncle Kaiser, with suppressed exasperation, turned towards me and whispered into my ear: *"Um Himmels Willen, Marie, was will der Mann eigentlich von mir?*—For heaven's sake, Marie, what does that man want of me, anyway?" Small wonder that I found it difficult to remain serious and act the part of an interpreter with the stolidity of a well-oiled automaton.

That same evening, while I was bidding Auntie goodnight in her boudoir, the Emperor came in and demanded: "Good heavens, Sissy, where did you pick them up? And what did you bring them here for?"

The Empress laughed: "Maybe they are not accomplished courtiers, but you should see what marvelous figures they cut on horseback."

"Perhaps, but if it can possibly be arranged . . . I would rather not eat with them, Sissy. It's too much of a strain."

After that, the English guests were transferred back to a side table, where they dined with the imperial retinue. They certainly had their peculiarities, especially when it came to their hunting clothes, which were so informal as to be almost outlandish. Despite the fact that both of them were extraordinarily good equestrians, when we brought them to the meet the first time, the whole hunting party had all they could do to suppress their laughter. I shall never forget the bewildered expression on Count Nicholas Esterházy's face when the Kaiser introduced his English guests to him. Count Aristide Baltazzi, Nicky's closest friend, was the only one who did not find anything odd about the appearance of the English couple. Partly of English stock himself, he had lived long in England and was accustomed to unconventional foreign ways.

A few days later, another English guest, Captain William "Bay" Middleton, arrived. He had been awaited patiently by Aunt Sissy. The Empress had told me much about him. She had met him the year before while hunting in England, and during the entire season there he had been her steady companion. Middleton had been a captain in the cavalry and enjoyed a great reputation as a "gentleman rider." His means, however, were modest, for, as Aunt Sissy expressed it:, "The poor devil has to live on his pension from the army." Captain Middleton was not to stay in the castle, but was given the exclusive use of a little lodge some distance away. While the royal *calèche* was down at the station, calling for Captain Middleton, Aunt Sissy said, as shyly as a young girl: "You'll soon meet Bay, Marie." And a happy smile diffused her face.

Her evident anticipation of Captain Middleton's arrival had aroused my curiosity to such an extent that, naturally enough, I was a little disappointed when I actually met him. Dressed smartly in a light gray traveling suit, he was a bulky man in his early forties with flaming red hair and a miniature mustache to match. His ruddy face was liberally sprinkled with freckles; his nose seemed a bit large. To offset these defects, his teeth gleamed with pleasing prominence and his blue eyes twinkled merrily, inviting sympathy.

"This is Captain Middleton, Marie . . . my niece and steady companion," the Empress introduced us. The Englishman extended a gigantic hand and immediately, in that handclasp, I felt as if I had always known him. There was that spontaneous contact between people attuned to each other.

Middleton turned to Aunt Sissy. His manner was at once respectful and unceremonious. "Why did you invite those people?" he asked, indicating the English couple.

Aunt Sissy threw the Captain a significant glance. "Why, I had to—for your sake. . . . Your visit will not arouse so much curiosity here as long as I have invited some compatriots of yours. You know there is a dreadful amount of gossip around this place," the Empress added frankly. "But there, don't worry—they won't interfere with us."

Aunt Sissy, however, was wrong; the English couple did

interfere. When we went out for a canter the same afternoon, the Empress motioned to Middleton to ride at her right side, until then the prerogative of the Squire, while his wife usually rode to the left of the Empress. The Squire tried his utmost to regain his old place of honor, availing himself of all the little equestrian tricks of which his consumate horsemanship was capable. Nevertheless, no matter how cleverly the Squire made his steed prance and rear and dance, Captain Middleton could easily cope with his artifices. At last, realizing that he simply could not budge his countryman, the Squire sadly relinquished all hope of regaining his place to the right of the Empress. He next maneuvered his horse between Aunt Sissy and his wife, thus trotting at the Empress's left. I noticed that he signaled to his wife to ride abreast of me, and I also perceived Aunt Sissy's annoyance. In the circumstances, it was absolutely impossible for her to exchange one single word with Captain Middleton without being overheard.

Suddenly the Empress seemed to lose all patience with the whole silly game. She murmured something to Middleton, and a second later she and the Captain galloped off as if their steeds had been stung by wasps. The Squire, taken completely unawares, was startled for a few moments, especially as his horse first reared and then raced after the Empress and Middleton. Meantime, while I was taking in this scene, the mare of the Squire's wife reared and joined in the race. I must admit that the English couple certainly knew how to sit tight in their saddles. A regular race developed, with the Empress and Middleton ahead, and the rest

of us following. Eventually we fell back, as the Englishwoman's saddlestrap had broken; soon we lost sight of the
Empress and the Captain.

Aunt Sissy and Middleton arrived at the castle much later
than the rest of the cavalcade. Apparently the two had taken
a detour. The Empress was so vexed with the English
couple that she was on the point of curtailing their visit. But
fortune favored her, for that very evening the Squire received a message that his mother-in-law was ill and that
they should return without delay. After they had left, in
great haste, to catch the night train, the Empress remarked
sarcastically: "I don't know whether it's his mother or hers,
and I generally don't approve of mothers-in-law,"—this was
a little dig directed at the Kaiser's mother, Archduchess
Sophie—"but here, certainly, is one mother-in-law that has
my blessing."

From then on, whenever we went on a canter, I knew
enough to remain behind while Aunt Sissy and Captain
Middleton rode ahead. It was easy to see that the suite of
the Empress was not very favorably inclined towards the
Englishman; especially Count Nicky Esterházy treated
him almost rudely. The only member of the court who really
befriended Middleton was Aristide Baltazzi.

"You know, Marie," Aunt Sissy said one evening after
supper—the usual hour when she became confidential—
"this animosity towards Bay is most exasperating. I am very
angry with Count Nicky. Since he became Master of the
Hunt, he has developed a jealousy directed against anything and everything regarding English sport. He even went

so far as to upbraid me because I enjoy hunting in England."

Aunt Sissy waxed eloquent in her abuse of Count Esterházy and the others while, at the same time, praising Captain Middleton.

"But, Aunt Sissy," I inquired naïvely, "why does that annoy you so much?"

The Empress seemed taken aback. "How stupid of you, Marie!" Then she caught herself. "Naturally, I don't want to see a special friend of mine slighted in my own house."

I shook my head in complete bewilderment. Despite all the pondering I did that evening, it was not until some time later that I learned the real truth. I did not know, then, that I was witnessing the prelude to an exalted love union—not only exalted because an empress was cast in the chief rôle. I was still too unsophisticated to peer beneath the surface of the glamorous life of a great empress. It was clear enough, however, that the nearer the date of Captain Middleton's departure, the more irritable Aunt Sissy became. Of course, she controlled herself admirably before the court, but when alone with me she abandoned her attitude of reserve.

"We shall really miss him, the good Bay," she sighed on the eve of Middleton's leavetaking.

I, too, regretted the visit was over, for the Captain had proved himself an excellent companion. He had formed the habit of addressing me as "little girlie"; an older brother could not have treated me any nicer. While he did not flatter the Empress, and at times even assumed an offhand manner, his behavior was always irreproachable. It was easy to see that he looked up to her as to a higher being not only because she was an empress.

The day before Middleton's departure was a Sunday. After dinner, the Kaiser shook hands with the Englishman and wished him godspeed. To all appearances, the Emperor liked Middleton, perhaps because of his snappy military bearing.

Contrary to custom, the Empress and Middleton inspected the stables in the afternoon, taking me along. The two lingered in front of the different paddocks while I kept at a distance. Although I realized that Aunt Sissy appreciated my discretion, I felt very awkward indeed. In order to leave the two alone as unobtrusively as possible, I remarked: "It's turning rather cold. Shall I fetch a shawl for you, Aunt Sissy?"

Her eyes flashed with gratitude. "Good girl," she approved. "Yes, fetch my shawl." As I rushed off, she called after me: "It isn't that cool yet. You certainly needn't hurry so."

I took the hint and returned no sooner than I thought absolutely necessary, to find Aunt Sissy with moist eyes, her long slender hand tightly enclosed in Middleton's. "I'll see you tomorrow before you leave, Bay," she nodded to the Captain. He bowed deeply, and without another word Aunt Sissy permitted me to drape the shawl around her shoulders. We left the stable, then, with Middleton remaining behind.

That night supper was partaken under a dark cloud. Aunt Sissy made no attempt to assume a cheerfulness she did not feel. No sooner had dessert been served, and despite the fact that the Emperor himself was honoring us with his society, she left the table.

When I saw her around noon next day, shortly after Middleton had been driven to the station, I found her in tears. I was petrified; never had I seen my proud, self-reliant aunt so unstrung before. "Dear Aunt Sissy," I entreated, "don't cry. You will see our 'red fox' in a few months again."

The Empress lifted her face, and her lips twisted in a tremulous smile. "You are right, Marie, I am acting like a silly child."

At that moment there was a knock at the door. The maid opened it, and I heard her whisper for a few seconds with the lady-in-waiting, standing outside. The maid returned. "His Majesty, the Emperor," she announced.

Aunt Sissy jumped up. "Under no circumstances must he see me like this," she cried, dabbing at her eyes. "Quick, Marie, stop the Kaiser. Tell him that I am trying on lingerie." Like a flash she had disappeared in her bedroom. Simultaneously there was a sharp rap at the door, and Uncle Francis entered.

I made my deepest curtsy. "Aunt Sissy is in her bedroom, trying on lingerie," I stammered. I was very nervous, but Uncle did not seem to notice my confusion. He held a telegram in his hand. As was his habit, he pulled his mustache somewhat impatiently, and then he said: "Sorry, I can't wait. Just take this wire to your aunt Sissy and tell her I would like to know what she has to say about it before I leave Gödöllö."

With that, he handed me a telegram, turned around and strode from the room. No sooner had he gone than I rushed towards the bedroom door and knocked carefully, whispering that I was alone. First the maid peered through a crack in the door; then the Empress came out. I handed her the telegram. She glanced at it and remarked ruefully: "Just think—all this commotion over that *Trottel!*"

The *"Trottel"*—dunce—was none other than the Archduke of Tuscany, who politely inquired whether Their Royal and Imperial Majesties would be gracious enough to permit him to pay his respects at Gödöllö a fortnight ahead of the originally agreed date.

"What do I care when that *Trottel* comes or whether he comes at all!" Aunt Sissy handed the message back to me. "Run over to Uncle and tell him that any time will suit me for the Archduke's visit."

"Shall I say the *Trottel?*" I asked mischievously.

"Ah, you're one yourself," Aunt Sissy laughed.

Life in Gödöllö was unpretentious and, in the fullest sense of that untranslatable German term, *gemütlich,* especially when the Emperor was away on affairs of state. Then we were "just by ourselves." The morning was usually spent out of doors, while many a cozy afternoon and evening hour was whiled away in the music room. Usually the party consisted of Aunt Sissy, myself, and one or the other lady-in-waiting.

One forenoon I received the Empress's order to come to the music room. The lackey who brought the imperial command offered me a little slip of paper upon which Aunt Sissy, in her almost illegible handwriting, had jotted down the titles of a number of songs. Among them was "The

Azra," "The Lorelei," and "The Lotus Flower," all compo-
sitions of poems by Heine, the German-Jewish poet whom
the Empress well-nigh worshiped.

Surprised though I was to be called upon for a musical
entertainment so early in the day, I was almost aghast when
I discovered that Aunt Sissy was not alone. The Empress,
ensconced in a deep chair, looked more like a young girl
than ever in a white flannel dress. The gentleman standing
in front of her was Count Nicky Esterházy. The way I
found the two reminded me of a little scene I had observed
only a week or ten days previously, but Bay Middleton had
been the cavalier then.

Count Esterházy advanced and bent over my hand for
the conventional kiss, while I sought to gain my composure.
There seemed to be some deviltry lurking in Aunt Sissy's
beautiful brown eyes as she looked from me to the Count
and back again.

"You are to sing just a few *Lieder* for us in a little while,
Marie," Aunt Sissy said. Turning to the Count again, the
Empress continued their conversation on horses which apparently had been interrupted by my entrance. I felt very
superfluous. Although I did not dare to show it, I was wild
with indignation. In the first place, I would have to sing in
the morning before I had a chance to practice; besides, I
resented this sudden command to act the part of an enter-
tainer.

At last all the equestrian questions in the world were settled between the two, and Aunt Sissy turned back to me.
"Let me see what you brought along." She looked at the

music. "Fine . . . but this one I want you to sing last," and she indicated "The Lorelei."

I sat at the piano, trembling with suppressed anger and, accompanying myself, I sang first "The Azra."

Count Nicky was lounging comfortably in a chair, not unlike a Turkish pasha. At his right was a little table on which stood half a bottle of champagne and a bowl of cookies.

As I turned to the next song, I heard Count Nicky remark to the Empress in Hungarian, of which I had a smattering then: "Really, she has quite a pleasing voice." His condescension only served to add fuel to my burning resentment.

Next I sang "The Lotus Flower." Again his complimentary remarks reached my ears. Hesitating a minute when I came to the last song, I complained that I found it difficult to go on, as my throat was dry. Immediately Count Nicky sprang to my side, offering a sip of champagne. I swallowed the sparkling drink and, with it, my hurt pride and anger.

Although I could not see the Empress from where I sat at the piano, I could watch the Count by glancing into a wall mirror out of the corner of my eye. I had hardly struck the first chord of "The Lorelei" when a remarkable change seemed to come over Nicky. He sat up straight. No sooner had I sung the first few bars than he began staring at me in a curious, hard fashion. He blanched, his eyes grew dark and unspeakably sad. I saw him turn his head slowly, and I knew that his eyes were piercing those of Aunt Sissy. Abruptly, then, he jumped up and, with long strides, made for the windows where he remained motionless.

The whole scene had a strange effect upon me, though I only vaguely surmised its import. I do not know how I managed to finish the *Lied,* but somehow I did. As I struck the last note, I found Aunt Sissy at my elbow, handing me my music.

"That was sweet, very sweet, Marie," she said, making it unmistakably clear that I was no longer wanted.

As I passed from the room, I caught one more glimpse of the Count standing so still at the window while Aunt Sissy remained in the center of the room as if rooted to the spot.

The door closed behind me. There was a lump in my throat; something uncanny seemed to have touched me. What could it be?

My curiosity aroused, I eagerly sought to fit together more and more fragments into that great jigsaw puzzle of pre-War days: Court Life. In 1876, at the *Hofburg*—the palace at Vienna—as well as at the imperial summer residence Gödöllö, near Budapest, the glitter and pomp were at their zenith. Next to Queen Victoria of England, my imperial Aunt Elizabeth was the most important personage of royal blood of her time.

Though as yet untrained to pry beneath the surface, I knew that the Empress-Queen was very unhappy. At times she would sigh and just look at me, stroking my hair with a gesture of touching tenderness. On other days she would be as happy and carefree as a young girl. The presence of certain people seemed to bring her solace. In Gödöllö, Aunt Sissy preferred the company of Count Nicky Esterházy.

More than once I caught her glancing first at Nicky and then at myself; more and more I found myself thrown together with the Count. It never occurred to me that my imperial aunt carefully planned these meetings for reasons of her own.

Once, when she did not feel well enough to partake in the hunt, she asked Uncle Kaiser to take care of me. I shall never forget the surprised face of Count Nicky when, in his official capacity, he came galloping up to the Emperor to report everything in readiness. He had expected to find the Empress with the Kaiser but found me riding beside Francis Joseph instead. Obviously Aunt Sissy's absence was a great disappointment to him. As soon as the opportunity presented itself, he sidled up close to me. He attempted to appear casual, but his voice vibrated with anxiety as he asked: "Why are you alone, Baroness?"

"Her Majesty has a slight cold," I replied. Count Nicky nodded, his large dark eyes taking me in sharply before he slowly turned his horse and returned to his post of duty.

No sooner was the hunt well under way than my mount stepped into a rabbit hole, throwing me. The cavalcade raced past me, with apparently nobody paying any attention to my predicament—a casual custom on these reckless rides. However, as I sprang to my feet, I found that Count Elemér Batthyány had observed my mishap and was leading back my mount by the reins. He dismounted and solicitously inquired: "Did you hurt yourself, Baroness?"

I laughed. "No, I just managed to get good and dirty, and I tore my sleeve. But that's all."

He whipped out his handkerchief and flicked the dust off

my habit, much in the manner one treats a child. "Why, Count Elemér, perhaps you'll even wipe off my face?"

"I shouldn't mind," he replied with a meaning glance.

We mounted our horses and followed the others, but did not catch up with them until we reached the railroad station. There a light lunch was served for the hunting party in the Emperor's dining car. I explained my little mishap to Uncle Francis, and he clucked his tongue commiseratingly. "Well, well, a bite of lunch will be just the thing for you. . . . What's left, anyway?" the Kaiser inquired from somebody standing near by.

"Just a few sandwiches, Your Majesty."

"What, no caviar canapés left?"

"Sorry, Your Majesty, all gone."

The Kaiser marched, without a moment's hesitation, to his own little table. He returned with a few caviar canapés and a small glass of wine on a platter which he graciously presented to me.

"*Guten Appetit*," he said smilingly.

On that same day I also met Baroness Helen Vetsera, sister of Aristide Baltazzi. The Baroness hailed from somewhere in the Levant. It was said of her that she was the mother of two strikingly beautiful girls, Hannah and Mary. When I shook Baroness Vetsera's hand that day, I surely could not foresee what a tragic rôle the younger of her two little daughters was destined to play in the drama of Meyerling which shocked the world thirteen years later.

In the evening, as usual, I went up to Aunt Sissy's boudoir to bid her good-night and relate to her all that happened during the fox hunt. I was so engrossed in my own adventures that only when I was on the point of leaving the room I remembered to tell her that Count Nicky had inquired after her. Aunt Sissy seemed surprised that I had almost forgotten to include this in my report. "But, Marie, why didn't you tell me that right away?" she asked with a touch of annoyance. Then a smile flitted over her face, but I guessed that it was not meant for me.

Little incidents of this nature could not fail to stir the most unsuspecting mind. Gradually I had to admit to myself that there might be some element of truth in the *Hofklatsch*—court gossip—revolving around the Empress and Count Nicky. Presently I witnessed a scene that amazed me in its striking implications, lending added weight to the rumors that already had reached my ears. I shrank from the obvious deduction brought home to me so vividly. However, the last shred of doubt was dispelled only a few years later, when Aunt Sissy herself frankly confirmed my conclusion. The Empress, smiling pensively, recalled the strange situation in all its details:

During a Hungarian lesson, which I took together with my little cousin, the Archduchess Valerie, her governess, Mrs. Scharak, brought word that Aunt Sissy wanted us in her suite. When we came upon the Empress, we found her with Count Nicky Esterházy. He hardly seemed to notice me; his attention was completely focused on Valerie. It actually took my breath away as I perceived the striking resemblance between his eyes and those of the child— round, long-lashed, and blazing with a dusky sheen. Never before, nor since, have I come across eyes such as those of Count Nicky and my cousin Valerie. The conversation between the man and child waxed so lively that a slight impediment in the child's speech became rather conspicuous. Startled, I recognized it as an identical handicap from which Count Nicky suffered! Valerie's governess, who formerly had been a trusted retainer of the Esterházy family, took in the scene between the Count and the little Archduchess with an expression of complete understanding. Once she furtively looked at Aunt Sissy, but the Empress avoided her gaze.

Aunt Sissy's deep attachment for Count Nicholas Esterházy became clear to me then; if I had dared, in that revealing moment, I, too, would have accorded the Empress a knowing glance. However, I had yet to surmise her purpose in throwing me together with him.

On the afternoon of a fox hunt, at Gödöllö, Aunt Sissy sent for me. Upon entering her suite, I found her engaged in a lively discussion with Mrs. von Ferenczy. The conversation was carried on in Hungarian, and although I could not understand every word, I gathered that Aunt Sissy had made a decision which her elderly lady-in-waiting disapproved. The poor woman seemed greatly distressed.

Abruptly my aunt turned toward me. "You don't know what fear is, do you, Marie?" Without awaiting my answer, she informed me that later in the evening Mrs. von Ferenczy would give me a little package. This I was to take over to the neighboring estate of Count Esterházy and deliver it to his trusted valet, returning without delay. This struck me as decidedly odd, but I knew better than to ask questions.

When night fell, a sealed envelope was handed to me by Mrs. von Ferenczy and I immediately started, on horseback, through the dark woods to the hunting lodge of Count Esterházy. I had my most dependable steed and sat astride as Aunt Sissy and I were wont to do when we went riding after dusk. It was so much more comfortable and safer than side-saddle.

I knew every tree in the neighborhood and soon arrived at the door of the little two-story building.

At my knock, the Count's valet, Peter, stuck out his head through an upper-story window. I explained my errand to him in my limited Hungarian: *"Vigyazz! levelet!"* —Here's a letter.—The man mumbled something about "waiting a minute," obviously mistaking me for an ordinary messenger.

The letter still in my hand, I waited, looking up at a row of windows illuminated by a green-shaded lamp. I concluded that either Count Nicky or his inseparable companion, Aristide Baltazzi, was at home.

A few seconds later a light flickered down the stairs, the door opened, and Count Nicky stood before me. His dark round eyes gazed at me questioningly. "Why, Baroness, dismount, won't you, please?" Count Nicky said, stroking the neck of my horse, all the while staring at me because I sat astride my steed. "Permit me to say so, Baroness," he said with a low bow, "you cut an even better figure riding astride than side-saddle." However, there was criticism in his voice, and very understandably so, because in the 'seventies it was unheard of for a lady to ride man-fashion.

I bent down to deliver the letter, ready to wheel around

and gallop home. I felt humiliated in the extreme. Why had Aunt Sissy chosen to place me in so embarrassing a position?

"Do come in for a moment, Baroness!" Count Nicky appeared altogether composed now. I noticed that he was dressed in a long black lounging robe that would have made a drab outfit but for one unexpected patch of color provided by slippers of a vivid green. Whenever I had seen him before, he had been attired in smart English riding suits or had worn his official hunting outfit.

I dismounted rather reluctantly and followed him into the house, still holding the letter in my hand. Once more I presented it to the Count. He accepted it, throwing it carelessly on a near-by table. Then he invited me to be seated, all the while eyeing me with unconcealed curiosity.

I sat down, fidgeting nervously because I could see that he intended to question me. He asked whether it had been "found necessary to dispatch a young lady on an errand in the dead of the night."

"That's just like her," he grumbled, more to himself than for my benefit. "A nice way to bring up a young girl, I must say! Sometimes she doesn't give a hoot if you break your neck. But that's like her. . . . I almost feel like writing a few lines to your mother advising her to take you home to Munich. The court is no place for an inexperienced young girl."

"Please don't do that," I pleaded.

He stared at me once more, plunging his dark eyes deeply into mine; then he slowly shook his head. I suddenly recalled that glance I had caught accidentally, some days ago, when Aunt Sissy had commanded me to sing "The Lorelei."

The valet meanwhile had brought refreshments for me, and Count Nicky asked to be excused for a few minutes in order to change into his riding togs. "I shall certainly not let you make that trip back alone," he said paternally. He must have divined my thoughts, for he promptly added: "Don't worry, I shall only bring you as far as the gate of the castle."

I pointed to the letter. "Is there no answer?" I knew there was no answer, but I thought the letter important, and I wanted him to read it.

"I am not in the habit of employing a young lady as a common messenger." Count Nicky bowed and left the room.

All through our nocturnal canter, he never uttered one word. When we reached the gate to Castle Gödöllö, he gripped my hand so hard I almost cried out in protest. "You are safe now," he reassured me. He lifted his hat. "Goodnight . . . Marie."

There was something in his voice that sent a shiver down my spine. It confused me so that I could not even reply. When I finally brought my horse around, he was gone.

Entering the castle, I found Mrs. von Ferenczy in a state of exasperation. Excitedly, she wanted to know what had happened to me, as I had taken so long. I did not offer any explanation; I merely complained that I was terribly tired and locked the door of my room. Despite the fact that I was exhausted, my nerves were too jangled to permit sleep. In bed I racked my brains to discover Aunt Sissy's reason for sending me on that nocturnal ride to Count Nicky. My mission struck me as pointless, and yet I realized that the

Empress always knew what she was about. She must be hatching some scheme but what, in Heaven's name, could it be?

A sudden thought jerked me into a sitting position: There was that sneering remark of Cousin Rudolf's: "Tell me, Marie, are they putting you on the marriage market?"

Could it be, I wondered, that the Count figured in Aunt Sissy's matchmaking plans for me?

Chapter Two

AN EMPRESS IN LOVE

We WERE still sojourning at Gödöllö when the first snow began to fly. One chill evening—it was 1876 and long before the era of steam-heated rooms—I entered Tante Kaiserin's boudoir for the usual good-night kiss. In the course of time this custom had become a more or less perfunctory bit of etiquette, varying only in cases when Aunt Sissy felt the urge to talk. Then she would invite me to remain while Mrs. von Feyfalik brushed her beautiful long hair. Tonight, however, to my unbounded astonishment, the Empress sent the hairdresser out of the room. I grew apprehensive.

While I secretly squirmed, Aunt Sissy came straight to the point: A marriage was to be arranged for me. Ah, it must be Esterházy, flashed through my brain. Aunt Sissy seemed to read my mind. She shook her head and, smiling a little, assured me: "No, it's not Nicky. . . . He'd never be the right man for you. I'm thinking of Elemér Batthyány."

And then I learned that Count Gyula Andrássy, at the suggestion of the Empress, had approached the Hungarian nobleman some weeks ago. Instantly I recalled Elemér's solicitude at the hunt when I had my little spill.

"Of course," Aunt Sissy continued coolly, "Elemér is considerably older than you, but from what I hear, he admires you greatly. He will make an excellent husband. Besides," the Empress pointed out, "with this marriage, that terrible feud of 1848 will be wiped out completely. Don't you see, Marie—the son of Ludwig Batthyány will become the nephew of the King of Hungary."

This was not Aunt Sissy speaking to me, but the Empress of Austria and Queen of Hungary. She was serious, almost stern, and there were fine lines on her usually smooth brow.

I knew that since 1867, shortly after the Compromise which reconciled the Magyars to the Hapsburg ruler, when she had accompanied the Emperor to Budapest, she had been greatly interested in establishing good relations with the Realm of the Crown of St. Stephen. As Queen of Hungary, the Empress had become an eager student of the Magyar tongue. After that first trip to the land of the *puszta,* she had made it a point to spend as much time as possible in Hungary, especially in Gödöllö.

I felt that Aunt Sissy was studying me from under those long eyelashes of hers and tried to check the sudden weakness that threatened me.

So I was to be Elemér's wife! Never had I dreamed of such a possibility. Still, I told myself that I could love him. Not solely because he was a striking personality, surrounded by a halo of romance, but for the very reason that appeared a drawback: our difference in age. Young men had never interested me. Today students of psychology would possibly diagnose this tendency as a father complex—and probably correctly so.

"In all likelihood, Elemér will propose to you on the next hunt. Naturally you must seem surprised." Having expressed her wishes, the Empress could afford to be my Aunt Sissy once more. She kissed me affectionately and rang for Mrs. von Feyfalik to continue with the nightly hair-brushing ritual.

Back in my own room there was no need to hide my feelings. I felt at once elated and stunned. That Aunt Sissy meant to marry me off did not take me unawares exactly. More and more of late, signs had been pointing that way. Only a few days before, Aunt Sissy, after introducing me to a mediatized prince, had remarked slyly: "That man might be a good match for you, Marie." The Prince's family was one of the oldest and richest in Europe, but this particular scion of the noble house was an elderly man with a wild grey mustachio, a tremendous beak of a nose, and a black patch over the left eye to cover an empty socket. Elemér Batthyány was perhaps not so much younger than this Prince and certainly not as fabulously rich, but then, I was still young enough to overlook material advantages. To me, at that age, Elemér seemed the nearest approach to a maiden's prayer. More than once I caught myself wistfully eyeing the finger on which I hoped to see Elemér's ring soon. To be sure, that finger was already encircled by a narrow band, made of Caucausian platinum. Inside, smallest Russian letters spelled the name GRISHA. He was a young Russian aristocrat whom I had never seen, the brother of a school chum.

One rainy afternoon, to the huge merriment of a houseful of girl friends, I had been "married" to Grisha in a mock ceremony with Nadja herself substituting for her brother. At her insistence, rings had been exchanged by mail between Grisha and myself, and I also had sent him my picture. Grisha was a junior officer in a regiment of Circassian cavalry in the far-away steppes of Siberia. That region, in the 'seventies of the last century, was still much too wild to boast photography or portrait painting, and I therefore never received a likeness of my "bridegroom." Of course, I romantically concluded from Nadja's ecstatic assurances that her brother was a veritable Adonis and the incarnation of all manly virtues. For some time my "long-distance husband" and I corresponded with each other. As letters were in transit from two to six months, however, according to the season, our correspondence gradually dwindled and eventually ceased altogether. By now Grisha seemed nothing more than a pleasant memory, while Elemér Batthyány represented exciting reality.

As a young girl will do, I began to weave daydreams with myself in the rôle of Countess Batthyány. Every morning, as soon as I arose, I anxiously scanned the sky, praying that no early frost would interfere with our next hunt.

My prayers were answered. A clear, cool day saw us at the meet, and it was during a short rest in some deserted neck of the woods that Elemér came toward me. There was always a certain hoarseness in his voice, but it was more noticeable than ever that day. He raised his eyes slowly and looked at me.

"Baroness Marie," he began hesitatingly, "will you always think kindly of me?"

I stared at him, astonished. Was this a proposal of marriage?

At the same moment the hounds had picked up the scent once more, and the hunt continued. Elemér kept beside me but remained strangely silent. I cast a furtive glance at him. Heavens, what had happened to the man? There was an expression of intense suffering in his eyes which made me compare them with the agonized features of the Redeemer, looking down at us from the little wayside shrine we were just passing. Never, in all my life, shall I forget those eyes.

We rode on interminably—or so it seemed to me. At last Elemér spoke again: "If only I did not have to leave here so soon—but I am going back to Budapest this afternoon. So it must be good-bye. . . . Perhaps we shall never meet again, and I shall never have a chance to say what I want to say so badly right now." He brought his horse close to mine. "Give me your hand, Marie." I extended my hand, and as we trotted on, I felt as if something irresistible were drawing me out of the saddle. Finally he released me. *"Kedvesem!"*—darling—was the last word he said to me in his native Hungarian. Then the distance between us increased and I found myself alone, pondering why Elemér had behaved so strangely.

When I entered Aunt Sissy's boudoir that night, I found her alone, as Mrs. von Feyfalik had already attended to her hair. Wearing a magnificent nightdress of purple, she looked beautiful and incredibly young, but there was something else which I noticed, despite the heaviness of my heart: while Auntie sat before her mirror, applying cream to her face, my eyes fell upon her slippers—vivid green in color.

"What are you staring at, Marie?" Aunt Sissy asked, following my gaze. "Oh, my green slippers." She laughed a little, as if to cover up her embarrassment. "Well, well, isn't accident a great aid to gossip?" It sounded sarcastic, but with Aunt Sissy one could only guess whether she was serious or not. "It seems green slippers must have impressed you greatly. Don't tell me that Nicky Esterházy received you"—she giggled a little like a schoolgirl—"in such unconventional attire."

"The Count came out in the garden wearing a long black lounging robe and funny green slippers that did not match at all."

"Just as mine don't match—although I have so many of them. Well, Marie, we crowned heads are, after all, only human. Now and then we act on an impulse." Thoughtful for a moment, Aunt Sissy suddenly adopted a flippant manner. "There are red slippers and blue slippers—why not green ones, too? And Nicky was always partial to that color," she added, as if impelled to do so against her own free will. "Even when he was younger and gayer, he affected green bedroom slippers whether they matched or not." The Empress grew pensive. "Would you believe it, Marie, Nicky was a real Don Juan once upon a time. Yes, he's had many a conquest in his day. There was one especially——" Suddenly she checked herself. "But it's you, Marie, who has a story to tell tonight. Quickly, tell me what happened? What did Elemér have to say to you to-day?"

I broke into tears. "Hardly anything. . . . He just said . . . good-bye," I sobbed.

Aunt Sissy gave me a few minutes to calm down, taking me into her arms and patting my shoulder solicitously. "Poor child, I would have saved you this disappointment, if only Count Andrássy had reported to me a little earlier." Then she explained: "You and Elemér had hardly ridden off when Andrássy came to me, greatly upset. Elemér's mother is still irreconcilable, and it seems she made a horrible scene. That nasty old woman threatened that if her son marries the niece of the King of Hungary—the man who murdered her husband, as she still refers to that terrible Arad trial—she will put a bullet through her head!"

There was a short pause; then Aunt Sissy sadly concluded: "And that's why Elemér must give you up."

So I had actually lost Elemér! I broke down again, sobbing my heart out.

"You poor child," Aunt Sissy tried to console me, "I never imagined that the old Countess would be so stubborn. God knows, I have done everything I can to reconcile the Hungarians with the House of Hapsburg. But somehow it seems that old women are always against me."

Although I was greatly preoccupied with my own grief, I knew that the Empress was alluding once more to the Archduchess Sophie, Kaiser Francis Joseph's mother—a difficult mother-in-law if ever there was one.

Aunt Sissy stroked my head, resting in her lap. Then she put her hand under my chin and, raising my head, she looked straight into my eyes. "Marie, this day has made you much older than your actual years. Let me warn you: there is no man in the whole wide world worth breaking a woman's heart. A man may think himself deeply in love, but he will always find consolation somewhere, somehow. . . . The woman . . . never!"

For days I went about, my mind filled with all the painful details of my short-lived experience with Elemér. Because I was young, I could not resist dramatizing the situation. I looked upon myself as the victim of an unhappy love affair when, in reality, it was only my girlish pride that had suffered. I fairly wallowed in my agony, probably the more so as I noticed that the Empress was sincerely concerned about me. Aunt Sissy finally achieved a cure around Christmas when she broke the news to me that she would hunt in England early in the new year; after first sending me home to Munich for a few weeks, she would take me along to London and Combermere Abbey.

"Shall we see Bay Middleton again?" I asked, studying her secretly. Recently, I had learned to look for "signs." Had I still been so childlike as weeks before, I would hardly have noticed the little flutter that agitated Aunt Sissy's eyelids now.

"Why, yes, Marie, so we shall," was all she said as she kissed me good-night.

During the few weeks at home in Munich, I was officially introduced to King Ludwig II of Bavaria. Of course I frequently had met him before, but only *en famille*. Now, however, I was received in audience. It was the first time that I saw the King in uniform, which made him appear extremely tall and broad-shouldered. At that time there was no indication that, in a short decade, the world would come to know him as the Mad King.

At a court ball, with *tableaux vivants* as a special attraction, I met Prince Herbert von Bismarck for the first time. Although by then I considered myself highly sophisticated, I remained completely oblivious of the fact that, in one of the scenes, the son of the Iron Chancellor had been cast in the rôle of my admirer at the suggestion of Aunt Sissy, and with definite matchmaking intentions on her part. To bring the Prussian Junker and myself together had probably been her only reason for sending me to Munich on a visit. However, I was still thinking too much of Elemér to take any notice of the Bismarck scion.

Meanwhile preparations for my trip to England were completed, and when Aunt Sissy passed through Munich, aboard the imperial special train, I joined her. She was accompanied by her lady-in-waiting Countess Festetics. Count Johann von Larisch acted as her "travel marshal," and he was accompanied by his veritable giant of a son, Heinrich. Mrs. von Feyfalik, two waiting women, and the trusted valet of the Empress completed the retinue.

A brown fog, through which gas lamps blinked feebly, covered London. We put up at the Claridge Hotel. Soon after our arrival there, the two Larisches reported to the Empress for duty. Of "the old Excellency," Count Johann, I had caught only a fleeting glimpse on board the channel steamer, when Count Heinrich had introduced me to his father. Heinie, as Aunt Sissy usually called him, was well over six feet, heavily built, and jovial. In later years I wondered if the Empress had been so gracious to Heinie because he somehow reminded her of Captain Middleton; Heinie, too, had beautiful white teeth he was always ready to display in a broad grin. Count Heinrich was not as much of a courtier as his father, who was the prototype of a suave diplomat of the old school. I knew that Heinie was married to his cousin Yetta Larisch, an older sister of Count George von Larisch. But that was about all I knew of the Larisch family at that particular time.

Heinie turned out to be very companionable, and the morning following our arrival he took me around London. Upon returning to the Hotel Claridge after lunch, I was commanded to appear before the Empress. When I entered her salon, I saw her seated beside a gentleman whom I first mistook for Captain Middleton, as I had been told that he had arrived in London to serve the Empress as her hunting guide. However, when I approached the couple seated before the open fireplace, I was greatly surprised to discover that Aunt Sissy's visitor was not Bay, but a heavy-set middle-aged man with a short beard and a gardenia in his buttonhole. Empress Elizabeth's caller was none other than Edward, Prince of Wales.

The heir to the British throne arose, bowed deeply, and after Aunt Sissy had introduced me as "my niece, Marie," we shook hands. As the Prince smiled at me, I could see that he had a way of taking in a woman at a single glance. He did not stay for dinner that night. Despite the fact that Aunt Sissy referred to him as "a charming fellow," she did not seem too regretful, perhaps because she was expecting

Bay Middleton. With the Hotel Claridge considered a
stronghold of strictest etiquette at that time, it would have
been impossible for the heir to the British crown and a mere
captain in the British army to dine at the same table.

Since there would be no chance of seeing Middleton alone
before dinner, Aunt Sissy called me aside and whispered to
me: "Give my love to Bay as soon as you see him." When
Middleton arrived, I gave him Aunt Sissy's affectionate
greeting. A broad smile appeared on his face, and he
stammered: "Why . . . why . . . thank you ever so much,
little girlie."

Next afternoon we went to Windsor to call on Queen
Victoria. At the station the royal *calèche* awaited us. Only
the Empress's *valet de chambre* had been taken along, but
even he remained in the private car while Aunt Sissy and
I drove up to the castle. We were received by a major-domo
in the amusing uniform of the Scotch Highlanders. No
sooner had we reached the first floor than Aunt Sissy, apparently no stranger in the castle, told me to wait and
stepped into a large room. Through the high open door I
caught just one glimpse of a small, stout lady in black, wearing a little white cap.

I settled down for a good long wait, but very soon the
major-domo reappeared, ushering me into the royal presence. I fought down my excitement, which was the easier
as the old lady smiled in friendly fashion at me, while her
white cap bobbed up and down as she nodded. She extended her hand, which I kissed respectfully. Then Victoria, Queen of England and Empress of India, motioned

me to sit down, inquiring whether I was glad to visit England for the hunting season.

After another gracious nod in my direction, the Queen once more turned back to Aunt Sissy, and while the two Majesties conversed, I noted how greatly the Prince of Wales resembled his mother. The Queen, however, seemed to be much more serious-minded than her son. Her short, thick neck especially attracted my attention. When the two Majesties arose, a few minutes later, I could not help comparing the tall slender Hapsburg Empress with the stout little woman who ruled the British Empire. Victoria gave the impression of being kind and capable, but certainly her appearance was not very "royal."

No sooner were we settled in the *calèche* on our way to the station than Aunt Sissy put her hand on mine and said: "Thank Heaven that's over. Tomorrow we shall go out in the country for a real good time."

On the morrow we arrived at Combermere Abbey, a tremendous castle-like edifice, dark but not too forbidding, covered with ivy and surrounded by an extensive private park of wonderful old trees. It was the typical setting for a Walter Scott story.

Day after day, guests would call, among the first of them the Prince of Wales. As the heir to the British crown was to dine with us that night, it was necessary to postpone the dinner for a later hour than usual—a change of schedule which upset Aunt Sissy considerably, as she disliked to eat late. She believed that such a meal threatened her lovely, slender figure.

Aunt Sissy instructed me shortly before Edward arrived:
While the Prince visited her on the first floor, I was to remain in the lower hall until I heard her call me. To pass
the time, she gave me, very suitably, Walter Scott's *Ivanhoe*
to read.

"Remember, when I call you, Marie, I want you to come
immediately." As I was never in the habit of keeping my
imperial aunt waiting, her strict injunction surprised me.
However, as always, Aunt Sissy had her own reasons for
this.

Promptly the Prince of Wales arrived and ascended the
stairs rather asthmatically. The old Count Larisch accompanied the royal visitor as far as the door to the Empress's
suite. While I thumbed the pages of the Scott novel, I heard,
from time to time, the soft laughter so typical of Aunt Sissy.
Suddenly she called me. In all haste I dropped my book and
rushed upstairs. There stood the Empress, at the head of the
staircase, pressing her handkerchief to her mouth as she
was wont to do when trying to stifle her laughter. Halfway up the stairs I met the Prince of Wales, who stopped
for just a second to say a friendly word. However, His
Royal Highness seemed extremely preoccupied.

As soon as the door was shut after Edward by a flunkey,
Aunt Sissy broke out into unrestrained laughter. Tears of
mirth coursed down her cheeks.

"No, no, Marie, don't ask me. I couldn't tell you—and
if I could, you wouldn't understand, anyway."

I had my own theory. Most likely, the Prince of Wales
had told the Empress a funny story of the kind he used
to pick up on his frequent trips to Paris. No doubt, Aunt

Sissy had felt called upon to pretend that she was shocked. Yes, that would account for the Prince's manner at leaving.

It was not until Aunt Sissy dictated her poems to me, some years later, that I found the key to this scene in two stanzas, each with an English refrain, entitled:

MEMORIES OF LONDON

We sat together, Prince Edward and I,
In cozy tête-à-tête;
He made such ardent love to me:
"Elizabeth, it's fate!
My dear, what do you say?" he urged—
This man of great affairs;
I drew away and murmured then:
"There's somebody coming upstairs."

We paused . . . but all was still, and so
He resumed his amorous quest;
His boldness was amusing, for
'Twas more than a regal jest!
"My dear, what do you say?" I mocked;
It took him unawares. . . .
In turn, he blushed and rose to say:
"There's somebody coming upstairs."

The "somebody," of course, was I; that the Empress had instructed me, in advance, to await her signal of distress proved that she knew Edward, the man, very well.

At dinner that night Aunt Sissy, looking more beautiful than I ever had seen her before, cast mischievous glances

first at the Prince of Wales and then at Captain Middleton.
Here, at Combermere Abbey, the code of strict etiquette
was relaxed so that it was possible for the heir to the British
crown and a mere captain in his army to dine at the same
table. I had been placed between Count Heinie and Bay,
and I 'remembered how both of them, in the course of the
evening, repeatedly asked me whether I could account for
Aunt Sissy's extraordinary gayety.

"Oh, I suppose His Royal Highness told Her Majesty an
amusing joke," I finally ventured.

"Aha," exclaimed Count Heinie with a smile.

"So—that's it?" Captain Middleton muttered.

During our stay at Combermere Abbey, Bay Middleton
was the Empress's constant companion. Unless there were
visitors, he was commanded to come to her suite almost
every afternoon. "We discuss horses and the like, and we
mustn't be disturbed," Aunt Sissy explained these visits to
me.

All too soon those wonderful days at Combermere Abbey
were drawing to an end. About a week before our leavetaking, Aunt Sissy, as if on the spur of the moment, proposed a little trip incognito to London "just for one day."
She said that she had heard about a new cosmetician and
that she would like to see what this woman had to offer in
creams and lotions.

Her trusted *valet de chambre* was sent ahead to reserve a
small apartment at the Hotel Claridge with the instruction
that the Empress was coming to London incognito and that
no word must leak out in the press. I was overjoyed when

Aunt Sissy told me that Count Heinie and I were to go along. For baggage, we were not to take more than a suit-case each. The whole trip would be in the nature of an "excursion," and the only servants at our disposal would be one of the waiting women and the *valet de chambre* who had preceded us to London.

Without arousing any undesirable attention, we arrived at the Hotel Claridge early in the afternoon. As soon as we had changed into fresh clothes, two hansom cabs were ordered for us. The Empress and I climbed into the first, while Count Heinie followed us in the second in lonely splendor. Soon, however, we paused before a modest hotel; a tall man in a light overcoat rushed out and joined Count Heinie.

The Empress noticed how I took in the incident and smiled in amusement. "Well, Marie, there are all sorts of surprises in store for you today. First, we are going to the Crystal Palace to see the vaudeville show."

"But, Aunt Sissy, I thought we were to look up that cosmetician?"

"Oh, forget it, Marie. You know I never use any of those commercial preparations."

By that time I had learned not to shake my head, otherwise I would have done so then. Had not Aunt Sissy expressly come to London to consult that cosmetician? . . . and yet now she was not in the least interested. I was still puzzling over the turn of affairs when our cab stopped in front of the Crystal Palace and Count Heinie assisted us to alight. Behind him, as if appearing by magic, stood Captain Middleton. In a daze I watched Aunt Sissy take Bay's arm

while Count Heinie offered his arm to me and we followed
them. I noticed that the Empress had pulled down her veil
when she turned to us and remarked that we easily might
become separated in the crowd. It would, perhaps, be a good
idea if each couple would go their own way, later meeting at a bar which Heinie and Middleton seemed to know
very well. No sooner were these arrangements made than
the Empress and Middleton disappeared from our view.

My face must have betrayed some anxiety for Aunt Sissy,
because Heinie turned towards me and said: "You know,
Baroness Marie, you are really very, very young yet."

His words sounded entirely too condescending to my ears,
and I stiffly retorted: "I beg your pardon, Count, but I shall
be seventeen in a few months."

"What a ripe old age!" my huge escort exclaimed mock-
ingly.

Throughout the performance I tried to discover Aunt
Sissy and Captain Middleton somewhere in the audience,
but I could not locate them. To add to my uneasiness, when
we reached the appointed meeting place after the performance, Aunt Sissy and Captain Middleton had not yet
arrived.

"I wonder what happened," I murmured nervously.

For answer, Count Heinie shot another such indulgent
glance at me as before; then, to relieve me of my obvious
anxiety, he started to tell me amusing anecdotes, and he told
them very well indeed. Nevertheless I could not help consulting my watch now and then, and in my mind I began
to formulate some course of action should the Empress of
Austria-Hungary actually be lost in London.

Count Heinie remained unperturbed. He emptied a full beaker of ale while I sipped at a tiny glass of *crème de menthe.*

At last the door opened, and Aunt Sissy and her escort came toward us. The Empress did not seem tired at all. She was in the best humor, and without sitting down she proposed: "Let's go somewhere for a bite." Under no circumstances would she return to the hotel "so early."

I was aghast. This certainly didn't sound like Aunt Sissy, who was usually so very careful to keep sensible hours.

Count Heinie, with a deep bow, suggested in a half-whisper: "Would Your Majesty graciously accept my invitation for a little supper?"

His boldness startled me. I expected a frown from Aunt Sissy, but, to my great surprise, her face was wreathed in smiles as she accepted. Heinie explained that he would take us to a very exclusive little restaurant where the Empress could depend upon remaining incognito.

"Very well, let's be off," agreed the Empress. "Suppose they take us for cocottes, Marie? But that shouldn't worry us on a night like this, now should it?"

I was dumfounded. Aunt Sissy seemed an utterly changed person; true, she was still imperial, but somehow she seemed so human.

The greatest surprise was still in store for me. A few hansom cabs were parked outside. Without hesitating a second, Aunt Sissy stepped into the first, followed by Middleton. She closed the low doors and smiled at Heinie and me mischievously. I was so startled that my escort literally had to lift me into the cab, all smiles at my helplessness. Heinie

talked incessantly, repeating time and again that the poor
Empress was certainly entitled to a little freedom occasionally—a taste of that freedom which other mortals enjoyed
every blessed day of their lives. "Being an Empress does
not mean that she shouldn't have her fling for once," he
wound up.

It dawned upon me that Aunt Sissy was certainly having
hers tonight and making the most of her rare moments of
liberty. At the restaurant she, who never dined late at night,
consumed one caviar canapé after another with great gusto.
She even went so far as to drink champagne with it. When
fried chicken was served, the Empress helped herself to a
larger portion than I had ever seen on her plate before, par-
taking of more champagne with the poultry. Finally the
Captain arose and took his leave.

It was in the so-called wee hours of the morn when Aunt
Sissy and I arrived at the hotel, followed in a second hansom cab by Count Heinie, riding in lonely splendor once
more.

The next morning, driving to the station, the Empress
asked me: "Well, Marie, what kind of a time did you
have?"

"Simply great, Auntie, only there were so many surprises
they almost took my breath away. I must have acted rather
stupidly."

"Well, you'll learn, Marie, you'll learn," Aunt Sissy said,
throwing me a glance full of meaning. "You know, once in
a while I like to go my own way, without dragging a whole
trail of pompous chamberlains and liveried lackeys behind
me. And our running into Bay Middleton—that certainly

was funny, wasn't it? If some people would only know of it, my, wouldn't gossip unhinge their jaws!" Aunt Sissy expressed herself colorfully in the Viennese vernacular. She threw her arm around me and hugged me for a second: "It was wonderful, Marie, simply wonderful!"

One last surprise awaited me. When we returned to Combermere Abbey, none other than Captain Middleton stood at the front gate. Later Count Heinie told me—probably so that I should not make a *faux pas*—that Bay supposedly had visited somewhere in the neighborhood the day before and had returned on the night train. There was a merry twinkle in his eyes as he imparted this information.

Our trunks were packed for a short stay in London before our return home. For the last dinner at Combermere Abbey, the Empress donned a simple lilac-colored crêpe-de-Chine gown in which she looked ravishing. When coffee was served, Aunt Sissy asked me to sing a few songs, among them "The Last Rose of Summer."

Aunt Sissy, who sat between Middleton and Count Johann von Larisch, arose after a few moments, and with only a nod to all of us she rushed from the music salon. As usual I followed her to the staircase to kiss her good-night, but, contrary to custom, she beckoned to me to follow her upstairs. Once in her room, the Empress broke into wild weeping, oblivious of the presence of her waiting woman. I indicated to the servant to leave us alone and drew Aunt Sissy to me in a tender embrace. It was my turn now to play comforter. She shook with sobs, and was far more unstrung than months ago when Bay had left Gödöllö.

Gradually the Empress regained some of her composure. Reclining upon a chaise-longue, still crying softly, her voice was so stifled with tears as to be almost inaudible. "Tomorrow, everything will be over . . . back into captivity again . . . into that terrible monotony of a prison existence. . . . Here, at least, I am not watched all the time. Nobody spies on me. The servants are trained to see nothing. . . . Why, oh, why can't I break my neck? Why can't I dash in my skull so I may have peace at last?" Again she broke out into hysterical sobs.

I racked my brains how I might best console her. Being with Auntie day and night, I had come to understand what she meant by The Curse of the Crown. She simply craved little human interludes from time to time. They were like mileposts on her life's journey, encouraging her to continue along the thorny road of royalty.

"But, Aunt Sissy," I finally ventured, "remember that Valerie will be so happy to have you home again."

Intuitively I had hit upon the right thing.

"Ah, yes, my darling," she murmured, jerking into an upright position; she swallowed hard a few times and then dried her tears. "Valerie will be so happy . . . she is all I have. . . . I have nothing . . . nothing else in this world."

Then she changed completely. Anxiously she glanced in the mirror. "Heavens, I've cried myself into a red nose, and look at the hour! You, too, should have been in bed long ago. Don't forget, tomorrow will be a very strenuous day."

The next day we were to leave early in the afternoon. Luncheon was to be served, as usual, promptly at noon. At

eleven o'clock Captain Middleton was formally conducted
to the upper hall to take leave of Her Majesty because he
would not accompany us to London. However, when I came
downstairs for luncheon at five minutes of twelve, I found
Count Heinie pacing back and forth nervously. So far there
had not been the slightest sign that luncheon would be
served on schedule.

"What shall I do if Middleton doesn't come down on
time?" he whispered to me.

His evident agitation surprised me, for he was invariably
complacent. "Go upstairs and fetch him," I advised.

Count Heinie shook his head. "No, I can't do that," he
demurred. "Couldn't you go up?"

"Certainly not. Aunt Sissy gave me no such orders."

Heinie resumed his nervous pacing while the footmen
and waiters stood at their posts like so many statues. "I don't
know what to do, I don't know what to do," he mumbled,
consulting his watch again and again. Suddenly he straightened up and walked out of the room. I looked after him.
I certainly did not envy him his ticklish job. Recalling the
scene of the night before, I feared that Aunt Sissy would
take her last tête-à-tête with Bay very much to heart.

Casually I flipped pages of a magazine to hide my dread.
At last Heinie came downstairs again, Middleton trailing
behind him. I looked at the Captain, and although, at first,
I felt like laughing, my throat suddenly contracted. Poor
Bay was the very picture of utter woe. To all appearances
he had cried. His usually proud bearing had given way to
one of utter dejection. Bay seemed a broken man. The

change in him was so obvious that I carefully looked around to see whether anybody else had observed it. But the well-trained servants never seemed to see anything amiss.

Another half-hour passed before the Empress's *valet de chambre* came to announce that Her Majesty would not appear for luncheon. Aunt Sissy only joined us when the carriages were already before the door to take us to the station. She stepped into the hall, every inch an empress, addressing a few friendly words to the major-domo and graciously nodding to the rest of the servants lined up in front of the gate.

In the carriage, she turned to me and, with a deep sigh, remarked: "Play-acting, my dear child, is the sad lot of those who wear a crown."

At the station in London the Austro-Hungarian ambassador came to pay his respects. Everything was very formal. In Calais, after a smooth crossing, the Empress kissed me good-bye. While I was proceeding to Munich, she was off for Amsterdam to undergo one of her occasional mysterious cures—this time a massage treatment—and we would not meet again before the summer at Feldafing.

Back in Munich, I soon discovered that while there were still plans under way to marry me off, Prince Herbert von Bismarck was no longer considered "eligible." The reason for his elimination was the strong objection on the part of King Ludwig II, who, as the head of the royal family, meanwhile had been consulted. His Majesty was firmly opposed to any member of his family marrying the son of the Iron Chancellor, an objection that sprung from the old

Wittelsbach-Hohenzollern jealousy. Through the political astuteness of Prince Bismarck, during the Franco-Prussian war, the royal Bavarian house had lost out against the Berliners. King Wilhelm of Prussia had been proclaimed German Emperor at Versailles and not King Ludwig, as the southern states had hoped.

I was told that when my father, at the suggestion of Empress Elizabeth, mentioned Prince Herbert as a possible candidate for my hand, King Ludwig thundered: "I would rather see your daughter dead than married to a Bismarck." The unfortunate King, a few years later—alas, much too late!—was to appeal to the Iron Chancellor to save him from his so-called friends.

No sooner had their latest scheme fallen through than Tante Königin—Aunt Maria—erstwhile Queen of Naples and the Two Sicilies, invited me to visit her in Paris for a few weeks. I was overjoyed. I knew that she had a very tender spot for me, perhaps because I looked very much like her. Always she called me her "little girl," even in later years when I had children of my own. Her voice, whenever she spoke to me, seemed to take on a special note that never failed to touch me deeply. As a child, I instinctively felt Tante Königin's attachment for me. Of all my crowned and uncrowned aunts, I felt the most strongly drawn to Aunt Maria, even more so than to Aunt Sissy. I loved Aunt Maria as dearly as I loved my mother. For me she was restfulness personified. Contrary to her sister Elizabeth, who was much more vivacious, sarcastic, and witty, Queen Maria was invariably even-tempered. Her dark, soulful eyes never failed to make a deep impression upon me, especially after I heard the story responsible for their sorrowful expression. Not only had Queen Maria been forced to enact the part of the Heroine of Gaëta during the harrowing days when her husband lost his throne to the newly united Italy; destiny decreed, also, that she play the leading rôle in a love tragedy. While the first part of the drama had been written in the pages of history, the second part has remained untold until now.

Aunt Maria was the last "picture bride" of royal blood. Never since she was sacrificed on the altar of dynastic considerations has another princess been married off in so absurd a fashion.

It was in fall, 1858, that discreet inquiries were made by King Ferdinand II and Queen Maria Christina of Savoy, to ascertain whether Duke and Duchess Maximilian of Bavaria were prepared to give their daughter Maria in marriage to Francis, Duke of Calabria, Crown Prince of Naples and the Two Sicilies. Both royal families scarcely knew each other personally; the young people had never even met. Nevertheless my grandparents answered with an unconditional yes, because the Crown Prince was considered a very desirable match. On his paternal side, Francis was a Bourbon; on his mother's side, he was related to the Sardinian royal house. Most important of all, he was the heir apparent to an old and honored kingdom, constituting a considerable part of beautiful Italy.

Aunt Maria was never consulted in the matter, merely told, and no sooner had word of her "assent" reached Naples than Count Ludolff, trusted minister of King Ferdinand II, appeared in Munich to tender the official proposal of marriage. He was received by my grandfather with great ceremony. The Count presented to the then eighteen-year-old Princess, on a purple velvet cushion, a miniature of her future husband, five years her senior. The picture showed the Duke of Calabria in the smart uniform of the Hussars of the Guard, looking extremely impressive. My Aunt Maria never conceived the idea that she should be asked; she was satisfied that her parents knew what was best for her; moreover, her future husband was, to all appearances, a very fetching young officer.

Early in 1859 my aunt and her unseen betrothed were married by substitutes, as was then the custom for royal unions in the Bourbon family. Maria, Duchess of Bavaria, thus became the picture bride of Francis Maria Leopold, Duke of Calabria and Crown Prince of Naples and the Two Sicilies. King Maximilian of Bavaria and the Queen led the bride to the altar, with the King's brother substituting for the absentee groom. Five days later Aunt Maria left for Naples, accompanied by her brother Ludwig and some gentlemen and ladies-in-waiting.

At that time the liberation movement in Italy had developed to the extent where it was quickly approaching its ultimate consummation. When Ferdinand II died in May, 1859, the Crown Prince clung precariously to the royal scepter for another eighteen months. He had to leave his country when Garibaldi's "red shirts" advanced on the capital. The royal pair fled to Gaëta, but it proved impossible to hold the fortress. In the heat of the bloody battle Aunt Maria rushed on errands of mercy through the rain of bullets and grapeshot, from casualty to casualty, thus earning the epi-

thet of Heroine of Gaëta. After the fortress finally capitu-
lated on February 13, 1861, the royal pair found a sanctuary
under the protection of Pope Pius IX.

What did it profit Aunt Maria that German princesses,
expressing their appreciation of her striking heroism, sent
her a laurel wreath of pure gold? Not only was she now a
queen without a throne; she was also a woman without love.
While the strain of the great historical drama in which she
had played such an important part had lasted, she was
spared the full force of the artificiality of her marriage to
the King. But when all the excitement subsided, she discovered the appalling emptiness of her life. Only then she
awoke to the realization that Francis II was by far not the
good-looking, dashing officer the miniature had made him
out to be. Besides, the defense of his throne, during the last
two years, had left the King little time for honeymooning.
After he had been deposed, he became sickly and morose.
While Aunt Maria was still longing for romance, Francis's attention was completely absorbed by political intrigues aiming at the restoration of his rule.

At this difficult juncture in their marital relations, the
young woman of twenty-one fled into the arms of a fascinating Belgian officer. Later Aunt Maria left the King to
return to her native Bavaria, presumably suffering from
some pulmonary ailment. In reality she retired to the Ursu-
lines' convent in Augsburg to give birth to a love child,
Daisy. But before tongues could be set wagging outside intimate court circles, a reconciliation between the Queen and
the King was effected.

Now, in spring, 1877, when I journeyed to Paris to visit

Aunt Maria and Uncle Francis, sixteen years had passed since that interlude. The deposed royal couple meanwhile had grown to regard each other with a kindly, if somewhat resigned, tolerance. When I arrived in Paris, chaperoned by Mademoiselle Bertha, I did not expect Aunt Maria and the King to meet me, as it was very late at night. Nevertheless the royal couple awaited me at the station. Uncle Francis was extremely friendly, and Aunt Maria her usual beloved self. I felt immediately at home as we drove up to an old-fashioned but cozy dwelling; its very simplicity was impressive. Despite the late hour, a *souper* was served, and I could see how time had healed old wounds. Aunt and Uncle had grown very much attached to each other, after almost two decades of married life. Always ailing, the ex-King was on a very strict diet, and every bite of food he consumed was watched by Aunt Maria. If ever Uncle Francis ordered a dish not on his diet list, the ex-Queen, like any good wife, would admonish him, putting her hand on his arm: *"Assez, cher ami! je t'en prie!"* And the King would desist, a bit regretfully—like any other husband. After all the curious young girl's ideas I had entertained about these two, this little domestic scene touched me greatly.

The very first day of my Paris sojourn, Aunt Maria took me on a long drive into one of Paris's beautiful suburbs. There, in a comfortable cottage, I made the acquaintance of Daisy, a girl of my own age. Standing before a mirror, trying on each other's cloaks and hats, as young girls will do, we were both struck by the fact that we looked a good deal alike. To such a great extent did family resemblance manifest itself in us that we easily could be taken for sisters. To be sure, while I was robust, Daisy seemed extraordinarily frail—a quality which rendered her loveliness the more appealing. I felt drawn to her irresistibly from the first moment I met her—much more than I expected, considering the girl was, after all, only a cousin.

Daisy proudly showed me a painting, depicting a dashing young officer. Remembering that my aunt had been a refugee in the Ecclesiastical States, I recognized the colorful uniform as that of a captain of the papal zouaves. *"C'est mon père!"* Daisy explained to me. I did not dare to question her, for I did not know how much or how little I was supposed to know of her origin, especially as Aunt Maria, when speaking of Daisy to me, always alluded to her as "a sweet young girl friend of mine." Whether Daisy knew the ex-Queen was her mother, I am not at all certain; she always addressed her as *"Ma chérie."* Later, I grew bold enough to ask Auntie for Daisy's full name. The ex-Queen explained calmly: "Her father was Count de Lavaÿss, member of an old Belgian family."

And then we talked about something else. . . .

I had come to Paris unaware of any marriage plans on the part of my royal relatives. As a matter of fact, even when Tante Königin took me to the best *modistes* and most expensive *couturières,* I thought that all these preparations were for the approaching races, to which Uncle Francis always referred as "that great exhibition of horses and women." However, at the very last minute, Aunt Maria admitted to me that she was not only dressing me up for the races, but also to make the best possible impression on the young Duke of Norfolk whom I would meet. To marry me off to the secular head of the English Catholics was the pet idea of King Francis II. Without saying it in so many words, he nevertheless made it very clear to me that the Duke of Norfolk would be a brilliant match.

"Why these incessant plans?" I pleaded.

Aunt Maria shrugged her shoulders. "Of course, Aunt Sissy would be so glad to see you married,"—and after a little pause she added: ". . . happily, I mean."

"Don't I know it?" I came back bitterly. Then and there I determined that the man of the Empress's choice must be my choice also.

Softly Aunt Maria explained to me that in case I should find myself interested in the young Duke, she and Uncle Francis would take me to London for the "season." However, if these new marriage plans should come to naught, I would return to Munich and join Aunt Sissy at Feldafing later.

On our way to the race track where I was to meet the Duke of Norfolk, Uncle Francis made it a special point to inform me that the English nobleman was the possessor of the precious necklace of Mary Stuart, Queen of Scots. I did not dare to show it openly, but by now I was actually amused by all these frantic machinations, watching them with an air of detachment amounting to indifference.

The Duke turned out to be a rather nice young chap. Apparently he had neither a clear idea of who I was nor did he, in any way, know of the plans in which he played so prominent a part. We shook hands . . . and that was the end of it.

If, on that day, I could have looked into the future, I would have thanked Aunt Maria and Uncle Francis on bended knees for troubling to introduce me to the Duke of Norfolk. I would have made myself as agreeable as possible to become his duchess. But foolishly I snubbed the rather pleasant young man, and instead of becoming the protected chatelaine of stately Arundel, I inadvertently took a hand in steering myself towards the cliffs of matrimonial disaster.

Instead of the necklace of Mary, Queen of Scots, I was to wear a crown of thorns.

Chapter Three

THE COMMAND TO MARRY

$\mathcal{I}$T WAS summer, 1877, and once more I was back in Feldafing on Starnberger Lake in the Bavarian Alps, near Munich. Upon my arrival I was happy to hear that, for the next few weeks, I would be the only steady companion of my imperial aunt. Bent upon making her sojourn there as *gemütlich* as possible, the Empress never permitted more than an actually necessary retinue to accompany her to the mountains. Her only lady-in-waiting had just been sent on a vacation, and so it was I who walked with her every morning before breakfast. Sunshine or shower, we would start on a strenuous hike promptly at seven o'clock, returning in time for the *petit déjeuner* which was served at ten. The Empress was convinced that only these walks, and her canters in the afternoon, made it possible for a woman of forty, and the mother of four children, to preserve her remarkably youthful figure. A few years later, Aunt Sissy gave up breakfasting altogether and submitted to various strict diets, all in the name of vanity.

My paternal grandmother, Duchess Ludovica of Bavaria, was a steady breakfast guest at Feldafing. From the near-by Castle Possenhofen, the old lady would come to visit her imperial daughter, accompanied by her trusted chamberlain, Baron von Wulffen. Weather permitting, the top of the vehicle was let down; in the back of the carriage sat the old Duchess, surrounded by four or five very frisky dogs. Opposite her, on the narrow front seat, almost completely buried under a rich assortment of umbrellas, reticules, and woolen shawls, rode the Baron. Every morning it was my task to run downstairs and lead Grandma to the table where Aunt Sissy breakfasted, her wonderful chestnut hair cascading gracefully over her shoulders.

Towards evening, when a cool breeze blew down from the near-by glaciers, the Empress and I would go for a short canter, our usual goal being a little lake, romantically surrounded by tall, dark green hemlock trees. On these excursions Auntie usually wore one of her black-and-white riding habits, which more than once made the Emperor remark dryly: "Sissy, you look exactly like a zebra in that outfit."

While Grandma's visit was a daily routine, the call paid the Empress by her royal cousin, King Ludwig II of Bavaria, was an event extraordinary. Not only because the King hardly ever visited anybody, but because of the stage setting which surrounded his call. Known to history for his love of luxury and pageantry, the King arrived in an enormous, highly ornamented *calèche,* drawn by four milk-white steeds and preceded by an outrider. I watched the splendid procession from a window. The horses were wrapped in a

cloud of foam when the carriage stopped in front of the
mansion. The King had insisted upon driving up the steep
mountainside at top speed. Without lifting his slouch hat,
just nodding curtly, he stepped from the carriage into the
house.

That day I caught only one more glimpse of Ludwig II,
when he left about two hours later. Settling himself in the
rear seat of his carriage, he gazed up at the balcony where
the Empress stood and doffed his hat with inimitable *gran-
dezza.*

Two days later Aunt Sissy commanded me to accompany her to Castle Berg. There was no need to dress for the
occasion, as I would wait for the Empress in the beautiful
park surrounding the château. I therefore wore a riding
habit and was mortified when a lackey appeared to usher
me into the royal presence. Not only was I unsuitably
clothed but, to make matters worse, I had accumulated
practically all the dust on the road.

My heart pounded furiously as I followed the lackey into
a drawing room. However, no sooner had I put my foot on
the mirror-like waxed floor than all my fears fled. I struggled
to control myself from bursting into wild laughter, for
there was His Majesty, ensconced in a wide armchair, his
face almost entirely covered by poultices. "He's got a terrible toothache, poor man," Aunt Sissy whispered. Under the
stern glance which accompanied this information, I quickly
lost all inclination for hilarity.

The King stretched out his hand; but when I tried to
kiss it, as etiquette demanded, he would not let me. He
mumbled something, but what it was I shall never know,

because of the yards upon yards of bandage which framed his face. Then, with a gracious nod, he pointed to the piano.

"You are to sing for His Majesty, Marie," the Empress advised me. I was simply stunned. Not only had I neglected to practise for days, but my throat was parched from the dust of the trip. If Aunt Sissy guessed my confusion, she preferred to ignore it. Instead, she continued: "His Majesty wants you especially to sing the part of Elsa in *Lohengrin.*"

I certainly admired Wagner, then at the beginning of his glorious ascent, in which Ludwig II acted as patron saint. That day, however, I wished the Great Richard had never been born, or at least had never caught the fancy of Bavaria's ruler. However, not one but two majesties had made their wishes plain to me—so I merely curtsied in acknowledgment of the command and stumbled over to the piano. I whispered to a lackey to bring me a glass of water and a few lumps of sugar, meanwhile fetching the *Lohengrin* music from a near-by table. I fervently prayed that the rumor prove correct that the King, despite his admiration for Wagner, was no real connoisseur in matters musical. I knew this to be true in the case of the Empress who, contradictory statements notwithstanding, was neither musically gifted nor did she ever touch a piano.

When, looking back now, I once more conjure up that distant day at Castle Berg, I still wonder how I ever succeeded in singing one aria after another in response to the enthusiastic applause of the King and his imperial guest. King Ludwig was so pleased with such musical treats as I had been able to offer that, upon leaving, he requested Aunt Sissy to bring me along again on her next visit to the château.

King Ludwig II *of Bavaria and his then fiancée*, Duchess Sophie *of Bavaria*.

Duke Ludwig of Bavaria, *father of Countess Larisch and brother of Empress Elizabeth—Gödöllö, 1876.*

When a week or so later the time came for a second audition in the royal presence, we drove up to Castle Berg in a ceremonial carriage. I accompanied the Empress without undue nervousness because, meanwhile, I had assiduously rehearsed a number of arias and *Lieder*. The King himself had seen to it that a glass of water and a few lumps of sugar were placed on the grand piano. He was very friendly and complimentary that day, listening to the whole program I had prepared and even requesting encores. Ludwig II seemed to be in one of his rare bright moods; his usually furrowed brow was almost serene. Not disfigured by poultices as on our last visit, His Majesty looked extremely impressive when he accompanied us to the door. He was a tall, good-looking man of proud bearing—altogether majestic in appearance. When he stood next to Aunt Sissy, the thought suddenly struck me: What a wonderful couple the two would make! At that moment the King turned to the Empress, and for the first and only time in my many years of association with Aunt Sissy, I heard her addressed by her full first name. "Good-bye, Elizabeth," Ludwig II of Bavaria said, bending over her hand.

I took in the scene wonderingly; doubtless my surprise was plain, for I felt Aunt Sissy's eyes upon me. On the way back in the carriage she put her hand on my arm and, with an emphasis the occasion did not seem to call for, she said: "Let me assure you, Marie, that there is one thing which will stand you in good stead in every situation, and that is to keep your mouth tightly closed. Silence is golden—an art that too few practise. Always bear that in mind, Marie!"

I was to hear this warning repeated so often that it finally became the very gospel of my life. Alas, twelve years later, this very dictum of my aunt's gave my life a cruel, never-to-be-healed twist.

A few minutes later, Aunt Sissy once more turned to me and said: "By the way, Marie, there's something I must tell you." The Empress hesitated just long enough for my heart to skip a beat, then went on, an imperious note in her voice: "If you wish to remain with me, Marie, it will be absolutely necessary for you to marry. As a single young girl, you may occasionally find yourself in an awkward situation. Moreover, unmarried as you are, you are not the proper chaperon for me. Of course, this makes little difference out here or in Gödöllö, but you know etiquette is much more exacting in Vienna. Only as a married woman would you be entirely satisfactory there."

Without awaiting a reply, Aunt Sissy proceeded: "I have taken the matter up with your father. Around the beginning of September, before your parents arrive at Gödöllö, I shall send you, together with the Countess Festetics, for a short visit to the Larisches in Silesia."

To remain silent was my only course, not that I was speechless with surprise, but because Aunt Sissy, as if to have it over with, continued to talk rapidly. She explained that a *mariage de convenance* was to be arranged between myself and George Larisch, cousin and brother-in-law of Count Heinie. The Empress considered the scheme a "brilliant idea." Although she spoke kindly enough, I realized that her words were an unmistakable command. As our horses trotted on, the even clatter of their hoofs sounded in my ears like the inexorable beat of Time.

Once more, then, I was to be "thrown on the marriage market."

I never opened my mouth until we reached Feldafing and, to all appearances, Aunt Sissy did not expect me to, either. Locking myself in my room, I slumped into a chair in a veritable daze. It struck me as ironical that Aunt Sissy should be the one to forge somebody else's marital fate. She certainly had married, not only according to her own choice, but actually against the wishes of her parents and the young Emperor's mother. The latter had decided that not she, but her older sister Helen, should wear the double crown of the Empress-Queen of Austria and Hungary.

Archduchess Sophie, mother of the young Kaiser, and sister of my own grandmother, was a somewhat over-energetic lady. It was her boast, and not an idle one either, that she was not only able to make up her own mind, but anybody else's as well. Thus she simply decided that Francis Joseph I was to marry Princess Helen. Then, as soon as the implicit agreement of the royal Wittelsbachs had been secured, she went blithely ahead and prepared the engagement of the young Emperor to Helen down to the smallest detail. Archduchess Sophie even went so far as to order the trousseau for the Empress-elect before the youthful Kaiser had been given a chance to speak to the girl. In Vienna the official announcement to be published in the *Wiener Zeitung* was already in type. All that remained was to arrange a supper for the young Emperor at Ischl, with members of both families present. There, Archduchess Sophie would announce the engagement of the Emperor to Princess Helen.

Everything had been considered carefully, even the fact that Princess Elizabeth was an irrepressible child; at that time, she was sixteen, three years younger than Helen. She had been entrusted to the care of a governess and was to remain in an adjacent room, so as not to disturb the engagement formalities by some precocious remark.

Princess Elizabeth felt highly indignant over this segregation from the rest of the family and did not hesitate to express her feelings very volubly and loudly. She protested emphatically against such treatment, her argument with the governess finally becoming so noticeable that the young Emperor rose from the table and strode into the adjacent room just to have a look at this girl who was disturbing the ceremonial peace. That impulse bore amazing consequences, for no sooner had the Emperor seen Princess Elizabeth than he decided he would not marry Helen.

There was quite some explaining to be done in Vienna during the next few days. The engagement announcement of the Emperor to Princess Helen, which meanwhile had been published in the *Wiener Zeitung,* had to be corrected and the lame excuse offered that, unfortunately, the imperial master of ceremonies had committed a deplorable blunder.

Incidentally, Helen, after being so suddenly jilted by the young Emperor, married the enormously rich heir presumptive, Maximilian von Thurn and Taxis, four years later, in 1858. As a mediatized princess, Aunt Helen certainly was much happier in her marriage than Aunt Sissy, wearing the crown of St. Stephen.

Just because the Empress knew the meaning of an unhappy marriage, it puzzled me that she should be so bent upon prescribing my marital fate for me. However, I consoled myself with the hope that Aunt Sissy's latest attempt at matchmaking would prove abortive once again. After all, it might be rather amusing to visit the Larisches; certainly, it would do me no harm to take a look at Aunt Sissy's "hand-picked" candidate.

The closer the date of departure for Silesia came, the more impatient I grew. By then I was actually looking forward, with great anticipation, to a few enjoyable weeks with the companionable Count Heinie; that his cousin George was my prospective fiancé did not disturb me very much. It would be simple enough; I need only treat him coolly.

Aunt Sissy, however, mistook my calm assurance for meek resignation. "It's always a good thing to swallow what you must eat anyhow," she approved, patting me maternally.

Accompanied by Countess Festetics and my maid Sophie, we arrived at Castle Solza early in September, 1877. The neighborhood was none too inviting, consisting mostly of coal mines, practically all of which were owned by the Larisches. At the castle I met Heinie's wife, Countess Yetta, looking like a mere slip of a girl and not at all like the mother of the three pretty children who trundled after her. The same evening I was escorted to Castle Freistadt, a few miles distant, where Heinie's father, the old Count Johann von Larisch, resided. I had met him on our trip to England, but I had never seen the old Countess before. Heinie's mother made a rather straitlaced impression at first, but I soon found out that she was only so unbending outwardly. There were also the young Countesses Francesca, nicknamed "Finschy," a sister of Heinie and almost as tall as her brother, and her cousin Marie, called "Mizzi," George Larisch's sister.

This young man who, by imperial command, was to play such an important part in my life, I had not yet seen. However, he arrived the next morning, looking even younger than his twenty-two years. He was small of stature, somewhat resembling his sister Yetta, although his profile was not as finely chiseled. His outstanding feature was his large mouth, which should have served as a warning to me.

The young man exchanged a few words of greeting with me—we both managed to appear at ease, although we knew why this meeting had been arranged—then he bowed politely and repaired to his uncle's study. Presently a stentorian voice was heard from that direction.

"Oh, that's Georgie shouting his head off," his sister Mizzi remarked. "Georgie always does that. No doubt Uncle has been scolding him."

"He certainly has a voice like the trumpets of Jericho," her cousin Finschy drawled. "And that's the very thing that Father can't stand. If he would only talk quietly, he would find that Father is the nicest fellow in the world, and that he could get anything he wants from him."

There was some more talk between the two girls, from which I gathered that George—or as they called him, "Georgie," with the last syllable long drawn out—was an unhappy sort of chap, generally considered "difficult" to handle. As his father had died while he was still a boy, the old Count Johann had been appointed his guardian. It seems the uncle was limiting his nephew, at that time a lieutenant in a regiment of the Imperial Guards, to a small allowance —a fact which invariably led to "scenes" as soon as George put in his appearance.

Not only George, but all the members of the Larisch family, seemed well aware of the reason for my visit. Early the next day Countess Yetta arranged for her brother George and myself to take a carriage ride together. As the young man proved rather stiff and silent, it was up to me to make conversation. Although I did not seek to make an impression upon this boy, the habit of sociability that plays so great a part in court life was strongly instilled in me. And so I indulged in the usual small talk of horses, hounds, and hunting.

"You love it, don't you?" he asked.

I enthusiastically replied in the affirmative.

There was a slight sneer on his face as he remarked: "Well, you are surely following in the footsteps of your imperial aunt. They say she loves horses so much that, frequently, she even sleeps in the stable."

I was so perplexed that I allowed several seconds to pass before I framed the reply: "Somebody must have been spoofing you."

"Perhaps," George agreed with more courtesy than conviction.

That marked the end of the conversation. All my life long I have regretted that I took his brief remarks—so absolutely characteristic of my future husband—lightly. It furnished leading clues to George von Larisch's character, a fact I discovered too late unfortunately.

I am sure that George was never intentionally unfriendly to me; he was merely reserved, just as he was with his sisters. Something appeared to weigh upon him eternally. He certainly did not try to make love to me; obviously, he did not even know how to flirt. He was simply an average young fellow with nothing special in his favor. I took it for granted that he would never mean anything in my life and expected to leave Solza as unattached as I had arrived. Certainly, whenever I thought of marriage, my fairy prince did not resemble George von Larisch. To tell the truth, the young man bored me to such a degree as to make him almost a nuisance in my eyes.

But something occurred that aroused a touch of pity in me. Again there had been one of those disagreeable noisy scenes, this time right at the dinner table. George, without asking his uncle's permission, had ordered one of his horses to be shipped to Solza. When, at the table, he politely informed his uncle about it, Count Johann became incensed. Never had I expected the old aristocrat to let go to such an extent, especially in the presence of guests. The more furious he grew, the louder George's voice trumpeted. The old Count continually reminded his nephew that he was filling the place of George's dead father and that, under no circumstances, would he permit George to do anything without first asking permission.

It surprised me that George, although making use of his stentorian voice now and then, remained comparatively calm, peeling a pear with admirable restraint. After all, it was not fitting to treat an army officer of twenty-two like a schoolboy, particularly before others. I felt genuinely sorry for the young man at that moment.

"Don't take that dressing down your uncle gave you too much to heart," I sympathized, when I discovered him sulking in a corner later. "My father sometimes treats me even rougher than that, but just the same, I don't let it bother me as you do."

"Your father is entitled to do so because, after all, he is your father," George came back bitterly. "Besides, I'm sure your father would never make it a point to humiliate you in public. Uncle Johann is not justified in keeping me so disgustingly short. It's my own money, and he is only supposed to act as administrator."

Suddenly George grew thoughtful. He shot a glance at me that I failed to interpret, but it appeared as if he were weighing the pros and cons of some scheme.

Three days before I was to leave Solza and join Aunt Sissy at Gödöllö, Count Heinie invited me for a morning canter. He seemed unusually solemn when he whispered to me that he had something to tell me. No sooner were we out of sight of the castle than he explained that, although it was somewhat embarrassing for him to speak to me so frankly, he felt called upon to do so. "You see, Baroness Marie, I don't want you to act blindly."

His words filled me with nervous dread. I remained tense and speechless, waiting for him to finish. Evidently he surmised my feelings, for he lost no time in explaining that the night before his father had had a very serious talk.with George, reminding the young man that his presence was solely for the purpose of becoming engaged to the niece of the Empress. Count Johann had reproached his nephew for having made no attempts to court me, preparatory to a proposal. He had pointed out that the whole Larisch family would be exposed to ridicule and worse at the imperial court if the Empress's plans were not realized. Finally he slyly had reminded the young Count that, with his marriage, the guardianship—so hateful to him—would be removed.

With a swift glance at my set face, Count Heinie continued to enlighten me. It seemed that the match already had been arranged last fall in Combermere Abbey, when the Empress had first spoken to Heinie about it. When he had remonstrated that George von Larisch would not make me a suitable husband, the Empress had lightly waved away his objections, remarking: "Well, after all, it is just an idea that may or may not materialize."

If, at that time, he had guessed that Aunt Sissy was absolutely determined upon it, he would certainly have raised stronger obstacles. However, Heinie felt reassured when, later on, rumors reached him that I had been invited to Paris to meet the Duke of Norfolk. He naturally concluded that the Empress had completely forgotten George's existence. But to his surprise and dismay, his father had curtly informed him that George and I were to meet at Solza, "by order of Her Imperial Majesty." Only one way out of the dilemma seemed feasible to him, and that was to let developments take their course. Perhaps, Heinie had reasoned,

George and I would really fall in love with each other. Now, however, he could not help noticing that not the slightest trace of interest existed between us, and so he considered it his duty to step in and, at least, warn me.

Count Heinie went on to say that, although his wife would be only too glad to see her brother married, even she had to admit that George was a "very difficult character." No doubt about it: any woman marrying him would be taking a great risk. Of course, George was a gentleman, a decent enough chap, but he had lost his parents when he was very young. It was Count Heinie's opinion that especially the long tragic illness of George's father, which he had watched as an impressionable youngster, had left its mark upon him. He was uncommonly morose for one so young and certainly ill suited to a lively girl like myself. In the twentieth century, he would have been classified as a neurotic. However, Dr. Freud's theories had not yet appeared on the Viennese horizon.

It was more than a full year later before I became acquainted with all the details behind George's sad childhood, spent under the same roof with a father addicted to the habitual use of narcotics. During agonizing months the adolescent boy had seen his father slowly die of a brain disease.

For a long time after Heinie had ended his melancholy recital, I was unable to do any more than just shake my head slowly.

"Of course, Baroness Marie," Heinie sought to reassure me, "Georgie will never propose unless you are altogether sympathetic to him. As a matter of fact, I'm not at all sure he will ask you in any case. George is very stubborn by nature, and it is most difficult to force him to do anything against his will. At any rate, if he should propose, I beseech you not to accept him immediately." The good-natured giant gazed at me pleadingly.

I was disconsolate. "But what can I do? Tell me."

"In the first place, don't say 'yes' right away. Ask for time to think it over." He hesitated for a minute. "Unfortunately, I can't take it up with Her Majesty, nor can I talk to my mother about it." An idea struck him, and his face brightened. "You can say that you want to go home to Munich and talk things over with your mother, can't you?"

I nodded eagerly. The smile which wreathed his face comforted me a little. At least, I would be given a respite and, once back in Gödöllö, I would speak my mind to Aunt Sissy even if it meant packing up and leaving, never to return to court again. I would not, under any circumstances, be forced into this marriage.

Two more days passed, and I was already congratulating myself on my lucky escape, since George paid no more attention to me than common courtesy demanded.

On the eve of our very last day at Solza, Countess Festetics came to my bedroom as I was preparing to retire for the night. I immediately sensed something in the air, because the Countess never visited me at such a late hour. The little lady-in-waiting seated herself on the edge of a chair and was so obviously uneasy that I was filled with foreboding. "My dear Baroness," she began, devoting what seemed an age to clearing her throat, "there are just a few words I would like to say to you."

Well trained, my maid Sophie recognized this as a signal to leave the room. Countess Festetics took a deep breath and then rattled on. She complained that, after all, I knew why she had taken me to Castle Solza at the command of Her Majesty, and that I absolutely must comply with Her Majesty's wishes. The day of departure almost had arrived, and the Empress was already waiting to be informed of the engagement. Unfortunately, I had spoiled everything by treating Count George indifferently to the point of snubbing him.

I could not keep silent any longer. "But, Countess, you don't expect me to propose to the young man, do you? I couldn't go that far even if he had positively bewitched me."

"That is not expected of you, Baroness, and it certainly will not be necessary, because Count Johann has spoken to his nephew. The young man will be only too happy over your consent. He hasn't approached you because you have a way of keeping him at a distance. However, now he intends to propose—and you simply must accept." The little lady-in-waiting was as excited as if she were fighting for her very life.

"I tell you, I won't! . . . I'm not going to be sold into marital slavery." I had read that phrase only a few days before in the latest Vienna novel, and it rolled off my tongue glibly.

Countess Festetics slowly, very impressively, arose from the chair. She stood directly in front of me, her eyes blazing. "Baroness Marie," she stated curtly, "I will not permit

you to make me the laughing-stock at court. Moreover, the
Larisch family will not stand for ridicule either."

I returned her gaze unflinchingly, and the next moment
she sank back into her chair with a deep sigh. Her head between her hands, she whispered: "Dearest Baroness, can't
you see that I can only bring you back to Gödöllö if you are
engaged? I can't return myself if I fail to fulfill the command of my imperial mistress."

Aunt Sissy's lady-in-waiting was wringing her hands by
now, the picture of utter despair. But my heart did not
soften toward her, for I had troubles of my own. My
thoughts turned to the advice Count Heinie had offered, and
I resolved to follow it. If George should propose, I must
fence for time, pretending that I wished to talk things over
with my parents.

Next day we drove over to the estate of the old Count,
where a formal luncheon was served. It was referred to as
déjeuner dinatoire by the Larisches, who had a weakness for
all things foreign. They spoke more English and French at
home than German and affected English and French cus-
toms. It was supposedly arranged to celebrate the recuperation of some distant relative from a protracted illness, but of
course I saw through this flimsy pretext. I also observed, my
alarm mixed with a certain amount of amusement at the
humor of the situation, that George was attempting to corner me. I knew that I could not postpone the issue much
longer and kept repeating to myself, over and over again, as
if committing a lesson to memory: "I must have time to
discuss it with my family." I was convinced that to gain
precious time would be an enormous advantage. It was all

like a bad dream from which I could not hope to awaken before talking to Aunt Sissy at Gödöllö.

There was a little mix-up in arranging the place cards at the table, and Countess Yetta asked me to assist her, for a few minutes, in rearranging them. She and I entered the dining room together, but a moment later she was called away and suddenly I was facing George Larisch. He had entered through a side door. I knew, then, that the fatal hour had struck!

He stepped over to me shyly and stammered: "Baroness . . . will you kindly . . . listen to me . . . for just a second?" He hesitated, and although I knew well enough what was coming, I stood there, completely petrified. Over and over, I repeated to myself those magic words which would grant me a breathing spell at the crucial moment.

Count George advanced half a step. "Baroness, I would like to ask you something." He was whispering now, whether from lack of courage or because he stood so near to me, I could not tell. The fact that he was not as tall as I, making it necessary for me to look down at him, made him appear somewhat ludicrous.

George halted, an agonized expression on his face. He heaved a desperate sigh, but before he could make a third attempt to unburden himself, the door to the dining room was flung wide open and Countess Yetta appeared on the scene. George and I doubtless looked as awkward as a loving couple taken unawares. Neither of us knew what we were doing. George had gripped my arm, and I stood half turned away from him. In that position, we must have looked as if we had been surprised in an embrace.

The Countess uttered a little shriek of elation and rushed towards us. First she threw her arms around me, and then around her brother; words gushed forth in a steady stream. At that moment, I was as near to fainting as I ever have been in my life and did not understand one syllable. I felt as if a spell had been cast upon me, and my struggle to throw it off was unavailing. It seemed like a clumsy scene from an amateurishly performed play. Such things could not happen in real life!

But they have a way of happening, just the same, I found to my sorrow. Presently we were surrounded by what seemed to me countless hordes of people. There was kissing and handshaking all around. Meanwhile, George had regained his equilibrium. More than likely, he was grateful to his sister for helping him out of an awkward situation. I only remember that I found myself sitting next to George at the table, that glasses were raised, that speeches were made, and that I tried to smile. I did not feel heartbroken. I merely felt as if the young girl sitting at the table were no longer myself, but just a marionette acting from some outside impulse.

I was awakened from my stupor by the blare of the Bridal Chorus from *Lohengrin*. It seems that the miners' band from the adjacent collieries had been held in readiness, and now struck up what, at that moment, was considered an appropriate piece of music.

This touch of stage setting aroused me from my inertia. Suddenly the whole situation seemed almost funny to me. I told myself that this was only a queer intermezzo, and that soon enough the whole nightmare would be dispelled. I felt completely relieved and even discovered that I was hungry.

Afterward, when demi-tasses were served in the adjoining
conservatory, Count Johann jumped up so suddenly that he
almost broke the fine Dresden china. "Great heavens, Countess Festetics," he addressed the Empress's lady-in-waiting,
"we must wire Her Majesty. . . ."

"So we must," the little Countess cried, rushing over to a
writing desk. A few minutes later, she read aloud: "I most
respectfully beg permission to report to Your Imperial Majesty that Baroness Marie has just become the happy fiancée
of Count George von Larisch."

Everybody nodded, duly impressed. The men sat stiffly at
attention, the ladies glowed with pride at their part in the
romance. To me, this was just another incredible scene in
an incredible play.

Countess Festetics came to me with the suggestion: "You
must wire to your parents now, Baroness."

"But what shall I say?" I asked, embarrassed.

The lady-in-waiting obligingly scribbled words on a telegram blank, and once again the message was read to the
guests: "Have just accepted Count George von Larisch's proposal and ask yours and Mother's blessing. Marie."

The fact that Countess Festetics had addressed my father
as His Royal Highness, as was his due, reading out the address in full, lent the proper pomp and circumstance to the
occasion.

I could not resist casting a sidelong glance at George. He,
too, seemed to appreciate the situation in its true aspect, for
he sarcastically remarked: *"Oh jeh, oh jeh, wie rührt mich
das. . . ."*—Oh my, oh my, how this touches me—he quoted

from Johann Strauss's *Fledermaus*—The Bat—then the latest hit in Vienna.

Well, I thought, at least the young man has a sense of humor. But even if George actually possessed some saving grace, the good impression was quickly and definitely destroyed that very afternoon. He told me that he intended to go to England, in a few months, to buy some horses.

"Will your stern old uncle grant his permission?" I asked, recalling the stormy scene of the other day.

"Uncle Johann won't have any say in the matter. In a few days he and I shall go to Vienna, where the necessary papers will be signed to release me from his guardianship." George made this statement with such evident satisfaction that it was clear to me why he finally had agreed to our marriage. It was the price he had to pay for freeing himself from the shackles of a guardianship he detested.

That evening at dinner, a whole sheaf of congratulatory wires were brought in and read aloud. There was, first, a telegram from Empress Elizabeth addressed to me, another from the Emperor, one from my parents, and many from friends of the family. It seems the news of my engagement had spread with alarming rapidity, despite the fact that it was still "strictly confidential and unofficial." However, what worried me most was that I had not even had an opportunity to deliver those words to my fiancé which I had memorized so earnestly in the hope that they would win me a respite.

When I arrived in Gödöllö two days later, Aunt Sissy embraced me warmly but made no reference whatever to the engagement. It was always her habit to ignore completely anything that might prove embarrassing—a simple enough procedure for an empress. My father just patted me on the back with the vague and inadequate comment: "Well, there you are." But my mother, with real understanding, inquired: "I hope you aren't unhappy, my child, are you?"

"I'm sure I don't know, Mother. Tell me, am I really and truly engaged?"

Mother shook her head at my bewilderment. "I wasn't consulted," she said. "I only know that Aunt Sissy showed us the wire and seemed very pleased that you are making such a marvelous match. The Larisches are a wonderful family, you know."

The Empress also had told Mother that, in a few days, old Count Johann and George would go to Vienna to draw up a marriage contract—a custom among the landed gentry. As soon as all legal arrangements were made, the engagement would be announced publicly.

To all appearances, the die had been cast for me. Nevertheless I resolved to discuss the affair with Aunt Sissy. But before I had a chance to do so, the Empress took matters in hand herself.

"With the Kaiser's permission, I have invited Count George Larisch to stay with us for a few weeks. He will probably arrive in two or three days, accompanied by his Uncle Johann. By that time I think everything will be arranged for your future."

Her words made me feel as if I were alone in a tiny boat bobbing up and down on an awfully big ocean.

This information was imparted during our usual morning canter. The Empress apparently did not expect an answer, but I would not have been able to make one in any case. I felt as if I were being strangled, and sat on my horse like a figure turned to stone. When I came home, I flung myself on my mother's shoulder, sobbing. Tearfully, I repeated what the Empress had said, adding that it looked as if I would have to see it through, after all.

Mother bent my head back tenderly and gazed into my eyes: "But, child," she sympathized, "did you ever believe that your engagement wasn't to be taken seriously?"

Time dragged miserably for me. Just when I was slowly regaining my spirit, something happened to rub salt into my open wound. Count Nicky Esterházy and his intimate friend, Aristide Baltazzi, came to Gödöllö for a few days. Nicky greeted me with an extraordinary show of indifference. He never offered a word of congratulation, although he certainly must have heard of my engagement through the usual channels of gossip.

When we went horseback riding that afternoon, Baron Baltazzi maneuvered to get alongside of me. As soon as there was sufficient distance between the Empress and Count Nicky, riding ahead of us, Baltazzi said: "My dear Baroness, tell me, are you really engaged to that Count Larisch?"

I affected surprise. "Engaged? Who told you?"

"Why, Her Majesty herself wrote Nicky some days ago. Of course, she added that the engagement was not yet official." Aristide stared at me; he cut an odd figure. He was a small man, and his diminutiveness was especially noticeable because he affected very big horses.

"But tell me, how did all that develop so quickly? Do you

know George Larisch well enough to become engaged to him?"

I answered with a few platitudes. Aristide scrutinized me so closely that I felt myself blushing. He took a deep breath before he burst out: "Well, I don't want to tell you what Nicky said about that engagement, and I certainly don't want to say anything about Count George von Larisch personally. He is a nice enough fellow from all I've heard. But under no circumstances could he be the right husband for you. I really can't understand why you couldn't wait a little longer."

I was piqued. "Exactly why should I wait?" I asked pointedly. Was he, perhaps, pleading for his friend Nicky?

"Well," Aristide confided, and there was an undertone of friendliness in his voice, "Elemér Batthyány was just about to return to Gödöllö. I hear he had a stormy scene with his mother, but had definitely made up his mind that he would not let her stop him from marrying you."

I was so astonished that I pulled in the reins. "You don't mean to tell me that Count Batthyány——"

"Exactly," nodded the little man on the big horse, his eyes flashing. "Too bad, too bad you didn't wait for him."

I felt like shouting: "They wouldn't let me wait." Tears filled my eyes. I spurred my horse onward.

Aristide had difficulty to keep up with me. "Please, Baroness," he implored, "don't give me away. I shouldn't have told you."

"I shall keep it a secret," I promised.

I wondered what had prompted the Empress to hurry my engagement with Count von Larisch. Hardly a year before, it had been her most sincere wish to wipe out, through my marriage with Count Elemér Batthyány, what she called "the last stain of 1848." I concluded that I simply had fallen victim to a combination of misunderstandings. Perhaps Aunt Sissy regretted that she had rushed me into the engagement with George von Larisch. That I might be right seemed the more plausible to me that night when, upon kissing the Empress good-night, she handed me a little box. Opening it, I found, reposing on velvet, a diamond brooch in the form of the letter E, surmounted by the imperial crown. The background consisted of stones in the Hungarian colors. It took me seconds to catch my breath. My obvious pleasure gratified her.

"That's all right, Marie dear, you are entitled to a little cheering up." She seemed on the point of unbending, but suddenly her manner changed. "It's rather late," she declared, pointing to the big grandfather's clock in the corner. Her warning recalled to my mind that, in the morning, the Emperor was expected at Gödöllö as well as the two Larisches—the old Count Johann and my fiancé, George.

The next morning His Majesty stepped into the breakfast room, his hand extended towards me. As I carried it to my lips, the Emperor put his arm around my shoulders and kissed me on both cheeks. "Congratulations, Marie," he said. "I hope you will be very, very happy." His voice rang with sincere affection.

As soon as the Emperor had withdrawn to his suite, a chamberlain, who had arrived together with the Kaiser, introduced the two Larisches to the monarch and then to my

parents. Uncle Johann, as I had to call him now, embraced
me, but George only kissed my hand. To all appearances, he
was ill at ease. The fact that he had been received in audience by Their Majesties seemed to have confused him. To
add to his bewilderment, there had been my parents. Mother,
however, soon found a way of putting George at his ease.
I noticed, with surprise, how quickly he engaged in an animated conversation with her. When Their Majesties withdrew, my father, in his rather unrestrained manner, remarked with an audible sigh of relief: "Thank God, it's
over and we can go upstairs and take it easy." George accorded him an appreciative glance.

To enjoy his comfort was not all, however, that enticed
my father to his rooms. He and Mother wanted to discuss
George, as I could plainly see.

"Nice fellow, this George, isn't he?" Father remarked,
once in our suite.

"Very nice indeed," Mother agreed. I could see she felt
relieved. George had certainly put his best foot forward.
Perhaps, after all, the others were right and I was
wrong. . . .

No doubt, George endeavored to be an attentive fiancé,
but he failed dismally despite Countess Festetics' pathetic
efforts to lend our engagement all the trimmings of a real
romance. In one of the salons she had arranged a number of
hothouse palms so that "the young lovers would have a
cozy corner." Willy-nilly, George and I had to sit there,
and it was in that "cozy corner" that George suddenly in-

terrupted himself while explaining the renovation work that was taking place at Castle Schönstein. We were to reside there after the wedding.

Remembering something, he dug into his vest pocket and brought out a little box containing a ring. Without even so much as looking at it, I began to put it on the ring finger of my right hand; George raised his stentorian voice to such a volume that my mother and Countess Festetics, who hovered near by as chaperons, jumped up, startled. It seemed I had made the mistake of placing the ring on the wrong hand, since European custom demands that the engagement ring be worn on the left hand, and the wedding ring on the right. George's foghorn voice made his small stature seem more incongruous than ever. Tears sprang to my eyes; it was fortunate that our "cozy corner" was so dark that nobody could see my distress. Not until I had reached my mother's room, later, did I examine the ring, a truly beautiful emerald.

"Green symbolizes hope, my little girl," she said.

The next forenoon was devoted to conferences between my father and the Larisches, or "negotiations," as Mother referred to them. Shortly thereafter the Empress sent for me and informed me that my engagement could be announced officially now, as "my future had been amply provided for." My grandparents and all my uncles and aunts were to receive telegrams from her. She would also order my trousseau immediately as a present from herself and the Emperor.

At dinner, in the great hall of the castle, my engagement was officially, and for the second time, celebrated. The ladies were in *grande toilette*, while the gentlemen all appeared in uniform, bedecked with medals. As the engaged couple, George and I had the place of honor between the Emperor and the Empress.

In the weeks that followed, George and I were supposed to become really acquainted with each other. Countess Festetics watched over us eagerly while George and I daily spent the prescribed time in the cozy corner she had so assiduously set aside for our particular benefit. In the evening Aunt Sissy usually asked me to sing songs of love and moonlight. In the daytime she made it a point to have George and me accompany her when she went horseback riding.

On one of these canters, George had occasion to come to the assistance of Aunt Sissy when her horse stumbled and fell. With a presence of mind I never expected of him, and with surprising strength, considering his slight physique, he succeeded in pulling the Empress out of harm's way as the horse struggled wildly to regain its footing. Aunt Sissy was covered with dust, and when George pulled out a handkerchief to brush her off, she drawled sarcastically: "You treat me exactly as if I were an old statue."

I thought of Elemér and the day I had that spill.

When the Empress preferred to walk, George and I were asked to give her horses a workout. On one such occasion we were threading our way through the trees. This is a trick that requires much practice, for one's mount must be under rigid control. George was apparently aware of the difficulty of the feat, because he objected strenuously. When I insisted, he refused to follow me, with the result that I rode home alone. I told Mother that I had lost George somewhere in the woods. "He'll be home soon," was her only comment as she turned to her newspaper.

I went into the adjoining room and had already changed for dinner when suddenly the very trumpets of Jericho seemed to fill the place. George was in the next room, complaining loudly about me. I heard my mother close the window so that everybody in Castle Gödöllö should not be in on our little family affair. I listened as George continued to give vent to his indignation. My maid Sophie was so unnerved that she shook all over. I stood with my dress unfastened, eager to rush into the adjoining room. However, Sophie was too upset to hook me up. If, at that moment, I had joined in the uproar, I am sure our engagement would have been broken off, then and there, and my life would have assumed an entirely different course.

While I stood helpless, waiting for my maid to regain her composure, I noticed that gradually, under the influence of my mother, George calmed down. When later, on my mother's insistence, I apologized to him for my rude behavior, he merely said: "Oh, it's all right. . . . I was only worried that you had lost your way." Of course this was merely an excuse, for he knew that the neighborhood was thoroughly familiar to me.

The same evening, Countess Festetics requested a word with George. I was not at all interested in what she had to say to him. However, the next morning, the Empress informed me in her most imperial manner: "Now, Marie dear, with the permission of the Emperor and your parents, and in agreement with your fiancé, we have decided that you shall be married here in Gödöllö on October 20th. In a few days George will leave for Vienna to wind up some business there. On the 18th he will return for the wedding, together with his Uncle Johann and other relatives. All arrangements have been made, and so you'll just have to get ready."

Aunt Sissy imparted these latest facts to me as if she were mechanically repeating lines. I was too astonished to utter a single word. I felt as if I suddenly had been shoved into freezing water and ice floes were closing above my head.

Somehow, what went on inside of me must have shown on my face. Aunt Sissy stared at me, then averted her eyes. At last I managed to say: "But that will give me only two weeks, Aunt Sissy."

I spoke quietly. The Empress smiled, very much relieved; probably she had expected a nasty scene.

"Why all the hurry?" Again my voice was calm.

Aunt Sissy affected an offhand manner. "Oh, it's just because it would be rather difficult for your parents to arrange for your wedding in Munich. You know, they haven't abundant means, and it would be very awkward if all the relatives could not be invited. On the other hand, here in Gödöllö we can arrange matters just to suit us. I hope you are entirely agreeable?" Her voice was soft, but her eyes signaled to me: "I won't permit any opposition."

At that moment I lost control of myself completely. I no longer looked upon the Empress as my adored aunt. "If my life is to be spoiled . . . if I must give up my freedom, then, of course, the sooner the better," I blurted out.

"I understand that all these developments almost take your breath away, but I really don't believe in long engagements. There is something unlucky about them. . . . Just look at your Aunt Sophie, who was engaged twice before she married," Aunt Sissy remarked coolly. She was referring to her youngest sister, the Duchess of Alençon, who originally had been selected to marry King Ludwig II of Bavaria. Before my mind's eye I saw her small fine face, animated by her expressive eyes. I remembered with what pride she had recently shown me her two beautiful little babies. In a protesting voice, I replied: "But after all, Aunt Sophie was permitted to make her own choice, and she finally found real happiness."

"You will find that, too—once you are married," said Aunt Sissy, an enigmatic expression on her face. Then she extended her hand in dismissal. Without venturing another word, I kissed it and withdrew.

Outside Aunt Sissy's boudoir I met Countess Festetics. "Please, couldn't you induce Aunt Sissy to postpone the wedding?"

The lady-in-waiting put her arm around me. "Now, be a brave girl," she coaxed. "Everything will come out all right in the end." She confided that plans had already been made for George and me to go to Paris first, then to London, and perhaps later wind up at the French Riviera. "The honeymoon trip is a present from the Emperor."

With only two weeks before the appointed day, preparations for my wedding were rushed at Gödöllö. As there was no possibility to have my trousseau ready in time, the Empress gave orders to assemble a temporary outfit for me from her own finery. Of course I thanked Aunt Sissy, although her kindness afforded me no pleasure whatever. The fact

that all the Empress's lingerie boasted a large embroidered
E, topped by the imperial crown, annoyed rather than flattered me. It would serve as yet another reminder of her
interference in my life.

"Well, at least you'll feel like an Empress wearing it,"
Countess Festetics said, determined to find good in all
things.

Meanwhile the press all over the world, especially the newspapers of the Dual Monarchy, were reporting the coming
marriage of "the Empress's favorite niece," pointing out
that Her Majesty herself was supervising the preparations
for my wedding. There were wood cuts of "the happy young
couple" in all the papers. It's a good thing that in 1877 moving pictures had not yet been invented. The strain of appearing properly joyous before a camera would have been
a little too much for me.

Day after day, wedding presents poured in upon me.
However, there was only one that really pleased me: a lovely
pin in the shape of an anchor, fashioned from emeralds and
diamonds, which Aunt Maria sent me, together with her
good wishes and those of the King of Naples.

One evening, shortly before the wedding, the Empress
brought the bridal gifts from the Emperor and from herself: a seven-strand pearl necklace with a diamond clasp,
and a good-sized ebony chest, filled to the very top with the
most exquisite old lace.

To my amazement Crown Prince Rudolf presented me
with a big black pearl—but then my imperial cousin always
doted on being unconventional. I thought I detected a smirk
on his face as he offered me the costly jewel. Surely he must

have known that a black pearl is generally considered an ominous symbol.

Relentlessly the days rolled by, and all too quickly my wedding day was at hand. I no longer recall it in detail, but I still remember that Mrs. von Feyfalik came in to arrange my veil. She was plainly scandalized when I asked her not to drape it loosely about my head, as the current style dictated, but to arrange it straight over my hair.

"Why, you'll look more like a novice entering a nunnery than a bride, Countess," Mrs. von Feyfalik objected, already addressing me by my new title.

"Please do as I tell you," I ordered, with all the firmness I could muster.

She complied, and after she had finished, I examined myself in the mirror. Mrs. von Feyfalik certainly had been right. I looked as severe as a novice, but far sadder than any girl who embarked voluntarily upon the cloistered life. I was, after all, embarking upon matrimony—but not of my own free will. That moment, I fervently wished I might really become a nun. But I was too hopeless to battle fate; sheer inertia prevented me from tearing off the loathsome veil and rushing off as far as possible. Mechanically I permitted the maid to put the wreath on me and adorn me with jewelry. When invited to look at myself in the mirror once more for final approval of my appearance, I refused, too sick at heart to care.

All that followed bore no reality for me. I remember entering the chapel and listening to the words of the priest. I dimly recall sitting at the table and being toasted by the Emperor.

The only scene that still stands out in my mind, with remarkable clarity, occurred in the vestibule, after Their
Majesties had withdrawn. The guests were seeing us off,
and the Empress's *calèche* awaited us before the low stoop.
A lackey was holding open the door to the carriage.

Suddenly the Kaiser stood right in front of me. Despite
the inclement weather, he had rushed out of the castle,
bareheaded. I tried to curtsy and kiss his hand, but he embraced me as if I were his own daughter, patting my shoulder fondly. "May you be very, very happy, Marie," the monarch whispered, as he helped me into the carriage.

My young husband followed, the lackey closed the door,
and the coach moved on.

Suddenly, to my breathless wonder, the Kaiser reappeared
on the other side of the carriage. He had run around behind
the *calèche* and now, once more, he extended his hand
through the window while the carriage was already under
way. His Majesty, the Emperor of Austria and Apostolic
King of Hungary, was running alongside the coach, pressing
my hand warmly and repeating over and over: "May God
bless you, my child."

There were tears in his eyes, as if he knew. . . . .

Chapter Four

STRANGE HONEYMOON

THE heavy, pigskin-bound diary which I thumb, now and then, as I piece together the story of my life, has many blurred spots on its faded opening pages—mute witnesses to the agonies I suffered during the lonely weeks of my "honeymoon." The diary, as heavy a tome as an old-fashioned Bible, yellow with black corners—colors of imperial Austria—was given to me, as a wedding present, by my little cousin, the Archduchess Valerie. The two tiny keys which unlock the volume, I still wear on a chain around my neck, together with a few holy medals, worn thin from age.

As I glance through its pages, I vividly recall a November afternoon, back in 1877: To all appearances, our "honeymoon" was to continue exactly as it had started. We either traveled with a crowd—only two's company!—or else I would find myself relegated to the rôle of premature grass widow. Although married hardly more than a week, my young husband had left me behind in the none too cozy sitting room of a second-floor suite in the Hôtel du Rhin in

Paris, while he, following his personal inclinations, had gone to Brittany.

Only a few hours after our arrival in the Seine metropolis, George and I, while window shopping along the Rue de la Paix, had run into the Marquis de S—— and his wife, formerly a Bohemian countess. It required no great degree of perceptiveness to realize that George was paying a good deal of attention to the Marchioness. Others, too, had noticed that my young husband was palpably smitten with her, judging from the not too tactful hints that were imparted to me. The Marquis and his wife had invited us to visit them at their country place in Brittany, but I had declined on the pretext of a heavy cold. My husband, however, saw no reason to keep me company, and so I found myself all alone in Paris. I rather liked having a few days to myself to find my bearings, as it were, but then it was the first time that George had deserted me. Later on, such interludes ceased to be of great consequence.

The first week of our married life had been neither hectic nor boresome, yet utterly different from anything I had expected. Leaving Gödöllö, we had stopped over in Vienna so that Joseph, George's old valet, might join us. My husband had contracted a slight cold and insisted that there was nobody in the whole wide world who knew more about looking after him in general, and wrapping his throat in compresses in particular, than this old retainer. George shook his head doubtfully when I offered my services. Many years later, when in charge of hospital trains during the Great War, I often was compelled to assume the duties of a physician. It was with no little amusement, then, that I thought back to this honeymoon when my young husband would not even trust me with the treatment of an ordinary cold.

Because Joseph was so absolutely indispensable, he traveled with us in the same compartment, babying George every minute of the trip. The valet was a quiet, dependable man, unobtrusive and discreet, yet his presence on our honeymoon necessarily changed the company of two into a crowd of three. Although George suffered no fever, he insisted upon interrupting our Vienna–Paris trip by stopping over in Munich. He had ordered Joseph to send a wire ahead in order to make suitable preparations for a night's stay under my parental roof. The result was that when our train rumbled into Munich, we were received by a veritable committee. My father's aide-de-camp, be-medaled and be-spurred, together with our old family physician, Dr. Wispaur, and a number of butlers and footmen carrying blankets and pillows, stood lined up on the platform. To be received by the ducal suite was an experience which George seemed to relish hugely. Dr. Wispaur immediately examined him in the first-class waiting room, which had been closed to the public temporarily. Although the physician politely assured George that, with proper care, he could continue right on to Paris, my husband nevertheless decided to stay in Munich overnight.

While we were stopping at my parents' house, I came to the conclusion that as long as Joseph was "chaperoning" us, I might just as well take Jenny along as my personal maid. And so, when we continued our trip to Paris, after two days, we traveled more with the ostentatious grandeur of potentates than in the blissful intimacy of honeymooners.

Paris seemed an utterly changed city. There was nothing to remind me of the happy days I had spent there only a few months ago with Tante Königin. Besides, King Francis and Queen Maria had already left for England for the season; everybody else, too, seemed to be away from the city. I congratulated myself that I had taken Jenny along, for, wearing the dresses that had once graced my mother's wardrobe, my maid looked sufficiently dignified to accompany me on my daily walks. Thus I could at least go shopping and to theaters and occasionally dine at one of the more conservative restaurants around the Place de l'Opéra. Together with Jenny, I went to Worth and Douçet to try on new gowns which George had ordered for me before he had left for the country. Among them was a bright sulphur-yellow velvet evening dress with a long train which had been the cause of a heated dispute. Despite the fact that I considered the robe much too loud in color, he had insisted upon buying it.

Although Jenny was a great help to me at this time, I felt terribly depressed. Perhaps it was just the reaction to all the weeks of excitement which had preceded my wedding. Then, too, brooding over my diary and jotting down in detail all the actual and imagined wrongs to which I had been subjected filled me with morose self-pity.

I finally reasoned myself into a state of mind where I became convinced that life had nothing more to offer and that an early end would not only be welcome, but the only solution open to me. And so I made two childish attempts at suicide by swallowing an overdose of some sleeping potion and by trying to smoke myself to death. The only results, however, were that from the one I contracted a condition for which the German *terminus technicus* is generally known all over the world as *Katzenjammer;* from the other I acquired a lifelong addiction to Turkish cigarettes.

At last, one rainy morning, George, in unusually good humor, returned to Paris, together with the Marquis and Marchioness de S——. In their party was another English couple. The husband was a dull taciturn man, and the wife was a buxom doll-faced woman who was in perpetual ill humor unless there were men about, paying homage to her. It turned out that she was the much-talked-of Barbara about whom I had heard a great deal. Even Count Heinie had spoken of Buxom Barbara with warm enthusiasm. Certainly George was completely under her spell, I noticed, but the fact neither surprised nor dismayed me.

That same evening the English couple joined us for *dîner* at a smart restaurant. I had gone along half-heartedly, never expecting that I would meet the Viscountess d'Avary, née Duchess de Monglyon. To me she became Rose immediately. The wife of a French diplomat, she was one of the few people I met in my long lifetime to whom I responded instantaneously. In a few days Rose and I became fast friends, and our friendship of many years in Vienna was to be renewed, decades later, in Florida, of all places. Five years older than I, and much more worldly-wise, she became my confidante and adviser. She possessed the gift of tact to a rare degree, as she proved only a few days after I had met her, in a situation which was as embarrassing as it was tantalizing.

Barbara's husband had gone back to London for a few days and had left his wife under our wing. The very first evening, my husband took us to the Café Riche for dinner, to be followed by a play later. Although I had disliked the idea of a party *à trois* at first, I was glad enough that George's attention was completely riveted on Barbara, when my eyes fell upon a familiar figure near by: Count Elemér Batthyány. Surely George would have noticed my confusion had he not been assiduously engaged in flirting with Barbara. Elemér, whom I had known only in riding togs, was wearing a Tuxedo, looking very handsome and every inch the aristocrat. For just a second his gaze met mine, but I could not bear his scrutiny. I bent over my plate and toyed with my food, feverishly praying: "Oh, let me be spared meeting him again!"

But we were to meet once more. A week or so later a member of the Austro-Hungarian embassy was giving a dinner. I surmised that Count Batthyány naturally would be there, provided he was still in Paris. Intensely disturbed, I opened my heart to Rose and confided the Gödöllö episode to her. As if guided by Fate itself, Rose was there the very moment our hostess sought to introduce me to Elemér.

"Why, you two know each other, don't you?" Rose broke into the strained situation. Then, cleverly, she engaged the lady of the house in a lively conversation, while Elemér bent over my hand ceremoniously. With an air of cool deliberation, he whispered in his native Hungarian: "You must excuse me, Countess, but really I can't talk to you. . . ." He bowed deeply and left me. I was not only disappointed; I felt piqued, for I had expected at least a show of friendliness from Elemér. During the evening my resentment grew as I perceived how studiously Elemér kept out of my way.

Eventually the grand piano was rolled into the center of the reception hall and I was requested to sing a few *Lieder.* First, I chose some Schubert songs. Applause greeted my efforts, and I curtsied my thanks. Suddenly I discovered Count Elemér, leaning against the door, at the far end of the room. As I sat down again to give an encore, I conceived a truly diabolical idea. Elemér had treated me curtly—now I would revenge myself!

On a near-by music cabinet there was a collection of Hungarian songs, some of which I knew. Among them was that old stand-by of Countess Festetics to which my imperial aunt could never listen without remarking that its saccharine sweetness nauseated her. I had never attempted the piece before, but I had heard it often enough to venture reading it off. It was the sentimental ballad of a knight who had jilted his beloved, the refrain reiterating accusingly:

> *You once said that you loved me,*
> *Yet now you spurn me.*

While accompanying myself at the piano, I glanced across the room from time to time. At last I had the sad satisfaction of seeing Count Elemér blanch, then quickly depart from the hall.

Some time later, as everybody made ready to leave, George came over to inform me that we must take Barbara home first, as she had no carriage of her own. I did not relish the idea of riding in a small coach with George and his buxom lady friend and was about to raise objections when Rose, with her inimitable tact, again saved the situation. She had come alone and now offered me a seat in her carriage. Naturally George was pleased and, with obvious relief, he hastily departed together with his inamorata.

As we waited for our cloaks in a corner of the crowded vestibule, I clutched Rose's arm in alarm; close by, Count Elemér was just being buttoned into his fur coat by his footman. When he turned around inadvertently and recognized us, Rose, with a sweet smile and in the most casual manner, asked: "Won't you be good enough to help the Countess?" So saying, she seized my cloak from the arm of a servant and fairly thrust it into Elemér's hands. Elemér had no choice but to drape it around my shoulders. Snuggling down deep into my enormous upturned chinchilla collar, I answered Elemér's inscrutable stare with my best Mona Lisa smile.

We were pressed by the surging crowd of homebound guests into a dimly lit corner of the vestibule. In the comparative privacy which the high standing collar of my cloak afforded, I suddenly felt. Elemér's eager lips upon mine. I closed my eyes . . . just for the fraction of a second. When I opened them once more, Count Elemér Batthyány was standing before me, calm and correct. He was pale—alarmingly so—while I felt I would swoon. Once again Rose was there at the psychological moment. "Here's our coach," she announced and, offering her hand to Elemér, she said ingratiatingly: *"Bon soir, Comte!"* then drew me away.

No sooner had the footman wrapped us up in our fur blankets and closed the door of the carriage than Rose turned to me and half laughingly, half disappointedly pouted: "Now, will you please tell me why you two behaved like plaster saints—not even talking to each other?"

I shook her arm in wild excitement. "But, Rose, Rose dear . . . he . . . kissed me," I sobbed, resting my head against her shoulder.

She patted me soothingly: "Well, well, just imagine . . . and I never even noticed!"

I had never known it before, but now I knew what a kiss could be like. Suddenly Paris—my whole life—seemed to take on a different aspect. . . . Heaven only knows what might have happened had not George informed me, a few days later, that we were leaving for London ahead of time. Barbara was returning to England, and the chance to travel in pleasant company was too good to miss, according to my husband.

I did not object; actually I was grateful to flee from Paris and the temptation it held for me then.

Our Paris sojourn had been hardly amusing; our London stay was to be nothing short of dismal. When we arrived at the Claridge, we had to be satisfied with the accommodation available, since we had come unannounced. Besides, the choice suites in the hotel were just being redecorated preparatory to the early arrival of Empress Elizabeth. I felt like leaving immediately for Brighton, but probably be-

COUNTESS LARISCH *at the time of her first marriage, wearing seven-strand pearl necklace given her by her imperial relatives.*

COUNTESS LARISCH *as a "child bride."*

cause Buxom Barbara intended to remain in London for some time, my husband was in no particular hurry to be off.

I spent a few thoroughly miserable days at the Claridge, all the while haunted by reminiscences of former, happier times. Without consulting George, I had written to my Aunt Maria who, together with King Francis, was staying at Torquay. I did not hear from Tante Königin for some time; then, one morning, Their Majesties' *valet de chambre* was ushered into the breakfast room. He brought the news that the Neapolitan royalty had arrived in London and would be glad to have us for luncheon. I was to reply immediately and naturally accepted with alacrity. Only after the messenger had left did I inform George of the impending meeting.

Despite the fact that the *valet de chambre* was still within hearing, George, in his annoyed surprise, rose from the table abruptly. Throwing down his napkin, he upbraided me in his overloud voice: "I am fed up with your aunt-worship. If it isn't the Empress you're running after, then it's the Queen. Well, let me tell you, I'm not going along."

"But Aunt Maria has always been so nice to me. It would be downright rude to decline her invitation. There is so much for which I am thankful to her."

"There is always something you have to thank somebody for, always somebody to whom you must cater. Very well—only I'm not going to have anything to do with these humiliating obligations. And that's final!"

The impulse surged strongly in me to sweep all the china from the breakfast table and hear it crash at George's feet.

With an effort I kept myself in check, merely retorting: "Have it your own way, then! You can stay behind and carry fat Barbara's parasol while I go and call on the Queen."

So saying, I stormed out of the room, choked with anger. I would show my husband that I could go my own way, too! But little was left of the happiness Aunt Maria's invitation had brought me.

I remained in my suite until it was time to dress and order the carriage. To my amazement, the lackey who came to announce the arrival of the coach also informed me that the Count awaited me downstairs. While I longed to greet George with some nasty remark, I feared that then he really might stay behind. If I could help it, I would not let Tante Königin even surmise my marital difficulties. Besides, George received me in a disarmingly peaceful manner, observing: "Well, I thought I would go along after all."

The former King and Queen of Naples and the Two Sicilies, living in rather modest quarters, received us warmly. I could not help gloating secretly as I noticed that George was visibly impressed when the King addressed him as *"Mon cher neveu."* Aunt Maria, too, was very friendly, and a lively conversation ensued for the better part of an hour. When we returned to the Claridge, George grudgingly admitted that the visit with the King and Queen had not been "too much of a strain."

Two days later we left for Brighton, but we found the seashore resort a bit forlorn at that time of year. Count Heinie von Larisch joined us for a few days, however, so I spent a pleasant enough Christmas. At the same time I eagerly looked forward to our return to London, since Empress Elizabeth was expected to arrive there within a few days.

Meanwhile I had discovered that George, when it came to "official matters" and "Her Majesty the Empress and Queen," would hardly ever offer any objections; however, as soon as Aunt Sissy played the part of a mere relative, my husband would try to interfere strenuously. To all appearances he did not like the possibility of my becoming a *Palastdame*—Lady of the Palace—nor did he care to consider a court position for himself.

We returned to London just in time to see the Empress step out of her private railroad car as slim and youthful-looking as ever and simply bubbling over with the joy of life. On the trip to the station George again had indulged in pointed remarks about the way I "everlastingly paid homage to crowned aunts." Nevertheless, when the Empress addressed him, his gratification was evident.

That Aunt Sissy, with her fine intuition, saw right through George, I learned that very same night when she received me in her dressing room. She resembled nothing so much as a picture right out of the pages of a fairy tale in her flowing, white lace gown, with its rose-colored silk slip imparting a soft lovely glow to her handsome figure.

The Empress opened the conversation: "Well, Marie, I expect you two have fought your way to a mutual understanding by now. Seriously, my dear, I really hope you are tolerably happy."

Aunt Sissy was unusually talkative that night. Reclining

in a low armchair, she stretched herself lazily, flexing her
form with the grace of a dancer. "You've seen Bay, haven't
you?" she inquired, a glint in her eyes. "No? Well, you will
very soon. But to get back to you and George. You know,
Marie, right now at the outset of your marital bliss"—there
was an unmistakable tinge of sarcasm in Aunt Sissy's voice
—"I dislike to step between you two and tie you down too
much with court duties. We'll come to some decision later.
Besides, you'll have to train him first."

I wondered whether Aunt Sissy had so much as an inkling of what it meant to "train" George. However, she did
not seem to be concerned with my difficulties just then. She
simply informed me of her general plans and told me that
George and I were to stay with her at Combermere Abbey
for some time. She was leaving London in a few days with
Countess Fürstenberg in attendance, instead of Marie Festetics, who had remained in Vienna, suffering from some
eye complaint. Another change in the retinue of the Empress was that this year, in place of Uncle Johann von Larisch, Prince Rudolf von Liechtenstein acted as the Empress's
"travel marshal." Countess Fürstenberg, somewhat hard of
hearing, was a pleasant enough woman, while Prince Liechtenstein was a brilliant and charming cavalier, although
generally too orthodox in matters of etiquette.

For dinner, on the evening of the Empress's arrival, Edward, Prince of Wales, had been invited. The English heir
to the crown was as friendly as last year, but he somehow
seemed a little more formal toward me. To him I was, apparently, no longer the imperial niece but Countess Larisch.

Nevertheless he greeted me with that merry twinkle characteristic of him.

Next day, as in the year before, I accompanied Aunt Sissy on her formal visit to Windsor, an assignment which conferred a great distinction upon me. "Of course, this time you need not make your bow again to Her Britannic Majesty if you do not wish it. Now that your curiosity has been appeased, you may wait outside, Marie. Or would you rather be presented once more?" Aunt Sissy asked when those amusingly attired Highlanders took us in charge at the entrance to Windsor Castle.

"I'll stay outside, Aunt Sissy," I agreed.

"That's exactly what I should like to do," the Empress remarked dryly.

Before Aunt Sissy left for Combermere Abbey, Crown Prince Rudolf arrived for a state visit. My cousin had just come of age and had been calling at other courts with an eye to picking a future empress for the Dual Monarchy. Rudolf, rather out of sorts when I saw him that evening, did not make the slightest attempt to conceal his feelings. Indulging in a yawn, vast enough to engulf me, he complained: "I tell you, Marie, this kind of 'inspection trip' leaves one dog-tired."

"Why don't you go to bed, then?" I counseled.

"You're not so wrong at that, Marie," he said, and off he went.

In general, he was not so "difficult" this time, and to my unbounded surprise he and George got along famously.

The Austro-Hungarian Ambassador was giving a dinner —a strictly formal affair—in honor of the Crown Prince,

The gentlemen were to appear in their dress uniforms, while *en rigueur* was the order of the day for the ladies. For the first time, I would wear that sulphur-yellow gown George had forced upon me in Paris, to be adorned by the seven-strand pearl necklace which the Emperor had presented to me upon my marriage. Just in time, I remembered that as long as this was a dinner in honor of Rudolf, I might as well wear the black pearl he had given me. Unlike my good mother, who had warned me never to wear that jewel, I was not superstitious. Almost the size of a small cherry, the pearl was set in an arabesque mounting of diamonds, which could be taken for a serpent as well as for a cabalistic symbol. Against the bright-colored dress, the gem showed up to great advantage.

On some pretext or other, Aunt Sissy had declined the invitation to the dinner and had commanded me to present myself to her in *grande toilette* before we left for the embassy. She was enchanted with my evening dress, considering it the height of good taste. When I told her that George, very much against my will, had practically forced me to buy it, she observed: "Your husband would make an excellent *tailleur pour dames*. He certainly has an eye for *chic*." Then, noticing the black pearl, she merely added: "So you are wearing Rudolf's present."

At the dinner I was seated next to Lord Beaconsfield. The famous statesman, better known as Disraeli, admired my black pearl. Later, as we lingered over our demi-tasses in one of the salons, the great man turned toward me. "Why, Countess," he stammered, "that black pearl of yours . . . it must have dropped out of the mounting!"

So it had; the precious jewel was missing! But the very next moment I discovered it in the saucer of my cup. I was glad my mother was not present, for she certainly would have interpreted the incident as a bad omen . . . and perhaps not incorrectly so, in view of all the heartaches which my cousin Rudolf was to cause me some twelve years later.

Returned to Brighton, George, to my astonishment, evinced great impatience because the promised imperial invitation for Combermere Abbey was somewhat slow in forthcoming. He was the more annoyed as an English friend of his had asked him to spend some time at Melton, and while awaiting the command of the Empress, he was unable to make any definite plans. I knew that Aunt Sissy had other guests staying with her just then, but I also knew that there would always be some small room available for me at the Abbey. I therefore wired to Prince Liechtenstein, inquiring whether I could be accommodated; if so, my husband could bring me there and then proceed to Melton. Immediately the reply came that I should leave without delay. Thus George and I arrived at Combermere Abbey next day, just as the retinue of the Empress was assembling in the main hall for luncheon.

When I stepped into the vestibule, Captain Middleton rushed over, his big hand extended in welcome, his ruddy face glowing happily. "Why, little girlie, how glad I am to see you!"

George stood immobile, taking in the scene. Bay caught my husband's glance and quickly guessed his identity. "I beg your pardon, Your Grace," apologized the Captain;

nevertheless, he still held on to my hand, pumping it so furiously that I expected my arm to drop out of its socket.

Mustering an air of poise which I did not altogether feel, I introduced Bay to my husband. The faces of the two men, as they shook hands, furnished interesting character studies. To all appearances George would have liked nothing better than to launch into one of his loud tirades; Bay—much taller and broader than my husband—had a half-embarrassed, half-defiant smile on his face. Fortunately, at that moment, the Empress appeared at the head of the stairs. Slowly she came down, step by step, her sand-colored riding habit clinging closely to her willowy figure. Only those of us who were initiated into Aunt Sissy's little secrets knew that it sometimes took an hour of tight lacing to encase her into the "sausage skins," as her imperial husband called these form-fitting suits.

Aunt Sissy ordered George to sit at her left, a command which pleased him until he discovered that Bay Middleton, in a matter-of-fact manner, took his place to the right of the Empress. All during the luncheon I clearly discerned that my husband was just bursting to voice his disapproval of the English captain. But the furrows on George's brow disappeared for a minute when the Empress, upon rising from the table, extended her hand to him and said: "My dear George, I'm so grateful to you for bringing Marie up here. I hope you will have a nice time in Melton, but do come back to us soon." George bowed deeply, bending over the hand of his sovereign. No sooner had Aunt Sissy left the hall, however, than he took me aside and, in a voice vibrating with suppressed anger, ranted: "Now will you

Captain William "Bay" Middleton

Rudolf, *at the time of his engagement.*

please explain to me why that red-headed bumpkin dares to call you 'little girlie'?"

Calmly—and I hoped with proper dignity—I replied that Captain Middleton knew me since my first days in Gödöllö. This explanation, however, only served to heighten George's anger. "Well, I declare!" he raged. "Things must have been pretty free and easy at Gödöllö. How brazenly that fellow planted himself right next to Her Majesty! It seems that place is reserved for him permanently. Of course, that doesn't concern me. But beginning right now, this fellow must treat you with all the respect that is your due as Countess von Larisch."

I was anxious lest Middleton, who was lingering at the other end of the hall, apparently waiting for a little chat with me, would catch the drift of George's harangue. Certainly the English captain was not the man to stand for any nonsense. A veritable giant, I hated to think what Bay could do to a lightweight like George if the rules and regulations of the Marquis of Queensberry should be suspended for just a few minutes.

Under the pressure of fear, a ready excuse sprang from my tongue. "Why, George, Middleton is known everywhere as an eccentric chap. He is very nice indeed, but manners he has none. Nobody ever takes him seriously, not even the Emperor. Whenever Middleton made a *faux pas* in Gödöllö, Uncle Francis would merely laugh and let it pass."

Of course, not one word of this was true, but I knew that if his Kaiser was willing to look upon this commoner as some sort of a court jester, George von Larisch loyally would subscribe to the imperial opinion.

Although my husband's anger subsided, once he accepted my explanation, I felt completely relieved only after he had left for the railroad station on his way to Melton.

Immediately upon his departure I was commanded to report to the Empress in her dressing room, where Mrs. von Feyfalik was administering the regular nightly scalp treatment. Upon entering, I noticed that Aunt Sissy's right hand was in a splint; she revealed that she had sprained her wrist during some gymnastics that afternoon.

"Well, Marie, I just heard George drive off to the station. What a wonderful idea of his to stay at Melton for some time!" My aunt looked at me quizzically, but I tried not to betray my own thoughts. "It will be splendid," she continued, "to have you all to myself for a while—just as in the old days." There was a wistful note in the Empress's voice. "Tell me, Marie, how did George get along with Bay?"

I related what had happened.

"What a loon!" she exclaimed, adding hastily, "of course, I don't mean George, I mean Middleton. Bay is a good-natured fellow, but he always acts like an overgrown boy." She sighed, "He gives me so much trouble."

Aunt Sissy did not look as if she were worrying greatly; on the contrary, she actually seemed to enjoy her predicament. "You haven't the slightest idea, Marie—all the talk that's flying about since I permitted Bay to watch me in the gymnasium the other day."

I was not surprised that such an incident should have set

tongues wagging, considering the daring costume Aunt
Sissy usually wore during those *Turnstunden*. I never saw
anything like it until almost fifty years later when, for the
first time, my eyes lit upon trim American girlhood surf-
riding along the Florida shore.

Mrs. von Feyfalik finished braiding Aunt Sissy's hair for
the night. After she left, the Empress said: "There is a letter
I want you to write for me. I can't very well do it myself
tonight—not being left-handed,"—she pointed to her injured wrist with a little smile. "Sit down there at the desk,
Marie, and I shall dictate it to you." With that, she put a
sheet of paper before me; the letter E, with the imperial
crest above it, was embossed in the left-hand upper corner.

"Dear Bemsel," Aunt Sissy began. I hesitated for a second,
and looked at her questioningly. "Yes, yes. Just write
B-e-m-s-e-l," she encouraged me, laughing. Then she went
on, relating some Combermere Abbey news. Not before she
mentioned family gossip did I surmise to whom Auntie was
writing.

"Why, Aunt Sissy, you are—you are writing to the Kaiser!"

"So I am, but go on now, go on," she urged, finally in-
structing me to sign the letter "Sissy." I was then ordered
to enclose it in a small envelope, seal it with lavender-colored wax, and stamp it with the imperial crest. Next, the
letter was inserted into a larger envelope, bearing the printed
address: His Apostolic Majesty, The Emperor and King,
Francis Joseph I.

Aunt Sissy correctly divined that I was still pondering
over that peculiar nickname. "You are wondering how

Uncle came by that name Bemsel? . . ." And then she explained to me that "in the days when we both were young and happy—once, perhaps, we really were"—the Emperor had occasionally scolded her for this, that, and the other thing. In the Vienna vernacular, good-natured nagging of that sort is called "penzen." Thus, from first calling the Emperor "Penzer," the nickname had gradually evolved into "Bemsel."

"It's a long, long time since I invented that name," Aunt Sissy said, and cleared her throat lest her emotions get the better of her.

The days spent in Combermere Abbey passed pleasantly as of old. Eventually George came back from Melton, but my apprehension that serious difficulties with Middleton might arise proved unnecessary. It so happened that at the time my husband returned, the Captain was breaking in a new mount for the Empress. This he did with such consummate horsemanship that George, himself a cavalryman, watched, spellbound.

"That Englishman is as crazy as a March hare," he commented, "but, Heaven knows, he certainly understands horses."

From then on George and Bay got along very well. They shook hands in sincere friendship when we left for Brighton a few days later.

After spending a few boresome weeks there and stopping in Paris just long enough for a little shopping, we returned to Munich. Upon our arrival we received a royal command to attend the next family dinner given by King Ludwig II.

On the night of the dinner Father was late and George was extremely fidgety as we waited to drive over to the residence. King or no King, Father's first consideration in life was *Gemütlichkeit;* he simply would not be hurried. When he finally put in his appearance, I saw that George longed to rebuke Father, but evidently thought better of it, considering that he was not only his father-in-law and a Royal Highness, but also the colonel of the Fourth Light Horse.

At any rate, we arrived at the royal residence at the precise moment the King entered the dining room. I had not seen the monarch since that last visit to Castle Berg and noticed that, meanwhile, he had put on considerable weight. Especially his face appeared changed, but his eyes were still as blue and as unfathomable as the mountain lakes of his realm.

George was presented to His Majesty, who addressed a few words to him. As Father had told me that the King's impediment in speech had become very pronounced of late, I was afraid George would have difficulty in understanding Ludwig. Fortunately the King just murmured a few words and then passed on to me. I strained every effort to catch his words, atremble with anxiety.

"Are you still devoted to your music, Marie?" came the unexpected question in a voice scarcely above a whisper.

Something prompted me to look directly into his eyes, and that same uncanny something made me answer: "Very little, Your Majesty. . . . I have no heart for it any longer."

I had spoken in a low voice, as if under a spell, and no sooner had I uttered the words than apprehension gripped me. How would the King receive such frankness?

His Majesty Ludwig II hesitated for what seemed to me an eternity. Then he bent low, and bringing his lips close to my ear, he murmured: "A great pity, Marie. There are hours which we will never forget." With that, he extended his hand. He referred, I knew, to my two visits at Castle Berg when I sang his favorite songs for him.

I think that I have never kissed anybody's hand as respectfully and sincerely as I kissed my King's that night. There was something about Ludwig II that baffled analysis —something unearthly. It seemed that the finger of Fate was already pointing the way to his tragic end less than a decade later.

When we reached home that night, Father, somewhat disappointed, remarked: "The King was very short with you, wasn't he?"

I did not reply, for I felt that what Ludwig II had said to me was strictly my own affair.

The family dinner at the royal residence constituted the main event of our Munich visit. Soon thereafter we left for Vienna, where, in February, 1878, I would make my official *début* in court society. I anticipated it with more than slight trepidation. Although I was niece to the Emperor, as well as to the Empress, I feared I might be regarded as a morganatic interloper, since court life in Vienna was full of cliques and camarillas. The lower the rung of the ladder of nobility to which they themselves clung, the more these crested snobs would let me feel my difficult status.

That Aunt Sissy was well aware of my precarious position and wanted to do her best to remedy matters, became clear to me soon. Shortly after my official presentation at court, she made me a full-fledged *Palastdame,* a rank best explained as honorary lady-in-waiting. A *Palastdame* was invariably a title for a member of the nobility who might be married and who received no salary; a *Hofdame*—a regular lady-in-waiting—was a paid position from which married women were excluded. A *Palastdame* ranked with a *Kammerherr* or chamberlain. At court functions, these two dignitaries would precede all other aristocrats, each *Palastdame* usually wearing her *manteau de cour* boasting a long train, while each chamberlain appeared in his official gala uniform, consisting of white trousers and a dark green dress coat, an enormous golden key of office embroidered on the left tail.

As far as I personally was concerned, the title *Palastdame,* for which the official certificate, with the usual bureaucratic delay in such matters, was not issued before many months, primarily was given to me so that I might have an official status at court as the Empress's niece and confidante. At the same time George was appointed imperial chamberlain. From then on, on every occasion of state, I donned the prescribed dress with its long court train while my husband wore his dress coat with its magnificent embroidery.

One wintry afternoon I came upon Aunt Sissy in a rather melancholy mood. She was locking some papers into her writing desk as I entered. There was the same unfathomable expression in her eyes that I had observed so recently in the eyes of King Ludwig II. The Empress, her thoughts ap-

parently far away, stroked my head and in a voice vibrant
with emotion, quoted Goethe's lines:

Of joyous days ye bring the blissful vision;
The dear, familiar phantoms rise again,
And, like an old and half-extinct tradition,
First Love returns, with friendship in its train.

My guess that Aunt Sissy was thinking of Combermere
Abbey and London was confirmed when she pointed to a
picture on the wall—a then popular English copper-plate
engraving of "Titania and the Ass." With a forced show of
gayety, the Empress exclaimed: "Look here, Marie, that's
Bay and I."

I merely nodded, without really grasping her meaning;
not so long thereafter, however, I was to learn all the implications of that picture.

Aunt Sissy, apparently plagued by some thought, that
far-away expression still in her eyes, pulled from her dress
an envelope which I recognized as one of Mother's. And instantly I recalled Father's repeated complaint to Mother
that he did not like her "to assume the rôle of a *postillon
d'amour*"; indeed, he had warned her that one day she
would "get into serious difficulties, relaying Sissy's *billets-
doux.*"

The Empress extracted a telegram from the envelope and
said: "I received this wire only today. You know, sending
it on by mail from Munich takes so much time." She paused
to dab at her eyes, then went on to explain: "Bay was thrown
badly during a steeplechase. Oh, I'm so worried about him!"

Auntie's eyes seemed focused in interminable distance. As if talking to herself she mumbled: "Bay's going to die some day from a riding accident . . . and I shall die by the water." A horrible sensation of fear gripped me, although I could not know, then, with what remarkable prescience the Empress had spoken in regard to herself.

With a visible effort she pulled herself together and began to rummage through the drawer of her desk. Finally she brought out a little box; this she unlocked, her eyes glowing all the while like those of a young girl. She held up a miniature of Bay Middleton painted on ivory.

"You know, Marie," Aunt Sissy confided thoughtfully, "you should have married Bay. Ah, then I could have had you two beloved ones with me always."

Whatever "honeymoon" I had had came to an abrupt conclusion upon arriving home.

"Home" was Castle Schönstein, situated in the Silesian plains. No sooner had I stepped from the railroad car than I realized what awaited me. We were met by a driver and footman whose brand-new uniforms contrasted strangely with the open, dilapidated calèche. The carriage, its springs as unbending as granite, rattled over dusty mud roads with much the same disconcerting noise as that of a child's half-empty savings bank.

The castle, at first glance, appeared to be a straggling group of ramshackle buildings. Unfriendly from the outside, Schönstein certainly gained nothing once inside its gates. After freshening up a bit, we proceeded to the dining hall. By then I expected the worst, so that the general gloominess of the room did not take me unawares. But to balance the picture somewhat, the table was set in the best of taste, while the service and food were exquisite.

"It's just a matter of management to make something of Schönstein," George declared with a touch of pride. I perceived that he took all the credit for the well-appointed luncheon table and successfully hid my smile. I remembered Aunt Sissy's remark that George would make an exquisite *tailleur pour dames* and decided that my husband surely possessed all the qualifications of a first-class majordomo also.

After luncheon, the old castellan escorted me through the manor. The more I saw, the heavier my heart grew. Alas, there was not one musical instrument in the whole place with the exception of an antique harpsichord, the strings of which were mostly missing. Practically the only livable room on the whole estate was what my guide, with an odd inflection in his voice, referred to as "the old Count's Turkish smoking den." I was in the act of inspecting this charming room when George appeared on the scene. He ushered me out with suspicious speed, at the same time throwing a glance full of fury at the castellan. As if to make me forget the smoking den, my husband insisted upon showing me through the entire ancestral picture gallery. In great detail he recited the history of the innumerable Larisches that covered the walls, the canvases faded and the frames cracked.

Probably the most dismal room of all was the one allotted to me as my bedchamber. I would not have minded its old-fashioned furniture had the general impression not been spoiled by grouping these antiques around a brand-new metal bed—an ultra-modern atrocity of the late 'seventies. This bed, I soon discovered, was the only piece of furniture which had been changed in the room since George's mother died there many years before.

I am not given to shudder easily, but the impenetrable gloom pervading that bedchamber filled me with the deepest depression. It actually gave me a creepy feeling at times, heightened by the fact that between the two very narrow but unusually high windows hung an enormous mirror which would produce the most startling reflections. Because the pier glass had not been resilvered for many years, it was very cloudy and lent a weird ghostliness to the face and figure of the person looking into it. To make matters worse, the mirror was broken; from one of the top corners a crack wriggled down almost to the middle, as if lightning had struck the glass.

My first idea was, of course, to have this queer ornament removed from the room. The castellan, however, explained that as the mirror was cemented into the wall, this could not be done without considerable difficulty. Besides, out of reverence to the late Countess, His Grace probably would object to the change.

I never bothered to confirm this point but, instead, tried to become accustomed to the trick mirror as well as to the rest of my uncongenial surroundings. Despite my best intentions, life became increasingly unbearable. The greater part of the time I was left to my own devices, while George visited near-by estates or made incognito trips to Berlin and Breslau. If only there had been a piano! I finally wrote to

Mother and had her send on my old zither, and with this native mountaineers' instrument to accompany me, I would sit by the hour, humming all the songs I ever had learned.

During George's absence, I wandered all over the castle. Through discreet inquiries here and there, I eventually pieced together the story of George's sad childhood along with the reason why he had hustled me away from his father's smoking den.

Old Count Leo Larisch, George's father, had traveled widely in the Orient and in the Far East. From his wanderings he had not only brought back to Schönstein a marvelous collection of smoking paraphernalia, including priceless chibouks and narghiles, but also the insidious habit of blending his tobacco with opium tablets. In the course of time, especially after George's mother had died, Count Leo became a drug addict and was isolated in a wing of the castle. George, an impressionable boy, had been made to visit his father by his well-meaning but thoughtless elders. On one such occasion Count Leo—then in the last stage of his illness—had lapsed into a paroxysm which affected the boy so deeply that he became violently sick for weeks. During George's illness his father died, but even then, with the source of his nervous collapse removed, the boy remained extremely morose. Later on, during years of strict, healthful army service, his condition improved; but he never could conquer it completely.

Although this information explained much of my husband's trying temperament, I am afraid I was too young at that time—barely seventeen—to make the logical allowances for it. Especially in my condition then—my first-born was to arrive in September—the Schönstein atmosphere was entirely too nerve-racking to promote complete understanding for George's "difficult" character. Perhaps not without reason, I felt sorry for myself, cooped up there, time hanging on my hands heavily.

After a dull spring and an even duller summer, my oldest boy was born. With the Emperor for godfather, the boy was naturally christened Francis Joseph. As a gesture of approval for perpetuating the family tree, George presented me with a grand piano. Now, at last, I had my beloved music, and every minute I did not spend with my little one found me at the piano.

Gradually I was becoming reconciled to the idea of remaining buried in Schönstein when, during one of the Count's frequent "business trips," something happened which unexpectedly liberated me from turning into a mummy while still young in years.

It was two months to the day since my little boy's birth. He was competently cared for by Thesi, perennial and hereditary nursemaid to the Wittelsbachs. I had Jenny for lady's maid, companion, and general confidante. She and I would sit up late at night, and then Jenny, never without trepidation, would return to her little room at the end of the long corridor. That night I had just locked the door behind her—a habit I formed at Schönstein which I never practised before nor since—when I heard a blood-curdling scream. A second later Jenny was pounding at my door madly. White as a sheet, and shaking from head to toe, she spluttered: "Spooks, Your Grace . . . spooks . . ." and then lapsed into fervent prayers.

"Nonsense, Jenny. You're getting old and foolish." I was not quite so calm, however, as I tried to appear. Finally I drew the story from her.

Jenny had continued along the dark corridor, carrying a candle in her hand. Suddenly she had noticed a streak of light emerging from behind the door of a narrow closet where, as I knew, Count Leo's collection of smoking paraphernalia was stored. "And then," Jenny concluded, incoherent with fear, ". . . and then . . . Your Grace . . . I swear, Your Grace . . . the picture . . . the picture . . . Your Grace . . ."

"What picture?" I repeated impatiently, no longer so self-possessed.

But all the information Jenny had to offer was to point down the hall.

"All right, let's see what it is!" I took a revolver out of the night table and, pushing along the nigh-paralyzed Jenny, we approached the closet. True enough, light seemed to be filtering through a crack.

"Somebody looked for something in the closet and forgot to extinguish the lamp," I spoke up firmly, nearly convinced of what I said. I opened the door, but the closet was as dark as a tomb. That very moment Jenny let loose another blood-curdling shriek; her right hand shaking, she pointed in the general direction above the door. "The picture, the picture . . ." she whimpered.

There were whole rows of pictures on the walls, part of

the overstocked ancestral gallery. However, there was only one which Jenny could mean, for it actually seemed alive now! It was a painting of one of the Larisches' great-grand-mothers who, as I had been told by George, had been too beautiful to be virtuous and finally had come to a bad end. There was a knowing smile on the face of the woman; her eyes shone alluringly and her full lips parted, clearly re-vealing her glistening white teeth.

I never could remember whether I screamed myself then, but I know that I let go of the candlestick. The light went out and, holding onto each other in a paroxysm of terror, Jenny and I groped our way back to my bedchamber through the dark corridor. There, still holding onto each other tightly, we waited for morning to come.

Finally, when day broke, I mustered up all my courage and marched back to the closet. There I found the candle-stick on the floor, and the door wide open. With the early-morning sun streaming in, the place had all the aspects of a neatly kept storage room. There was nothing spooky about it at all. I could not find the slightest explanation for the noc-turnal manifestation I had witnessed. Great-grandmother Larisch gazed from her frame as immovably lovely as ever. . . .

In later years I tried, time and again, to find a solution for that ghostly and ghastly incident, but I am as much at sea over it today as I was then.

It was too early for the servants to be up, and I warned Jenny not to talk about our odd experience to anybody. However, no sooner had George returned than I related the whole story to him. Apparently it brought back to him his unhappy childhood at Schönstein. He mumbled something about "this damned old shack . . ."

Three weeks later, I found myself installed in a cheerful suite at the Hotel Imperial on Vienna's famous Ringstrasse.

My husband had accompanied me to Vienna but left again to go "house hunting." He was resolved not to return to Schönstein, and proceeded to comb the neighborhood of Freistadt and Solza—old stamping ground of his family—for something suitable. As Aunt Sissy had just returned from hunting in Ireland and England, and was staying at the Schönbrunn Palace, I immediately asked to be received.

I found the Empress in high good humor, as effervescent as a young girl. With a teasing twinkle in her eyes, she told me that "somebody is sending his love to the little girlie." At great length she dwelt upon her equestrian exploits while in Great Britain.

When I finally seized a chance to tell Aunt Sissy why we had left Schönstein in such haste, she asked with mock seriousness: "Tell me, Marie, wasn't there a hook on which somebody once hanged himself in that castle?" Of the Ghostly Lady of the Portrait, the Empress remarked: "After all, you should have Mass read for that old grandmother so her soul may repose in peace. Remember, if it hadn't been for her, you would still be sitting in Schönstein."

If time had lingered agonizingly before, it flew much too fast now that I was so close to Auntie once more. All too soon, George brought the news that he had purchased an estate near Freistadt; the manor was being renovated in great haste.

Early in spring, 1879, we left the Kaiserstadt Vienna for Piersna. Our new home, tastefully redecorated under George's supervision, was a veritable paradise compared to Schönstein. It was situated on a little knoll overlooking the neighborhood. With my relatives and close friends for neighbors, I never had a boresome minute during the years I spent at Piersna. There, in September, 1879, my first daughter was born.

At Piersna, life seemed more bearable than ever before— or ever after, for that matter! No longer did unforeseen developments upset me, as they had in the past, or assume an air of tragedy. When, on my first canter after the birth of Marie Valerie, the new mount I was riding threw me so badly that I had to spend weeks in bed, I took it as a matter of course—although it should not have happened to so thoroughly trained a horsewoman as myself. And when, during the time that I was *hors de combat,* George invited Buxom Barbara "to keep me company," I just smiled knowingly. When my husband and his plump lady friend returned very late from a little joy ride one day because "something had happened to their phaëton," I wasn't the least inclined to indulge in a fit of jealousy. . . . With two lovely babies around, there seemed to be more important things in life.

The beginning of 1880 found me in Vienna once more, with George roaming away from home, very much to the gratification of Aunt Sissy. When I reported to her for duty at the *Hofburg,* I found her in her darkest mood. Perhaps there was something in the air of that bleak wintry afternoon that added weight to heavy hearts. I, too, fell under the spell of the hour, and before I knew why, I was telling Aunt Sissy all about George, confessing that married life had not been any too pleasant so far.

I remember how Auntie's lips slowly parted that day as if she were on the point of saying something very important. Suddenly her mouth narrowed to a thin line, and a hard expression crept into her eyes as if cautioning herself that silence was best.

It was easy enough for me, however, to divine Aunt Sissy's thoughts. I knew that my own marital revelations had set her thinking of the day, more than twenty years ago, when a barque of roses, assembled from the most perfect blooms that grew in the gardens of Schönbrunn, had conveyed the young Elizabeth down the Danube to Vienna, to become the Empress of the Dual Monarchy. Arrived at the capital, a gilded carriage, drawn by eight snow-white steeds, had brought her to the imperial palace. With unheard-of pomp and circumstance, the nuptials of the exalted couple were celebrated. Yet hardly before the wedding candles had been snuffed out, the young Empress had come to the conclusion that she had made a fatal error. Her illustrious husband concentrated all his interest on affairs of state, and if she so much as dared to offer advice, or made so bold as to inquire for information that would be vouchsafed any ordinary mortal, the Kaiser would scold her—*Penzer* that he was!

"Wild Sissy"—as her own mother had called her—in a spirit of daring, and perhaps fired by ambition, actually had succeeded in becoming the Empress-Queen of Austria-Hungary. Alas, she enjoyed but a precious short time of marital bliss. Almost from the very beginning of her imperial career, she collided with Viennese prejudices. Aunt Sissy's attempts to modify court etiquette, her extreme fondness for horsemanship, and her frequent hunting excursions to foreign countries scandalized Austrian society. Moreover, her predilections for Hungary and everything Hungarian offended German sentiment.

To make matters worse, not before two girls had been born to her—the first died in infancy—had fortune turned friendly and granted a male heir to the Hapsburg throne. But no sooner had the Crown Prince been tucked into his imperial cradle than the young Empress was exiled from the nursery by her formidable mother-in-law, Archduchess Sophie.

As Archduchess Sophie, daughter of King Maximilian I of Bavaria, was the sister of my grandmother, Duchess Ludovica, I had heard much of the redoubtable lady in my childhood. Without question, Sophie was a woman of great ability and strong character. During the years which followed the abdication of Emperor Ferdinand I, the widowed Archduchess was the most influential personage at the Austrian court. She had objected strenuously when her son expressed his intention to wed another Elizabeth, daughter of Archduke Joseph, Palatine of Hungary. This Elizabeth, widow of Archduke Francis d'Este-Modena, was far too energetic and self-reliant to suit the older woman. To settle the marriage question definitely, Archduchess Sophie had decided that, instead, Francis Joseph should marry Aunt

Sissy's older sister, Helen, who became Princess of Thurn and Taxis later.

Sophie never forgave Empress Elizabeth for interfering with her plan and hated her daughter-in-law from the very start. She had an insidious way of continually influencing the young Kaiser against his consort. Partly on account of the nervous strain imposed on her by such treatment, the young Empress, shortly after the birth of Crown Prince Rudolf, contracted a very serious cold which threatened to affect her lungs. Physicians warned Her Majesty to repair to a milder climate—advice she accepted with alacrity, since a definite alienation had developed between husband and wife. The young Kaiser, it seemed, again was resuming his friendship—platonic though it was—with the widowed Archduchess Elizabeth. Doubtless this other Elizabeth, at that time far more experienced than Aunt Sissy, appealed to the Emperor as an extremely sophisticated and witty woman. Although she meanwhile had remarried and now was the wife of Archduke Karl Ferdinand of Austria, there were persistent rumors that she exerted a great influence on the Emperor. In any case, she apparently raised as many difficulties as possible for his consort. Thus Aunt Sissy not only had her ever-interfering mother-in-law to deal with, but also the Archduchess Elizabeth.

From all I heard in the course of years, there is no doubt in my mind that it was primarily owing to the friendship between the Emperor and the Archduchess Elizabeth that the Empress ostentatiously left for Madeira after Rudolf's birth. On that trip she was accompanied by handsome young Count Imre Hunyadi as Chief Chamberlain. Later I

came to know more about this Adonis when Aunt Sissy
dictated to me her *Midsummer-Night's Dream* in which
Count Imre appears as the Fairy Prince Imo.

Not very long after Aunt Sissy's return from Madeira to
Vienna, she once more departed. This time, too, marital difficulties accounted for the trip. Together with her sister
Helen, she went to the island of Corfu in the Mediterranean, where, in later years, she built the Achilleion.

No wonder Aunt Sissy eternally sought to capture that
love which she had missed in her marriage; no wonder she
everlastingly ran away from the crown, as it were, seeking
solace in *affaires d'amour*. While these intermezzi were
rarely constant, they lingered in her memory. Among the
poems which Aunt Sissy dictated to me two years later,
there was one in which she describes herself as "Mistress
Bluebeard" and tells of the "eight scalps she stored away in
her treasure chest." In another, she says:

> *From my dear Hungary you came*
> *To be at your queen's side;*
> *You gave up splendid rank and fame—*
> *That cannot be denied!*
> *Indeed, it was a sacrifice*
> *You made in love's sweet name;*
> *And well I know it costs a price*
> *To play the old, old game!*

It was this paramour from "dear Hungary" to whom
Aunt Sissy entrusted me with a very delicate mission. Secre-
tive, as always, she did not reveal the identity of the person
to whom I was to take a small package and, trained as I was

in her school of discretion, I naturally did not ask any questions.

The Empress gave me my instructions a few days before I left for Munich on a visit to my parents. On a certain day I was to proceed from there to Mainz, a railroad ride of some six hours. The day prior to the trip I was to inform a certain Herr Peter Müller—a fictitious name, as I immediately and correctly suspected—of my imminent arrival by sending him, in care of General Delivery, the code message: "Sea gull's letter due on . . ." with the exact date inserted. Upon my arrival in Mainz on the morning train, I was to check in at a certain hotel under an assumed name. At exactly eleven o'clock I was to proceed to a second hotel, where an old man with a shock of white hair would receive the package and give me a letter in exchange. I was then to return to Munich without delay and deliver the letter to my mother. Aunt Sissy warned me not to let anybody know about my trip except my parents.

Neither Father nor Mother approved of this involved assignment. Father muttered angrily: "Another one of Sissy's crazy tactics. . . . Nobody can ever make head or tail of them!" Mother feared that, in some way, my husband would hear about the trip, which struck her as the sort of an errand "a woman of standing" should never undertake. She fretted that "somebody might see" me, and before I had covered the first lap of my trip, Mother's prediction nearly came true. At a way station, a captain of the Fourth Light Horse, my father's own regiment, made straight for my compartment. Fortunately he changed his mind the very last second and boarded the coach ahead of mine.

I rode all through the night. Arriving in Mainz in the
morning, I went directly to the hotel which Aunt Sissy had
designated and waited there until eleven o'clock. More a
modest inn than a hotel, it was definitely third-class and
greatly in contrast to the place where I was to meet Herr
Peter Müller at eleven o'clock; this turned out to be a fashionable caravansary. A venerable old lady ushered me into
a room where my eyes immediately fell upon the picture of
a sylvan scene. Although very familiar to me, I nevertheless
could not identify it at that moment. However, when Herr
Müller stepped into the room a few minutes later, I instantly knew the picture to be Count Nicholas Esterházy's
shooting box near Gödöllö. It was easy, then, to surmise for
whom Aunt Sissy's little package was intended. Herr Peter
Müller—none other than Count Nicky's trusted valet—
seemed a little startled when he recognized me. He bowed
deeply as he handed me a large envelope: "Here's the answer, Your Grace." I thanked him, and he opened the door
for me with another deep bow.

On the train back to Munich I took out the envelope and
stared at it curiously. It was not addressed and merely carried a lavender-colored seal, depicting a sea gull in flight.
Weighing it in my hand, I pondered what the envelope
might contain.

A few months later I learned the answer to this question
from Aunt Sissy herself, whom I met while at Ischl. "You
probably have been wondering, Marie, what that package
contained. . . . Well, I can give you one clue, my dear. It
was not a letter, but just a little miniature of somebody 'he'
loves. . . . Oh, not me," she added quickly. "In exchange

for this miniature, you brought back a photograph, showing the same person as a baby."

Putting together the various parts of this royal puzzle, I concluded that my trip to Mainz had served to exchange two pictures of my cousin, Archduchess Valerie. As always, in such exchanges of amorous contraband, my parental home had served the internuncio.

In Ischl, Aunt Sissy seemed to be given to very sentimental moods. This place, one of the fashionable spas of Europe and favorite summer resort of the imperial Hapsburgs and of the Austrian nobility, had been the scene of Aunt Sissy's great conquest. Here she had supplanted her older sister Helen in the marital intentions of Francis Joseph and managed to become engaged herself to the young Emperor of the Dual Monarchy. All this had occurred over twenty years ago, but there was hardly a walk on which I accompanied Aunt Sissy through the beautiful park surrounding the imperial residence when she did not allude to that surprising engagement dinner.

On all these strenuous walks, which proved the Empress as tireless as ever, she affected an ankle-length sports skirt. She never wore a hat but always carried a fan while I shouldered her heavy parasol. The nearest approach to this sun shelter I ever saw, in later years, were those enormous multicolored umbrellas so popular at beach resorts. Aunt Sissy's ambulatory "awning," with its wing spread of well-nigh five feet, was fashioned of écru silk lined with blue; in between was a layer of buckskin to shut out the sun completely. The parasol was opened whenever we paused for a short rest. An all too short rest, I thought it; usually it only served to give the Empress a chance to wipe her face with tissue paper. She subscribed to the theory that perspiration would mar her beautiful face with freckless.

One day Aunt Sissy guided me over an especially tortuous path to a narrow glade, high up on the mountainside and far away from everything. The Empress had not spoken one word during the entire strenuous climb; now she broke the silence as she sat on a tree trunk. "Tell me, Marie," she asked, a melancholy note stealing into her voice, "are you afraid to die?"

Her question startled me. "I . . . I really don't know, Auntie. I have never given it serious thought."

"Perhaps it's just as well. . . . But believe me, Marie, the less good fortune we encounter in this life, the easier it is for us to pass into the Great Beyond."

I did not relish the trend of conversation in the least and wondered why, on such a beautiful day, Aunt Sissy chose such a somber subject. Nothing could induce her to desist; apparently the Empress felt impelled to unburden herself.

"Marie," she whispered, "none of us has any luck. It's that curse that was laid upon us. Only when the very last of us has passed on will it be lifted."

The Empress's dire prophecy set me shuddering. My face must have revealed something of what I felt, because Aunt Sissy went on to explain: "To be sure, Marie, you don't know anything about it. I think, in our whole family, nobody is aware of it except your Aunt Helen, Aunt Maria, and your father."

My fear melted into curiosity as Aunt Sissy continued in a mournful manner: "I want to tell the story to you because you, too, come under the spell of that curse; it was laid upon all the ducal Wittelsbachs. And you also seem to have missed happiness. Such joyful moments as you may experience in your life you must snatch from fate . . . and you'll have to pay dearly for them, too. It will go on and on until none of us ducal Wittelsbachs remains, until our whole ducal line has perished. And that will be within the next hundred years!"

I listened, fascinated.

Aunt Sissy placed her gloved hand on my knee, her eyes glued to mine. "You see, Marie," she resumed, after a moment, "it was your grandmother who put the curse on us. Of course, she's forgotten all about it by now. And once she had uttered the dire words, she probably did not mean them to be taken seriously. But, Marie,"—Aunt Sissy's voice trembled—"the monk of Tegernsee . . . he heard it . . . every word of it . . . and since that very day, he's waiting, waiting, waiting for us. Whenever a member of the ducal Wittelsbachs dies, the wraith of that monk stands at the head of the bed. Not until the last of us has passed on will the monk be redeemed.

"It was in the year 1828 at Castle Tegernsee," the Empress continued, "when your grandmother Ludovica was married to Duke Maximilian of Bavaria, entirely against her own will. As I heard it told, her love had been plighted to Duke Miguel of Braganza. At that time, however, insecure political conditions prevailed in Portugal, and so Duchess Ludovica's parents decided that she should marry young Duke Maximilian instead.

"It was on her wedding day that the young Duchess, tearing off her veil, pronounced the terrible words: 'This marriage, and all that ever springs from it, shall forevermore lack the blessings of the Lord.' "

A wan smile appeared on Aunt Sissy's face now. "How lightly the impulsive young Duchess regarded her own words may be concluded from the fact that, in the beginning, her married life was really happy and blessed with children."

"But the monk, Aunt Sissy," I broke in, "what about the monk of Tegernsee?"

"Oh, yes, yes, I almost forgot the most important part of the story. You see, when the present Castle Tegernsee was still a monastery, a youth of noble blood was brought there to become a monk against his will. He had been enamored of a beautiful cousin of his who had been chosen to become the wife of his older brother. The girl married the older brother, but while she stood before the Lord's altar, pledging her troth to her future husband, she vowed that she would love the younger brother always. This young knight, who had meanwhile been forced to enter the monastery, flung off the cowl one day and rushed into the arms of his beloved. Alas, the two were caught! It is unknown what punishment the brother meted out to his wife, but the younger brother was brought back to the monastery and there immured . . . alive. You can find the whole story, Marie, in the chronicle of the monastery."

"But, Aunt Sissy, I don't see the connection between the poor monk and the curse uttered by Grandmother on her wedding day."

"Don't you know, Marie, that souls in purgatory are not

permitted to pray for themselves, but that they may do so for others? When the soul of that monk caught the hasty words of your grandmother, cursing all generations to come, he prayed to God for mercy. To be sure, the penitent monk could never avert the evil; but the privilege was granted him to stand beside each member of the ducal house in his hour of death and pray for those upon whom the curse had been laid. Only when the last of the ducal Wittelsbachs has passed on—only then, the monk will be redeemed."

I looked at her in amazement. "Heavens, Aunt Sissy, who told you that?"

The Empress arose. She stood proudly erect and spoke in a firm voice: "The monk himself told me." On the way home she referred to her story just once more. "Remember, Marie," she predicted, "the ducal line will have ceased to exist before another hundred years have passed."

It was at the beginning of the 'eighties that Aunt Sissy made that prediction. Since then, the ducal line of the House of Wittelsbach seems well on the way to extinction. Duke Ludwig Wilhelm, the present head of the ducal line, though married since 1917, is childless; the three sons of the late Duke Max Emanuel are not to be considered for the continuation of the ducal line because the oldest is mentally deranged, while the two younger brothers are unmarried. Thus it seems as if my grandmother's curse actually will be fulfilled, and the monk soon redeemed. I wonder, will he stand by my bedside when I am ready to pass on? . . .

That year, at Ischl, Aunt Sissy was given to Cassandra moods more than ever before. She complained of everything life had withheld from her since her marriage to Francis

Joseph and completely ignored the fact that she had entered the baneful sphere of the imperial court on her own initiative. She was sincerely convinced that it was the House of Hapsburg that had brought her nothing but ill luck. Doubtless it was in one of these moods that Aunt Sissy conceived the idea for her poem, "Hapsburg." When she dictated it to me in later years, one particular stanza impressed me so much that I still remember it:

> *Right you are, Hapsburg, to cover your head,*
> *Right to be wringing your hands.*
> *Do you think back to your offspring, now dead?*
> *They'll ne'er be ruling your lands!*

Today, looking back at what happened barely two years after this sojourn in Ischl, I believe what primarily ailed Aunt Sissy, at that time, was her stunted maternal instinct. In the course of years the Archduchess Sophie had succeeded in estranging Gisela and Rudolf from their own mother. Consquently, when Valerie was born in 1868, the Empress guarded her with jealous zeal, brooking no interference in her education. As for the Emperor, it was generally understood in court circles that he hardly had the right to exert paternal prerogatives over Valerie.

But despite the fact that this young daughter was her very own, Aunt Sissy still craved a child that might grow up outside the stifling atmosphere of the court she so detested. And although a woman in her forties then, the Empress was destined to see her dream fulfilled in the not too distant future.

Chapter Five

THE SECRET OF AN EMPRESS

*I*N SPITE of all the heartaches she had suffered in the course of her marital life, the Empress-Queen of Austria-Hungary was still one of Europe's most beautiful women when the imperial silver wedding was celebrated in Vienna in 1879 with great pomp and circumstance.

When I came to offer my congratulations to Aunt Sissy that morning, she looked at me quizzically and said: "You know, Marie, to be married twenty-five years is really bad enough. Why, I wonder, must people add insult to injury by celebrating such a sad anniversary?"

The imperial silver wedding was one of the rare occasions when my husband, still obsessed by wanderlust, for once returned from his rovings to the Kaiserstadt. During those years, we spent the winter months in an apartment in the heart of Vienna's Leopold district, a neighborhood not at all fashionable. Still, a few members of the Austrian nobility had established their winter residence there. I liked it well enough since, from my windows facing the Praterstrasse, I could watch all the coaches driving to and fro in Vienna's Central Park.

I was once more serving as amanuensis to my imperial aunt, and the little leisure time left to me was mostly spent in the company of my cousin Valerie. The young Archduchess had attained, by then, the *Backfisch* stage, that teasing tender time when a girl has outgrown innocent childhood but has not yet reached full womanhood; the "flapper" age, I later came to call it during my American sojourn.

My duties at court were rather strenuous at that time, but always interesting. If I had not known it before, the truth was brought home to me then that "uneasy rests the head that wears a crown." Not only political problems beset ruling royalty, but the intricacies of family life, subject to etiquette and political *raisons d'état,* must be contended with also.

His Majesty deemed it advisable that the heir apparent to the throne of the Dual Monarchy settle down and marry. I knew that cousin Rudolf was not at all in agreement with the imperial opinion, for he thoroughly enjoyed the free and easy life he was leading. However, it was the monarch's command that the Crown Prince must choose a suitable consort, and it was in this connection that I happened to witness a family scene between *Onkel Kaiser* and *Tante Kaiserin.*

One day I was consulting with Auntie about the imperial wardrobe when the Emperor burst into the room, evidently furious over some mishap. I was about to withdraw, but he remarked curtly: "Never mind, Marie, you might as well stay."

It seemed that Cousin Rudolf, accompanied by Count Bombelles, had "sneaked off to Switzerland." I could not understand, at first, why this was so terrible, but in the course of conversation the Emperor shouted: "It's unbelievable that he is running after that young woman again. I won't have it, I say!"

After the Kaiser had left, Aunt Sissy told me that "that young woman" was the Princess K . . ., morganatic daughter of a European potentate. Little did I realize then that more than four decades later, during my years in Florida, I would receive a letter from a man leading a simple farmer's existence in the Middle West, presumably the offspring of Rudolf's clandestine love affair with that fascinating young woman. Nor was I aware, that day, that the Kaiser's rage was so towering because, meanwhile, negotiations had proceeded to the point where the heir apparent to the Dual Monarchy was considered an acceptable candidate for the hand of Princess Stephanie, daughter of King Leopold II of the Belgians.

When Aunt Sissy confided this secret to me, one of state as well as of family, she shook her head thoughtfully: "I don't know, Marie. . . . I don't like this match at all. Belgium has been bad luck for the Hapsburgs before."

She was referring to Francis Joseph's brother, the ill-fated Emperor Maximilian I of Mexico, whose wife was the Belgian Princess Charlotte.

Eventually the dictates of dynastic interests proved strong enough to send the Crown Prince to Brussels to woo Stepha-

EMPRESS ELIZABETH *in her forties.*

nie in the prescribed, if unromantic, royal manner. Probably
because my cousin resented this match with a consort not of
his own choosing, he indulged in an extremely embarrassing
escapade on the trip to the Belgian capital. He had the poor
taste to take along with him, on that sober mission, one of
his mistresses, a woman known as *die schöne Fischerin*—
the beautiful Mrs. Fischer.

Rudolf's indiscretion became known at the court of King
Leopold and, although the monarch himself did not exactly
enjoy a reputation for unblemished morality, the scandal
assumed such proportions that the Belgian royal house was
ready to cancel all arrangements. It required innumerable
wires from the Emperor himself, along with the concentrated efforts of his special emissaries, to smooth over the
whole distasteful affair. Finally the glad tidings were spread
throughout the world that His Royal and Imperial Highness, Crown Prince Rudolf, had become engaged to Her
Royal Highness, Princess Stephanie of Belgium.

Even after the official engagement, Aunt Sissy, as well as
the Kaiser, was worried that the match would never be con-
summated. Their Majesties were plainly relieved when
Rudolf and Stephanie actually married in May, 1881.

Once again George's inborn restlessness induced him to
leave Piersna and move to Pardubitz, a neighborhood where
the Silesian plains are their plainest. Life was terrifyingly
monotonous there, and I was happy when the summer had
passed. Late in fall, 1881, I returned to Vienna, in pre-war
days the gayest of all European capitals next to Paris.

I found Aunt Sissy greatly changed. Her once peerless

complexion was sallow; she was then forty-four and actually looked her age. It seemed she was suffering severely from sciatica and planned to undergo a strenuous cure.

The first time I reported to her she said: "I know, Marie, that your handwriting is very poor, but can you take fast dictation?"

I assured her that I could, but Aunt Sissy did not reveal what was on her mind. However, a few days later, Mrs. von Ferenczy informed me that Her Majesty intended to have all her diaries and poetry copied, preparatory to assembling them in a volume. In those days typewriters had just been invented and were considered hardly more than an amusing toy. Since the Empress desired numerous copies, the only alternative was to set up her writings in type. The composing as well as the printing—so Ida von Ferenczy confided— would be done in a sub-basement of the *Hofburg* by a few trusted members of the nobility under the cloak of greatest secrecy.

Presently Aunt Sissy broached the subject herself. "It will be the work of several weeks, and you must not breathe a word about it to anyone," she warned me. "It will be hard work, and it brooks no delay. My cure starts in January, and all the work absolutely must be finished by that time. And so," Aunt Sissy continued, "I have written to your mother to send your cousin Henny Pecz. I know that she can be depended upon in confidential matters."

Henny Pecz, daughter of my mother's second sister, had found a home under my parental roof when, shortly after my marriage, her widowed mother had died. Henny, a teacher, was generally referred to in the family as "the little

schoolmarm." Although none too good-looking, she was a
girl of captivating charm.

"Henny will stay at some hotel in the neighborhood,"
Aunt Sissy unfolded her plan, "presumably as Ida's niece.
Nobody will doubt the relationship, since they both are
Hungarian. As for you, I think it best that you live right
here in the *Hofburg* with Ida, because I don't want your
husband to interfere in any way. Simply tell George that I
am engaged in literary work, but be sure not to mention the
printing arrangements which are under way. I want the
whole affair to appear as harmless as possible. Speak of it
casually to George, so that he will conclude it is merely another one of my whims."

That night, when I broke the news to George, the Empress's deep understanding of people was brought home to
me again. My husband shrugged his shoulders and said almost exactly what Aunt Sissy had expected him to say,
except that he did not use the word "whim" but referred to
it as "one of your illustrious aunt's crazy caprices."

Content in the knowledge that my children had the best
of care, I moved over to the *Hofburg* the very next morning
to share Ida von Ferenczy's apartment. Her suite was lo-
cated in an annex to the palace. This part of the enormous
compound of buildings forming the imperial residence was
connected with the main building by a long, low corridor,
its staircase so badly illuminated that, more than once, I
stumbled and fell.

Ida von Ferenczy, officially reader to the Empress, was the
pure Hungarian type with her black eyes and hair, olive
complexion, and wonderful white teeth. Unofficially she was

lady-in-waiting to the Empress; but outsiders would not concede her this dignity, although Ida had been longer "in waiting" than many others in Aunt Sissy's retinue.

No sooner had I moved into her apartment than Ida produced a great number of heavy paper bundles, made up of sheaves of sheets of different sizes and colors. Some of them were loosely tied together in small packages, and all the sheets were much thumbed. The imperial diaries and notes would be elegantly bound volumes, I had thought; actually they were just slim copy books, such as children use in school. The writing was in pencil; the scrawl even worse than my own. Ida, to all appearances, seemed very well informed about the material, which she assorted in little piles as I looked on.

"I suppose Aunt Sissy wishes to leave for England as early in January as possible," I remarked.

In an offhand manner, the reply came: "Her Majesty is not going to England at all."

"Oh, no? Where else, then?"

"She will go incognito as Countess Hohenembs to Château de Sassetot."

"What! For *la chasse au sanglier?*" I wondered aloud.

Boar hunting with a spear was the outstanding sport in that part of Normandy. "You don't mean to say such strenuous exercise is the proper cure for Aunt Sissy's sciatica, do you?"

With a half-suppressed smirk, Mrs. von Ferenczy murmured: "Well, it might be."

Months later I smiled, too, when I discovered the real reason behind this excursion to Sassetot. In questioning Ida, I certainly proved myself surprisingly unsophisticated for a married woman and a mother of two children.

During our conversation Ida picked out a few small packages of paper and laid them aside. The rest of the bundles she locked into a safe which stood in a corner of her bedroom. She then took the packages she had selected, hid them beneath her cape, and together we repaired to the apartment of the Empress. After exchanging a few whispered words with Aunt Sissy in Hungarian, she left us.

"Sit down, Marie," said the Empress, pointing to a chair beside her desk. She opened one of the small paper bundles, spreading the notes before her. Inadvertently I looked about me, remembering that, at Gödöllö, the Emperor frequently had entered his consort's boudoir unannounced.

Aunt Sissy read my thoughts; there was a roguish twinkle in her eyes. "Don't worry, Marie, nobody will surprise us here. Right now I am supposedly undergoing my sciatica treatment, and there are strict instructions that I must not be disturbed." Her face was wreathed in an impish smile.

Without further ado Aunt Sissy started to dictate. As soon as I had finished the first page, she looked it over critically. "Well, Marie, yours isn't exactly an example of perfect penmanship, but it will do. It's legible enough, and you certainly write fast. Remember, manuscripts for printing are written on one side of the sheet only."

Aunt Sissy continued to dictate for another two hours. She was so engrossed in her work that she did not notice how, time and again, I sought to relieve the cramp in my hand by spreading my fingers.

At last she stopped. "Hard work," she complained. "Believe me, this is an awful strain on my throat."

I felt like adding: "And it certainly is not easy on my poor wrist." I ventured the suggestion: "If you will give these sheets to me, Aunt Sissy, I am quite sure I could read them."

"Decipher my scrawl?" She seemed rather doubtful.

"Well, I could go over them first, and wherever I cannot make out the words, I could consult you."

Aunt Sissy nodded. "That would be an idea. Talking for so many hours on end is a terrible task." She cleared her throat. "I'm as hoarse as an old rooster already." She handed me a sheaf of papers. "Go on, Marie, see whether you can decipher them."

I went over the notes carefully and found I could read almost everything.

"Yes, that's what we'll do. I'll dictate to you whatever you cannot read. It will make things much easier all around. I think I'll do the same with Henny. You both can do the recopying in Ida's apartment."

As if driven by something, Aunt Sissy launched upon her literary labors with an almost terrifying energy. Suddenly she did not seem ailing any longer, merely impatient.

Henny arrived the next day, and thereafter my cousin and I were chained to our desks for many hours each day.

It may be because I was so naïve and unsuspecting in those years that Aunt Sissy selected me, a married woman, to transcribe certain parts of her writings which apparently seemed to her too personal for Henny's eyes. Taking down her dictation, or copying it, I succeeded in reading between the lines only occasionally. Interesting as the work was, it would have held greater significance if, during those late fall and early winter days of 1881, I had known what I came to know afterward.

The first collection of fairy tales and poems which Aunt Sissy dictated to me was entitled *A Midsummer-Night's Dream*. Here, the implications were obvious enough in the story of her early youth and of her surprising engagement to Francis Joseph. At the conclusion of the first part, Titania changed herself into a sea gull, and this sea gull in turn, on a Christmas Eve, became a little princess. . . . Aunt Sissy's birthday was the 24th of December.

When I transcribed these chapters of the Empress's writings, I was greatly charmed. The impression created by the second part of *A Midsummer-Night's Dream* was something of a shock. In dealing with her days at Madeira, Aunt Sissy's cynicism was strikingly apparent. She had a way of squaring accounts with people she disliked and frequently proceeded with a ruthlessness akin to cruelty. Time and again a character appeared in her story whom she had dubbed "the green dung beetle." This rôle had been assigned to one of the courtiers, groveling at Oberon's throne—in reality, none other than His Apostolic Majesty, the Emperor and King.

I could not help giggling when Aunty dictated that little episode to me, and my amusement grew when she explained: "That green dung beetle, my dear, is none other than Count Grünne." The very name of the then Imperial Master of the Horse, sounding very much like *grün*—green

—had inspired Aunt Sissy's flippancy. "Imagine, Marie, that green dung beetle had the amazing effrontery to offer himself as 'consolation.' It was shortly after Rudolf's birth, when I first learned of the Kaiser's interest in a certain Polish princess." It seems that Count Grünne had spied on the young Empress continuously while at Madeira, reporting all her doings to the Emperor, who at that time was not treading the narrow path of virtue any too firmly.

Entitled "The Scandalous Chronicle of Queen Titania," this second part of the Empress's *A Midsummer-Night's Dream* told of a love adventure, its scene laid in Fairy Island. Titania, of course, was Aunt Sissy herself. In Elf Imo, I immediately recognized that much-famed Adonis, Count Imre Hunyadi, who had accompanied the Empress on her trip to Madeira. The story, in its conclusion, sadly related how King Oberon insisted that Queen Titania return home without delay. Subsequently Count Imre left the court and retired to his Hungarian estates. He married a very buxom girl who presented him with seven children in good time. I met him once, when he was an old man, during the races in Budapest. He came to pay his respects to the Empress. Immediately I was struck by his beautiful eyes, so beautiful, in fact, that I almost fell in love with the superannuated Adonis. A pure-strain Magyar, the years had not lessened his charm. Long afterward, recalling the scene at the race track, I remembered the mischievous twinkle with which Aunt Sissy had glanced from Imre to Count Nicholas Esterházy, who had been standing near by. Nicky had been Imre's successor in Aunt Sissy's affections, but at the time of the race-track meeting, Nicky, in turn, had been succeeded by Captain Middleton. Of course, all this only became clear to me many years later. But the scene at the Budapest race track impressed itself on my mind so indelibly that even to-day I can conjure up that picture in all its minute details.

Practically all of the Empress's stories and poems referred to her love affairs—sometimes slyly, sometimes openly—even revealing the paternity of Cousin Valerie. There was especially one poem, written in 1868, before the birth of Valerie, when Aunt Sissy fervently prayed for a son. She hoped that, one day, he might be King of Hungary, once the realm of the Magyars would separate from the rest of Austria and become an independent kingdom. Always, this had been Empress Elizabeth's dream.

The poem was entitled:

OH, FOR A KING OF HUNGARY

Oh, for a King of Hungary,
To free it from its chains;
My eyes long so to see the day
He'll rule the Magyar plains.

For Hungary her heroes died—
It was the price they paid
To make their land a mighty one;
Nor were they e'er afraid!

It is a King the pusztas need,
A man of brain and brawn;
Some Magyar proud, of noble birth,
Who'll never cringe nor fawn.

He'll share your ev'ry joy and pain;
New Freedom he shall bring;
Ah, would the day were close at hand
That you might have this King!

Count Nicky Esterházy, who Aunt Sissy had hoped would found a new Magyar dynasty, played an important part in the Empress's poetry. In her *Book of Dreams,* he repeatedly appears as a vampire, a creature for which my entire family seemed to have had a strong predilection. In 1856, when a young man, my father dabbled in writing; he penned a terrifying tale about one of those blood-sucking bats. When I read it first, it impressed me so much that I still treasure the original manuscript which Father gave me for a present. From him and other relatives, especially from Aunt Sissy, I heard so much about vampires that I eventually came to look upon this beast as a domestic pet of the House of Wittelsbach.

In her introduction to her *Vampire Cycle,* the Empress elucidates:

The most famous scientists have written learned pages on the subject of vampires, a creature which, according to human conception, is frequently represented by that much-feared South American bat of whose habits the most divergent stories are abroad. It seems that nobody yet has been able to ascertain why the attack of a vampire never arouses its victim, be it man or beast, so that the victim perishes without ever knowing what destroyed it. The vampire never bites—it "kisses." Softly, caressingly, the terrifying creature sucks the lifeblood from its victims.

In dictating her vampire tale to me, Aunt Sissy at last provided me with an explanation for that strange scene which occurred in Gödöllö in 1876 when she requested me to sing "The Lorelei" for Count Esterházy. It seems that a few weeks before the birth of Valerie, in 1868, Nicky had left for a short trip to inspect a maternal estate on the bank of the Rhine where he owned a little chalet. While there, he became infatuated with the seventeen-year-old daughter of the sexton. The girl was as golden-haired as the Lorelei of folklore. On St. John's Night, when, according to old Teutonic custom, bonfires were lit on the mountain tops to ward off sickness and ill luck, the romance had come to a culmination.

All this the Empress discovered months later when, by mere chance, she found a picture of the golden-haired girl in Nicky's room. Under the Empress's urging, Count Nicky confessed the affair and admitted that he had just received a letter from the girl, pleading that he come to her assistance without delay. The Empress assumed that the girl was just a clever schemer. She was beside herself with jealousy, and when Nicky proposed to visit the girl, she strenuously objected, insisting that he must send his trusted valet Peter to offer the girl a settlement.

A few days passed while this point was argued between the Empress and Count Esterházy. By the time Peter finally arrived at the Rhine, the girl had died. From the reports the valet brought back, the Empress concluded that she had been mistaken in believing the girl to be a cold, calculating flirt. Conscience-stricken, Aunt Sissy poured all her agony into the tale she dictated to me. There Aunt Sissy appears as the Lady in Black who brings roses to the girl's grave, while Count Nicky is personified by a vampire whose kiss carries destruction.

Aunt Sissy everlastingly reproached herself for her interference. Then, again, her jealousy would flare up violently. Once, in order to hurt Count Nicky, she sent him a music box; the instrument had but one cylinder, which played "The Lorelei." She knew that she could fling Nicky into the deepest abyss of remorse by reminding him of that tragic romance on the bank of the Rhine. And it was for this purpose—although I do not know what prompted her revengeful spirit that particular morning at Gödöllö—that Aunt Sissy had requested me to sing "The Lorelei."

Aunt Sissy told me, not without a slight tinge of unconscious triumph in her voice, that Nicky never again visited the little chalet, nor did he ever marry.

Now, after years of piecing together the puzzle of Aunt Sissy's confusing conduct, I am sincerely convinced that, despite outward appearances, the late Empress Elizabeth is not to be regarded as frivolous. She was neither a Messalina nor a Catherine II. As with King Ludwig II, individual incidents of Aunt Sissy's life should not be scrutinized under the microscope of psychological research. Rather, her entire life should be studied sympathetically against that background of mysterious symbolism in which she, as well as her "spiritual brother" Ludwig, revelled. Contemporary probers of the soul probably would classify the late Empress-Queen as a high-strung woman, suffering intensely in the artificial, rarefied air of those lofty heights where royalty supposedly dwells. Innately bubbling over with *joie de vivre,* her high spirits were tragically harnessed to the yoke of rigorous court etiquette. She was extremely unhappy in her marriage. With advanced ideas beyond her time, she could not fathom why an occasional glimpse of happiness might not be hers.

Not only was Elizabeth an empress, but she was a beautiful and highly gifted woman. It was, therefore, much easier for her than for many others of her sex to attract men to her side. Again and again Aunt Sissy tasted the tantalizing draught of life's bitter-sweetness, and it is this quality which pervades practically all of her poetry, regardless of its literary value. It is especially discernible in those poems in which, directly or indirectly, she refers to the Emperor. There are three stanzas which I shall always remember because they illustrate so graphically this characteristic of the Empress:

> *I beg of you, my Oberon,*
> *Cease all recriminations;*
> *Oh, why the strife and why the grief?*
> *Desist from lamentations!*

> *Please let me have my freedom, dear,*
> *Unto the fullest measure;*
> *I love to dance in moonlight's gleam.*
> *Don't rob me of that pleasure!*

> *Now, I beseech you, Oberon,*
> *Go dally 'midst gerania*
> *With Melusina . . . but the Ass*
> *Belongs to me, Titania!*

To Aunt Sissy, geraniums symbolized "the sort of woman who glories in cake-baking and lives in a little house surrounded by a little garden"—a type that evidently elicited the Emperor's approval. In her poems Francis Joseph invariably is pictured sympathetically. Although the Emperor never completely understood Aunt Sissy, he always was ready to forgive and forget. To all appearances the Empress appreciated the exemplary good-naturedness with which Francis Joseph overlooked certain indiscretions. To be sure, the Kaiser was no hero in the eyes of the Kaiserin; as a matter of fact, the only heroic character in her *Midsummer-Night's Dream* was that of the Eagle, easily recognizable as King Ludwig II of Bavaria.

There were many other pieces of poetry and prose besides the *Midsummer-Night's Dream* tale, all frankly biographical. Mostly written in the style of Heinrich Heine, whom Aunt Sissy sought to emulate, they described the Empress now as a female Flying Dutchman, and then again as a woman Ahasuerus. One of the poems expressed Elizabeth's contempt for thrones and nobility; in one of the stanzas of the poem, she satirized Francis Joseph's meeting with the Czar with withering scorn. Portraying the Czarevna as Peacock, she introduced the Czar as Orang-outang. They foregathered at Kremsier for the avowed purpose of benefiting their peoples:

> *At last they depart once more through the gate,*
> *While we stay behind, as wise as of late,*
> *And though they may seem as smooth as fine silk,*
> *Protect us, dear Lord, from Czars and their ilk.*

We worked faithfully, day after day. As soon as a sheaf of pages had been transcribed, I had to sneak down to the sub-basement to a small but complete printing plant, including a book bindery. The locked door to the sepulchral work-shop was usually opened to me by a tall bearded man who bowed deeply but never uttered a word. Like all the others, he wore a black mask and a long black smock so that I could never identify him.

Everything went along smoothly until one Sunday morn-ing when the Empress sent for me at the unearthly hour of seven o'clock. I dressed hurriedly and, within fifteen min-utes, appeared before my imperial aunt.

"Look here, Marie, on what terms are you with Count Wilczek?"

Count Hans Nepomuk Wilczek, then a man in his forties —a *chevalier sans peur et sans reproche* if ever I met one— was distinguished for his exploits on bloody battlefields and in the icy wastes of the polar regions as well as on the waxed floors of aristocratic mansions. He always had treated me with utmost courtesy, honoring me with his friendship and confidence.

"On the very best, Aunt Sissy. In fact, the Count some-times calls me Little Goose."

The Empress smiled a little. "Good," she nodded. Then, with a show of excitement, such as I had seldom witnessed in her before, she told me that among the pages which had been copied on Saturday, and which were now locked away in the printery to be set up the first thing Monday morning, there had been certain sheets; these, on second thought, must not go into print.

"By the way, Marie, who copied the pages about . . ." And Aunt Sissy mentioned a name which repeatedly occurred in the material she wished to withdraw. "You or Henny?"

"I copied them, Auntie."

The Empress appeared relieved. "I'm glad it was you. It's not suitable reading for a young, unmarried girl like Henny."

"I thought so, too." The words slipped off my tongue glibly.

"Why didn't you say so, then?" the Empress demanded impatiently. "If you had been a little more careful, you would have known that it is not material I should like to see in print."

Her Majesty's rebuke stung me. I could have defended myself easily, for, in copying her notes, I had run across material more than once which seemed too indiscreet to appear in cold type. But this was not the time for idle talk.

Aunt Sissy instructed me to rush over to Count Wilczek and ask him to retrieve the pages from the printery immediately. I knew, then, the identity of the "tall one" who generally unlocked the door of the printing shop for me. I was to return with the sheets, recopy a few pages, and renumber the entire sheaf. Next, the sheets were to be restored to the printery once more so that everything would be in order for the aristocratic craftsmen on Monday. Of course, all this had to be accomplished with speed as well as secrecy.

On the face of it the task seemed simple enough. Of course, it might be awkward to explain to the household my early-Sunday-morning visit to Count Wilczek. Suddenly

Countess Larisch *and the young* Archduchess Valerie. *Gödöllö, 1876.*

I had an inspiration. A year before, returning from an arctic expedition with Dr. Julius Payer, the Count had brought along a number of Eskimo dogs and had presented me with one of them. My excuse for calling would be that the dog was desperately sick and I wanted to know how to treat it. This was the story, at any rate, which I poured into the butler's ears. He left me alone in the vestibule, for a moment, and then returned to escort me to Count Wilczek's study.

Count Wilczek's bearded face beamed upon me kindly. "Well, is that all that worries you?" he asked a trifle quizzically.

A glance at the door assured me that it was tightly shut. Quickly I divulged to the Count what I really wanted, confident that my mission would terminate successfully.

But we struck a snag and a very difficult one, too. It turned out, to our dismay, that a serious obstacle confronted us, since Count Wilczek had no access to the printery. The key was in the hands of an anonymous co-worker who always visited his estate over Sunday. Even if the Count actually recovered the key, it would be very late in the night before he could retrieve the pages Aunt Sissy demanded, and at that ungodly hour he could not very well come to the *Hofburg* annex to deliver the package to me. What, then, were we to do?

The Wilczek mansion stood in Herrengasse, right around the corner from the *Hofburg*, its rear removed from that of the *Hofburg* annex by only a few yards. From my third-floor bedroom, in Ida von Ferenczy's suite, I could look down into the second-floor *bureaux* of the Wilczek residence.

The Count finally evolved the idea that he would immediately rush out of town to procure the key to the printery. As soon as he retrieved the manuscript, he would take it to his office and step on the window sill. I was to "stand guard" behind the curtain of my bedroom and reach out for the manuscript as soon as the Count appeared on the ledge of the office window. Simple, indeed!

The whole procedure was not nearly as reckless as it sounded, considering the Count's astonishing record at mountain climbing and his other feats of daring. We agreed that, at eleven o'clock in the evening, I would "mount guard" and wait for the Count's appearance on the window ledge.

It was with this report that I returned to Aunt Sissy. She was grievously disappointed when I failed to bring her the manuscript. On the other hand, she knew that the Count could be relied upon to procure it. "I suppose we must hope for the best," was her final comment. "By the way, it might be just as well not to tell Henny all the details. Just see that she is ready to give you whatever assistance you require. Let her stay with you tonight instead of going back to her hotel."

Later, when I saw my cousin, I informed her that Her Majesty had decided to eliminate a few paragraphs in her manuscript and that we would make the necessary changes as soon as the pages were brought by Count Wilczek. As this might be late at night, I advised her to go to sleep in the next room; I would call her when I needed her.

During the day I repeatedly went to the window of my bedroom to look down into the Wilczek offices; each time I felt a nervous qualm. The chasm between the two houses seemed too wide even for a man of such amazing athletic accomplishments as Count Wilczek. We both were tall, but, surely, our arms would not be long enough to bridge the gap.

With a heavy heart I began my vigil behind the hangings, waiting what seemed an eternity to me. I fretted over the possibility that the Count had not obtained the key, and I hated to think of the scene Aunt Sissy would make if I had to admit defeat.

At last the chimes of the near-by St. Stephen's Cathedral proclaimed it to be midnight. Almost at the exact stroke of twelve, I saw the Count climb out on the window ledge. Balancing himself precariously, he extracted a sheaf of papers from his inside coat pocket. I bent down as far as I dared, but the distance was still too great, despite the fact that the Count stood on tiptoe. Suddenly he seemed to be losing his balance! I froze with fear. Before my mental eye, I already saw the Count tumbling to his death. . . . I cannot recall whether I covered my eyes with my hand or whether I turned away in fright, but the next minute I noticed two strong hands holding onto the frame of my bedroom window. A second later Count Wilczek, known for his predilection for entering and leaving his own house through a convenient window instead of the conventional door, had pulled himself up as far as his shoulders.

"Come on, Countess," he said coolly, "give me a hand."

In another moment he stood in my bedroom. I uttered a

little cry of astonishment, at the same time stepping back
and overturning a chair.

"Careful, careful!" the Count admonished me, putting a
finger to his lips.

The next moment, the door to my bedroom opened. In
its frame appeared Henny, ghostlike in her long trailing
nightgown, her hair done up as usual in little pigtails. "Oh,"
she uttered, aghast, her eyes almost popping.

"Sh, sh!" I warned her. "Can't you see, it's Count
Wilczek? He's brought us the manuscript."

"Yes, it's he," the Count chuckled softly, "and in his
stockinged feet, too." For the first time, I noticed that the
Count, in the manner of experienced mountain climbers,
had undertaken the little house-to-house excursion without
his shoes so as to assure a firmer hold.

"Well, ladies," he addressed us, "with your kind permission, I shall now withdraw." Sitting on the window sill,
he swung himself around quickly. "If I may ask you to
lend me a hand . . ."

"Why, Count, surely you're not going back that way?" I
demanded.

"How, then, shall I get out of the *Hofburg* at this hour
of the night? Just give me your hand."

At that moment Henny displayed unusual presence of
mind. While the Count lowered himself from the window
sill, she resolutely held onto His Excellency by the collar
of his coat, and the very second he said "Now!" Henny
assisted him with a gentle shove in the direction of his office
windows. For a split second the Count hung between
heaven and earth; then, to my enormous relief, he landed

safely on the window ledge. He clung to the frame to regain his equilibrium; after a friendly wave of his hand and a whispered "good-night," the intrepid Count disappeared from sight.

Once the excitement was over, Henny verged on hysterics.

"No, no, you mustn't," I checked her firmly. "There isn't any time for it. We have lots of work to do—so put on something warm, and let's get busy."

I thumbed through the manuscript and quickly extracted the pages which Aunt Sissy wished restored to her and which Henny was not to see. Then we sat down, and while my cousin copied one page, I renumbered the rest of the material and did what editing was necessary. It was two o'clock in the morning before we crawled into our beds, frozen and utterly exhausted.

Exactly as on the preceding day, the Empress sent for me at an unearthly hour.

"Did you get it?" she demanded breathlessly as I entered her boudoir.

I handed her the withdrawn pages.

"Thank God," exclaimed Aunt Sissy and added: "Tell me all about it."

The Empress evinced no great surprise when I described the Count's bold exploit. "I knew I could depend on Wilczek. There's nothing he can't do. As for his window acrobatics, he's done something like it before. That's the way he courted his wife while she was still my lady-in-waiting. But tell me, Marie," Aunt Sissy teased me, "what do you think people would say if they knew you received Count Wilczek in your room last night?"

"Didn't I have Henny for a chaperon?" I protested laughingly.

"Ah," pointed out the Empress with her most mischievous smile, "perhaps she was merely a little glowworm, lighting the way."

Another dramatic incident occurred before Aunt Sissy left for Sassetot. On the eve of her departure, she had a charcoal stove brought up to Ida von Ferenczy's little alcove kitchen. There, sitting in front of the gleaming embers, with Ida and myself standing ready with big pitchers of water in case of fire, Aunt Sissy tore up her original writings, page by page, together with the galley proofs of the book. The Empress was wearing an old raincoat and had covered her beautiful hair with a red silk kerchief. Mrs. von Ferenczy and I were dressed in tremendously large pinafores. The scene had the weird aspect of a witches' kitchen.

The cremation of the papers took hours and hours; to describe what the room looked like after the *auto-da-fé* would defy even a Dante's pen. Finally all the copies in my own handwriting were wrapped into paper on which I was told to write a few lines to the effect that these documents were the private property of my mother, Henrietta von Wallersee.

Then the Empress gave me the package with the instructions: "I want you to take this to Munich as soon as possible. Not one solitary shred of these papers must remain in the *Hofburg*. As long as either the Emperor or I am alive, all this is to be kept secret. Will you swear to that, Marie?"

I nodded, deeply stirred, especially as Aunt Sissy concluded the whole scene with the dire words: "To be prepared as for the final journey"—it had the ring of a quotation—"is always a wise plan for us mortals."

I never discovered how many copies of the Empress's books were struck off in that secret printery. Some of them, I know, were entrusted to Count Hans Wilczek; others were given to Prince Rudolf Liechtenstein with the instruction that they could be released to the general public sixty years after Aunt Sissy's death. The Prince, who kept this mission secret up to his death, provided in his last will and testament that his books be placed in trust with the Municipal Court in Brünn, now in Czechoslovakia. Liechtenstein also stipulated that, after the 10th of September, 1958 —six decades following Aunt Sissy's assassination—three men were to read the imperial writings and decide whether they could be published then without desecrating the memory of the Empress.

I know of five others who received one or more copies of Aunt Sissy's books. Some of these "trustees" have disappeared into oblivion since the World War, and it seems more than doubtful that their copies will ever see the light of day. That nothing has been heard of these copies so far indicates that they probably have been lost.

I saw Aunt Sissy but once again before she left for her "cure" at Château de Sassetot. She kissed me more tenderly

than ever; for a keepsake, she gave me a brooch of white
enamel and gold, with a sea gull fashioned from precious
stones.

Shortly after her departure I journeyed to Munich, taking along the papers she had entrusted to me. Mother received them frowningly and lost no time in locking the
package away. She shook her head uneasily, murmuring the
while: "I really don't know . . ." It was to be many years
—not until after Mother's death—before I would see that
parcel of papers again.

Weeks later, while still staying under my parental roof,
Father received a telegram from Sassetot early one morning. He took it up to Mother's room directly after he had
read it, and when I inquired about its contents, he most unceremoniously closed the door in my face. After the better
part of an hour had passed, he and Mother came downstairs. To all appearances they had something important to
impart to me. They looked at each other uncertainly, and
I could see that neither of them was eager to break the news
to me.

At last my father cleared his throat. "You see, Marie,
Aunt Sissy . . . Oh, well, she's had some sort of riding acci-
dent." My father stopped abruptly, palpably embarrassed.
He gazed at Mother as if inviting her support.

"My dear," Mother said simply, putting her arm around
me, "your Aunt Sissy is the happy mother of a little baby
girl."

"A baby girl," I echoed in astonishment. "Why, Mother!"
Suddenly I realized the truth behind Aunt Sissy's "sciatica"
and I felt extremely concerned for her. After all, she was a

woman of forty-four, and many years had lapsed since last she had enjoyed the blessings of motherhood. Now I understood why Aunt Sissy had been so bent upon assembling and editing her writings before journeying to Sassetot. To think I had never so much as suspected the real reason behind her journey! My deplorable lack of sophistication brought a rueful smile to my lips. "But tell me, Mother——"

"Never mind the details now," broke in Father. "The point is that Aunt Sissy wishes your mother to hurry to Sassetot and take the baby discreetly—you understand, very discreetly"—the frown on Father's forehead deepened—"to Vienna. There the child will be entrusted to foster parents who have been selected already. Of course, Marie," my father added significantly, "this whole baby incident is Her Majesty's private affair—a strictly personal matter concerning the Empress alone!"

There was an awkward pause. Father, who was pacing up and down the room nervously, suddenly seemed to remember the real reason for drawing me into the secret. He stopped directly in front of me and assuming an off-hand manner, he said: "Now, Mother doesn't speak French, which would complicate matters considerably. I have therefore wired to Aunt Sissy, asking whether you may go in your mother's place."

It was late that afternoon before a telegram arrived saying: *Envoyez Marie avec Jenny.*—Send Marie with Jenny.

Meanwhile, Father had lost no time. He had obtained a passport for me under the name of Countess Irma de Nágy-Tamasa, an incognito I could assume easily, since Nágy-

Tamasa was one of my husband's Hungarian estates. Together with Jenny, I left for Fécamp by way of Paris and
Rouen, careful to speak nothing but Hungarian on the
train. At Fécamp we were called for and immediately
driven to a villa in the neighborhood of Château de Sassetot. There I was received by a lady belonging to the oldest
English aristocracy, whom I knew to be a very intimate
friend of the Empress. She was famous for her string of
thoroughbreds, some of which she had brought with her
from England. It therefore seemed plausible enough that
the Empress should have suffered a "riding accident," as
Vienna newspapers of March, 1882, reported.

I saw Aunt Sissy for just a few minutes, also the wee
baby girl. In attendance was a most capable, if somewhat
mysterious, woman, always referred to as Frau Sari; also
the imperial private physician, Dr. Wiederhofer, together
with Professor Braun, a well-known Vienna specialist.
Everything seemed serene enough, and definite plans were
made for me to conduct the baby, together with the wet
nurse, back to Munich. There Mother was to meet me and
proceed with nurse and baby to Vienna.

Suddenly everybody and everything was thrown into
utter confusion. It seemed that Dr. Wiederhofer, alarmed
because the Empress ran a slight temperature after the birth
of the child, had informed the Emperor that Her Majesty
had fallen off her horse, but that there was no danger.

Uncle Francis Joseph, who had not seen Aunt Sissy for
a few months, had been greatly upset over his consort's "riding accident." He had decided to rush to Sassetot without
delay, incognito. As a matter of fact, he was already on the

way. This unexpected development necessarily changed our plans. While Professor Braun, with nurse and baby, left hurriedly for Vienna, Jenny and I were taken back to Fécamp so that the Emperor should not find us at Sassetot and suspect something.

Today, in retrospect, it seems incredible to me that the Emperor noticed nothing amiss. Indeed, it was precisely this fact which lent a piquant touch to the whole affair. I remember that on the trip home I thought of the situation as *a Hetz und a Gaudi*, as we Bavarians call it, for, despite its innate gravity, there was an undeniable aspect of amusing and thrilling excitement.

No sooner did I arrive in Munich than Mother departed for Austria. She had meanwhile received a letter from Aunt Sissy, requesting her to proceed to Vienna. There she was to assure herself that the baby girl was receiving the very best of care in the house of her foster parents in Mödling, a suburb of Vienna. After Mother's death I found this letter among her papers. It furnished details of the child's birth and concluded: "Thank God that everything went off so satisfactorily."

Although the child was not born in Château de Sassetot proper but near by, my parents and I, in the course of years, came to refer to her as the Girl of Sassetot.

This Girl of Sassetot—the child for whom Aunt Sissy had hungered as "one all her own"—was to become the mother of Elissa Landi of screen fame. For the time being, however, little Caroline was to remain "The Secret of an Empress."

When I saw Aunt Sissy again, after the Sassetot "accident," she never mentioned it with so much as a single word, although I was with her almost daily now. I was kept very busy with court functions and other duties. That season was an especially lively one, as Aunt Sissy had decided to stay in Vienna throughout the entire winter, contrary to the year before, when her ailing condition and her sojourn in Sassetot had kept her from all court affairs. During the season 1882–3 she even attended a number of court balls— "mass meetings," as she termed them derisively. The first of these I shall always remember because of two amusing incidents.

Part of the official headdress of an imperial lady-in-waiting consisted of two silver-embroidered lappets, fastened to the tiara. These dangled loosely—and, to my mind, grotesquely—on either side of the face. It always had seemed to me that the only suitable place to exhibit them was where my husband carried his embroidered golden key of imperial chamberlainship—on the tails of his green dresscoat. When I scrutinized myself in the mirror, before leaving for the ball that night, the lappets struck me as looking more ridiculous than ever. Therefore I directed my maid to pin them behind my ears with diamond-studded hairpins, first curling them up, snake fashion.

Certainly I was not aware that I was committing a heinous crime against etiquette. When I entered the cloakroom, however, I attracted the astonished stares of the other *Palastdamen*. They could not have been more taken aback if I had appeared in a pinafore, or in my nightgown. One and all earnestly assured me that I must never dare to appear before Their Majesties with such an unconventional head-dress.

Convinced of my social error, I hastened to make the necessary change when I heard the arch-chamberlain knock three times on the floor of the ballroom with his staff of office. It was, I realized, the signal announcing the imminent entry of Their Imperial Majesties.

Willy-nilly, I had to remain as I was, feeling more and more crestfallen at the half-disapproving, half-commiserating glances of the others. When I passed the Kaiser, making the prescribed deep genuflection, Uncle did not notice anything. But when I curtsied before Her Majesty, Aunt Sissy looked at me quizzically. I felt relieved at her final comment: "Well, Marie, it's not entirely in order, but it's very becoming indeed." She smiled and added in a lowered voice: "After all, what's the difference how these washrags are worn?"

Then she nodded graciously—and I drew a deep breath. However, I still felt uncomfortable, no longer on account of those lappets but because of my shoes. I was wearing a pair of slippers which the shoemaker had brought only that afternoon. They were more than a little too tight, and with every minute my agony became more unbearable. Something had to be done about it!

I withdrew behind one of the large columns and removed my shoe. What a relief! Suddenly somebody alarmed me with the whispered warning: "The Kaiser is coming!"

According to the rules of etiquette, I had to line up with the other ladies, notwithstanding that one foot was shod while I held the other slipper in my hand. As His Majesty was holding *cercle,* addressing a few words to each of the ladies, I somehow managed to slip into the shoe, but my foot was so swollen by then that I could wriggle into it only halfway. The Emperor beckoned to me to step forward. Limpingly I sought to obey the command, with the result that I almost toppled over as I made my curtsy. My foot hurt me excruciatingly.

At first I thought Uncle was oblivious of my little mishap, for he conversed in friendly fashion; but presently he interrupted himself: "Tell me, Marie, why are you making such faces?"

I had never feared the Emperor; he had always treated me graciously. So I simply told him the truth.

"Well, well," my Uncle sympathized, "that's what you get for being vain. Now run along and see that you get your shoe on properly." He nodded kindly and passed on to the next *Palastdame.*

Once again I drew a deep breath.

Generally, Aunt Sissy seemed to be in a much mellower mood that winter. Now and then she even mentioned Rudolf with real warmth. She was seriously worried about the Hapsburg family tree, for Rudolf had been married nearly a year and a half and was still denied the blessings of paternity.

"What a world this is!" Aunt Sissy complained one day, a touch of bitterness in her voice. "There are so many people who do not want children—and naturally they have them. And here, in our own family, where so much depends on an heir——" She broke off the sentence with a deep sigh, then exclaimed: "Thank God I did not arrange Rudolf's marriage. As a matter of fact, I was against it. But the Kaiser absolutely insisted on this match with Stephanie. I can't help shivering when I think of those Belgians. . . . I'll never get Maximilian out of my mind."

Aunt Sissy grew thoughtful. "I remember the day when Maximilian left for Mexico with that doll-faced Charlotte clinging to him so doggedly that I couldn't so much as say one word without her hearing it. You know, back in 1867, political affairs were very dark. We received nothing but contradictory information from Brussels, Paris, and Mexico. Personally, I put more stock in the news from across the sea. Those reports were very pessimistic, and unfortunately bad news is always true news. How I prayed that somebody or something would make the situation entirely clear to Max, but he was in the power of those Belgians irretrievably. Charlotte was his Angel of Death. It was but natural that a tragedy ensued. Max was sacrificed on the altar of politics and lust for power."

I listened, wide-eyed. Aunt Sissy seemed almost unaware of my presence as she resumed her painful reflections: "To be sure, his brothers were properly stirred—the Kaiser conventionally moved. But the Kaiser, as always, was thickheaded about it. It seems he can carry off anything with dignity—even the murder of his own brother! Poor Max, he was indeed an innocent victim. Nobody appreciated his high mental gifts. Perhaps *he* should have been the Emperor of Austria. He really would have been a ruler by the grace of God. If only I could have talked to him before he heedlessly rushed into his undoing. But then Max was a dreamer who simply wouldn't believe that people can be low and mean and false. He would perceive a spark of good even in a criminal and would do everything to aid him."

Aunt Sissy's gaze was that of one entranced by mental pictures conjured up from the past. Suddenly her eyes narrowed. "Of course, there was this Belgian goose, this woman who had been foisted upon him. Ignorant, arrogant, vain, lusting for power, it was she who dragged Maximilian into his undoing—just so she could wear an imperial crown. Do you know, Marie," Aunt Sissy confided, her eyes flashing, "that once Charlotte had the idea of becoming Empress of the Dual Monarchy? It was during the years when Rudolf was an ailing babe. But Fate fooled her there. After that disappointment, she was more anxious than ever for Maximilian to go to Mexico. She was perfectly satisfied for him to risk everything if only she could become an empress. What good did it do her later when she threw herself at the feet of Napoleon? She, who always had been so haughty and proud, humiliated herself in the end. Small wonder the woman became insane—but certainly not because of her love for Max!"

I did not dare to move, but waited breathlessly for Aunt Sissy to continue.

"Max was actually forced to accept the imperial crown." Aunt Sissy made the statement with all the assurance of one who knew. "I shall never forget the terrible scene between the Kaiser and him right here in the *Hofburg*. . . . Finally poor Max gave in. He was all worn out when, at last, he said: 'May God give me the necessary strength to do my duty!' It sounded like a prayer. Then and there I had a pre-

sentiment of the tragedy to come. I studied Maximilian's
wan face; he looked the picture of death itself. I felt like
screaming. And that Charlotte woman, do you know what
she did? She smiled . . . smiled, oh, so smugly!"

I shall always remember those words of the Empress. I
recall them daily as I gaze at Uncle Maximilian's picture on
the wall of my room.

After that outburst Aunt Sissy never again mentioned the
tragedy of the golden-bearded Emperor from the sands of
Miramar, but I knew that she thought of him often.

Her bitterness toward the Belgians was somewhat as-
suaged, however, when she learned, shortly thereafter, that
Stephanie would be a mother in September; that month
was to mark the birth of Princess Elizabeth.

All during that season, I was kept breathless with court
functions. My first rest—albeit an involuntary one—came in
March, 1883, when I was laid up for some weeks. Thrown
by a horse, I had sustained very bad contusions. Because I
was still ailing from former equestrian intermezzi—my
shoulder blade, as well as my collar bone, was in a rather
weakened state—the doctor prescribed a few weeks of rest
in bed. During that period, to my uneasy surprise, the Empress sent for George. I was greatly relieved when he returned and told me that he had "arranged with Aunt Sissy
to have me accompany her to Amsterdam," where the Metz-
ger method of massage was very much *en vogue* at that
time.

"I turned that trick neatly for you, didn't I?" Aunt Sissy
observed with a mischievous wink when I met her on the

day of departure for Holland. The Empress seemed in a merry mood once more; that she was traveling incognito, as Countess Hohenembs, probably accounted for it.

In Amsterdam we occupied a comparatively modest suite at the Amstel Hotel. For weeks our time was well taken up between the massage cure and long walks. Aunt Sissy and I usually returned afoot after the treatment, the Empress attired in a somewhat bizarre costume. This consisted of an extremely tight-fitting short dress which revealed the tops of her high-laced shoes. With it she wore a tiny hat which rode precariously on the curly waves of her chestnut hair. In her hand she carried a light-colored leather fan for relief against the rays of the sun. As we usually returned from the massage treatment around lunch time, we attracted the curious stares of workaday folk swarming out of the shops for their midday respite. The glances and remarks to which we were subjected by hoi polloi upset me, but Aunt Sissy scarcely seemed annoyed.

One day, spying a hunchback in the crowd, she seized my arm in excitement. "Look, look, Marie," she exclaimed.

Before I could dissuade her, she made straight for the unfortunate man to touch him for good luck. It was just another example of her growing superstitious beliefs. The next thing I remember was that somebody, somehow, had knocked the fan out of the Empress's hand and that a crowd of people were thronging about us, using Dutch expletives which clearly conveyed their threatening meaning to me, although I did not understand the language. Fortunately a horse-drawn street car happened to stop in front of us just then. Quickly I drew Aunt Sissy into the tram, trembling with nervousness. The Empress, however, laughed with the roguishness of a naughty child. "I touched the hunchback just the same!" she said.

After this experience I suggested to Aunt Sissy that a plain-clothes lackey follow us in future. She thought over the idea, then decided: "No, Marie, potentates are just people, after all, aren't they? I admit that people *en masse* frighten me, and that I dislike curious crowds. Still, I feel like extending my hand to each single individual."

It was sentiments of this sort which, after her tragic death —a direct result of Aunt Sissy's habit of moving among people in the democratic Haroun-al-Raschid manner—induced certain historians to make much of her "imperial liberalism." To be sure, the Empress scorned the narrow-mindedness and self-sufficiency of the average potentate. She sneered at the by-the-grace-of-God idea, realizing that it fell indiscriminately upon good as well as bad monarchs. Her opinion, often expressed to me, was that human beings must not be ruled with despotism and cruelty, but with intelligence and feeling.

"Rulers," Aunt Sissy expounded, "must be sensitive to human needs and must never forget that they, too, are humans among humans. No monarch should misuse his power. It should be of the utmost importance to him whether his people love or hate him. Why, after all, should the people show any love for us? We have everything in abundance while most of them are poor, many actually starving!"

The Empress shook her head emphatically. "No, I don't want any flunkey clinging to my heels if I can help it." The only concession Aunt Sissy would make was that, in future,

on our way back to the hotel, we would take a route leading
through a better neighborhood.

"We are liable to run into some old friends here," Aunt
Sissy hinted one morning with a mysterious smile.

Therefore I was not especially surprised when, a day or
so later, Captain Bay Middleton stepped up to me in the
lobby of the Amstel Hotel. His right arm was in a sling,
and so he offered his left hand. His face wreathed in smiles,
he greeted me with the same nonchalant friendliness of
former days: "Howdy, little girlie?"

He told me that, once again, he had suffered a very bad
spill and had come to Amsterdam for massage treatments.
Considering that he had broken his collar bone for the third
time and fractured his shoulder blade for the second, it was
small wonder that he did not look at all well. His face was
so thin that his prominent nose appeared more conspicuous
than ever.

Bay remained with us until the end of our stay, which
flew by all too soon. As if aware that, for the next three
years, holidays would be few and far between for me, I
thoroughly enjoyed every minute of it. In the years ahead
I was to add branches to the Larisch family tree; a second
daughter was born to me in September, 1884, a second son
in February, 1886, and yet a third in September of the following year.

Pages, too, were added to Aunt Sissy's diary and poetry.
The Empress's new writings were not prepared for print
this time, but merely copied into a heavy tome which could
be locked. I transcribed into this volume all the material
Aunt Sissy had collected on slips and sheets of paper during

her foreign travels. Most of it had been jotted down in Greece, which Her Majesty came to love more and more.

The book was almost half filled when Aunt Sissy gave it to me. I discovered, to my surprise, that some notes had been transcribed in a firm masculine handwriting. Despite all my comparisons of this handwriting with others, and all my pondering over it in later years, I never learned who had served as Aunt Sissy's amanuensis before me.

Chapter Six

FAREWELL TO LOVE

Summer, 1886, found my husband planning to spend the season at some North Sea resort while I intended to take my children to the Bavarian mountains. There, in the neighborhood of Starnberger Lake, my mother had spent the two previous seasons. Traunstein, an unassuming little village, seemed the logical place for a family holiday. Aunt Sissy lent her approval to the idea because she would be in Feldafing, on the opposite shore of the lake, ". . . and it will be easy for you and your mother to come over to see me."

My mother's house was outside the village, and directly opposite was a similar abode which my children and I would occupy for the summer. The place was truly idyllic and promised days full of peace and serenity. Anxious to start our vacation soon, it was decided that we would leave the Monday after Whitsuntide.

Thunderstorms had prevailed over the week-end, and heavy clouds of fog veiled the mountain tops when, on that memorable Whitmonday morning, we arrived at the railroad station to board the train for Traunstein. The depot was full of commotion, with people crowding around a public notice which had just been posted. It stood out against the black background as if framed by a wide mourning band. The bulletin contained only a few words. . . . His Majesty, King Ludwig, together with his physician, Dr. Bernhard von Gudden, had drowned in Starnberger Lake.

The shocking news left me in a daze; then, suddenly, a thought shot through my brain: Aunt Sissy! . . . and just now she was in Feldafing!

The trip to Traunstein was the worst ordeal I can remember. When, at last, my brood and I arrived in the evening, I found Cousin Henny at the station. She reported that Mother, upon receipt of a telegram from Father, had rushed back to Munich. Of the King's tragic end, she knew no additional details; merely the fact that he had drowned.

Despite the exhausting trip, I could not fall asleep that night. Hour after hour I listened to the chimes of the historical little chapel of Ettendorf near by.

Mother returned that night; she had been in Feldafing, where she had found Aunt Sissy prostrated with grief. Father had remained with his imperial sister, seeking to console her. The letter we received, next morning, was addressed in his handwriting, although the message it contained was written by Aunt Sissy herself. I had great difficulties in deciphering her writing, since it was more illegible than ever. Slowly reading it aloud to Mother, we hardly could believe our ears: An intricate plan had been worked out by the Empress in every detail; so intricate, in fact, that Mother wrung her hands despairingly and cried: "Oh, Lord, Lord, it can't be done, it can't be done!"

I knew my Aunt Sissy better. "Mother, it simply has to be done!"

There was a short pause; Mother jumped up abruptly. "Then I must return to Munich immediately."

"So you must. . . . And, Mother," I consoled her, "with all the servants on vacation just now, nobody will discover that Aunt Sissy stayed in Munich overnight, so don't let it worry you."

Mother, still doubtful, murmured: "I can't understand that Aunt Sissy at such a moment——" Energetic headshaking finished the sentence.

"Probably she had made arrangements long before this terrible accident at Starnberger Lake."

"Just the same, just the same . . ." Mother was completely distraught.

I myself felt none too easy when, after Mother had left, I proceeded to execute Aunt Sissy's plan. Although I was never given to asking questions where the Empress's affairs were concerned, I could not help wondering why, precisely now, she was so eager for a clandestine meeting with Bay Middleton—her very last, so she had written. Well, no doubt the tryst had been arranged long before the lake tragedy occurred. But why, I wondered, could not the Empress postpone her meeting with the Captain? After some meditation, I concluded that Aunt Sissy was so eager to meet Bay in the shadow of the old chapel at Ettendorf the following night because she felt that just in this moment of bereavement he was the one person she knew who could offer her real consolation.

I induced our old family physician, Dr. Wispaur, who always summered in Traunstein, to fetch Captain Middleton from the station next day, keeping him in his house until nearly midnight. On the afternoon of that same day, Aunt Sissy, after spending the night in Munich, had arrived together with my mother; but there was hardly any chance to discuss the lake tragedy with her. In the dead of night, the two of us walked in silence to the Ettendorf chapel. There Aunt Sissy waited on a little bench while I went back to Dr. Wispaur's house for Middleton. I found him the very picture of despair and shrank from adding to his woe by following Aunt Sissy's strict order. But I had no choice, and so I gently informed him that I could take him to the tryst only after he had given me his word of honor that he would not make a "scene." He was to bear up like a man, especially since the Empress had just sustained such a terrible shock. If he promised all this, she would allow him five minutes.

However, it was nearer twenty-five minutes before Aunt Sissy called me; I had been waiting under a tree at the other end of the chapel. Middleton staggered toward me like a drunken man; he clung to me for support, sobbing his heart out.

I petted him as I would a child: "Now, Bay, be brave . . . there, there, Bay. . . ."

At last he pulled himself together, even remembering to shake hands with me; then, slowly, he lumbered off in the direction of Dr. Wispaur's house. I knew the physician would put him on the train from Salzburg, passing through Traunstein between four and five in the morning on its way to Munich.

I knew, too, that this night had seen the close of a roman-'tic chapter in Aunt Sissy's life.

Breakfast, next morning, was indeed a sad affair. Hardly a word was uttered until Aunt Sissy finally blurted out: "Those cowards hunted him to death. They have killed Ludwig!"

"They" were the enemies of the King, members of a court camarilla who had been backed by considerable wealth. They had plotted the elimination of Ludwig and of his brother Otto, seeking to put the government of Bavaria into other hands. The royal family itself was very much in the dark about these political machinations; perhaps, in the past, they had never taken the intrigue seriously enough.

Ludwig had always been considered an eccentric extraordinary. This Wittelsbach, from his very youth, had indulged in whims and fancies—inherited traits which had never been curbed sufficiently. When he became ruler of Bavaria at the age of eighteen, it was too late to change him. Ludwig's behavior, at first merely odd, turned into morose moodiness when his engagement to Empress Elizabeth's younger sister, Sophie, was terminated. Doubtless he loved Sophie dearly, probably because she resembled her imperial sister so much. He showered Sophie with presents and had an ornate gilded bridal coach built which elicited shouts of admiration and wonderment when it rolled through the streets of Munich from the wheelright's shop to the royal residence. There it was to be kept until the nuptials.

There were two versions of King Ludwig's broken engagement to Aunt Sophie. According to one rumor, Ludwig came to the conclusion that Sophie, after all, was just Sophie and not her sister Elizabeth. The other maintained that the same court camarilla which conspired against the reign of the ruler was also responsible for his broken engagement; "they" had untruthfully informed the King that Sophie was very flirtatious and, even then, was involved in an affair with some courtier.

It is very likely that Ludwig's disappointment in love contributed to his insanity. At any rate, it is an undisputed fact that, thereafter, his behavior became increasingly erratic. His inborn aversion towards women—which had partly disappeared under the influence of Sophie—soon grew into a veritable obsession. All these unfortunate inclinations of the King were assiduously nurtured by his enemies, who seemed to favor the maxim that the goal sanctifies the means.

When a high-strung man, from his earliest years, is continually catered to by scheming sycophants, it is not surprising if, eventually, he succumbs to hallucinations. Small wonder, then, that at Neu-Schwanstein King Ludwig arranged spiritualistic séances and midnight banquets where he imagined himself entertaining the ghosts of Julius Cæsar and Louis XIV. He invaded the mystic realm of occultism to such an extent that, in June, 1886, he was officially declared *non compos mentis*. Prince Regent Luitpold decided that it would be best for the King to be transferred to Castle Berg, where he would remain under the surveillance of Dr. von Gudden and Lieutenant Colonel Baron Karl Theodor von Washington.

I knew Baron von Washington very well from his frequent visits to my parents' home. He was a grandnephew of
the great George Washington, son of the son of the latter's
brother John, who had settled in Holland. This brother,
Jacob by name, entered the Bavarian service and, in 1829,
was created a baron by the King of Bavaria, after reaching
a top rung of the military ladder. Karl Theodor was Baron
Jacob von Washington's third son, born in 1833. He was a
retired Lieutenant Colonel in the Bavarian army and Royal
Bavarian Chamberlain when he was drafted, as it were, by
the Prince Regent as the deranged King's sole gentleman-in-
waiting at Castle Berg.

Where I had sung for him ten years ago, the unfortunate
monarch dwelt as if in a glass house. There were peep-holes
in the doors and walls, preparations which had been made
against Ludwig's virtual incarceration.

He had just arrived at Castle Berg, and there was not the
slightest inkling that he planned to escape. Together with
Dr. von Gudden, he went for a walk on the afternoon of
Whitsuntide, during a temporary lull in the rainstorm.
When neither of them had returned by eight o'clock, Baron
von Washington became greatly disturbed. Presently a
search was instigated, with the result that, at midnight, in
the flickering light of a stable lantern, the bodies of the
potentate and his physician were dragged from the lake.
Meanwhile another rain squall flooded the neighborhood,
creating a dismal picture if ever there was one.

In the light of what Empress Elizabeth told me and what
I pieced together from information received from my father,
there is no doubt in my mind that King Ludwig had at-

tempted a break for freedom. It was the monarch's intention to reach the near-by Villa Hornig, owned by the Master of the Royal Stables and one of the few who had remained absolutely loyal. Villa Hornig was situated outside the park of Castle Berg, adjacent to the shore, but divided from the royal estate by an iron fence. This extended into the lake for some fifteen feet. There the lake was very shallow, the ground consisting of easily shifting sand. However, there were many unexpected holes at the bottom of the lake, in general a very treacherous body of water—a fact well known to the natives. To all appearances the King had waded into the lake, intending to walk around the fence which protruded into the water. When Dr. von Gudden rushed after him to hold him back, the two had slipped on the shifting sand into one of the unexpected holes and were drowned. It is probable, too, that the King, as strong and powerful as Dr. von Gudden, fought with his physician—a theory confirmed by the fingermarks on the doctor's throat.

I am firmly convinced that the King did not contemplate suicide, but merely escape. His insanity notwithstanding, he knew that Villa Hornig was headquarters for facilitating his flight across the Tyrolian border. Once on Austrian soil, Ludwig would have been safe, because the Tyrolians loved him; moreover, those who conspired against the King would no longer be able to put their hands on him.

Staying with her mother at Castle Possenhofen in Feldafing, on the opposite shore of the lake, the Empress's protection would have been solicited for the fleeing king. As soon as Ludwig regained his liberty, she was to be informed. However, under no circumstances was Aunt Sissy to know about Ludwig's proposed flight any earlier, for fear of embroiling her in international difficulties.

From what Aunt Sissy told us that morning at breakfast, I know she had no idea that King Ludwig had been kept a virtual prisoner. Along with other members of the royal family; she had never imagined that the King would be treated so cruelly by Dr. von Gudden.

"That this physician, in cold blood, could tell the King to his face that he was incurable, was unspeakably brutal," Aunt Sissy declared that morning between half-stifled sobs. Although she admitted "that something had to be done" about Ludwig, she abhorred the ways and means which were employed. Far from opposing the dethronement of the King in principle, she opined at the breakfast table: "Poor Ludwig would have been fortunate to be relieved of all worries and duties and become a free man. He always would have remained a king in the fullest sense of the word. I'm certain I could have made that perfectly plain to Ludwig. Why didn't they let him live a quiet, simple life as any bourgeois family permits an insane member to lead?"

Because of her innate mentality, the Empress was capable of understanding the illustrious visionary. Her eyes held a melancholy expression as she quoted from *The Winter's Tale:*

> *No settled senses of the world can match*
> *The pleasure of that madness. Let 't alone.*

Years ago, I was asked to write a book about King Ludwig. Numerous documents, absolutely dependable, were put

at my disposal for the purpose. As it was before the Great
War, I did not feel that the time was ripe, then, to uncover
that royal tragedy. Meanwhile I have come to the conclusion
that truth is the only real cloak of Christian charity. Unfortunately the material which was offered to me then is no
longer available today. In the words of the man who submitted it to me, it has been "confiscated by certain people."
However, I remember that this material contained the last
voluntary confession of a dying man who, tortured by his
conscience, had supplied most of the documents upon which
I was to base my book. These primarily consisted of confidential letters exchanged between those immediately surrounding the King and state officials. Among other facts,
the correspondence revealed that a letter had been "caught
en route" in which the unfortunate King had appealed to
Prince Otto von Bismarck for help; he who had once so
despised the Iron Chancellor had addressed a virtual suppli-
cation to him.

Much has been made of the fact that the King spent untold millions, building palaces and castles, and that in this
way he practically ruined himself and Bavaria financially.
This has been offered as yet another proof of the King's insanity. Even if this be so, it is well to remember that these
selfsame fairy-like castles and palaces still entice visitors to
Bavaria. Thus, in the long run, they have actually proved a
good investment.

In December, 1886, George and I were in Vienna for our
Christmas shopping. We were at the breakfast table when a

letter was brought to my husband. He read it with palpable excitement, then rose from the table abruptly. "We must leave for home at once."

"I should say not! I haven't done half my shopping yet," I retorted.

George waved my objections aside. "I tell you, we've got to. . . . We've got to," he reiterated. With trembling hands he folded the letter back into the envelope and thrust it into an inside coat pocket.

"We'll do nothing of the kind," I protested vigorously. But George's face was so full of agitation that the next moment I added, in a softer tone: "Tell me, what's happened? Why do you want to change our plans all of a sudden?"

George came over to me. Instead of raising his voice angrily, as I expected, he surprised me by blurting out guiltily: "Why, Marie, Marie, if we don't leave this very minute . . . there will be a scandal!"

His words alarmed me; observing my apprehension, my husband would say no more. I had to exert all my powers of persuasion for the better part of half an hour before he dug into his coat pocket for the letter and handed it to me.

"Well, here you are, then," he said, assuming an air of bravado.

The letter was written in a rather childish scrawl and not exactly in the best style, either. But its clarity, in stating the case, was truly admirable:

DEAR GEORGE:

You are sadly mistaken if you think you can leave me in the lurch. You see, I discovered your real whereabouts although you wrote to me you were going to England. If I don't hear from you, I'll blow your brains out and then kill myself.

GRETCHEN.

I glanced at George; he was deathly pale. "And she'll do it, she'll do it," he almost whimpered.

I am afraid I took recourse to rather inelegant language. "Will you please inform me who the devil this . . . this hussy is?"

In halting fashion George revealed that, on one of his "excursions," he had met "two charming ladies," the older already an accomplished actress, the younger, Gretchen, aspiring to become one. And now Gretchen's theatrical career was forever ruined.

"Ruined by what? By whom?" I questioned sharply.

"Through me . . . me," the culprit confessed.

My icy stare demanded more details.

"Why, you see, Marie, she had a . . ."

"Ah, a baby? Well, isn't that fine!"

"No," George corrected me—and I had never seen him so meek and miserable—"No . . . not one, but two. . . . Imagine, Marie, twin girls!"

I was stunned for a few seconds. "So that's the reason she wants to shoot you," I murmured finally.

"You see, she thinks her career is completely spoiled for her now and . . ."

"Well?"

"She demands twenty-five thousand guilders for damages."

"Oh . . . blackmail!"

"Listen, Marie. I assure you Gretchen is really a decent girl. The money is coming to her. To tell the truth, I repeatedly promised it to her. I would have kept my word, too, but you know how things are with all our money invested in property. . . ."

There was a lengthy pause. I thought the matter over while George watched me out of the corner of his eye.

"Well, I think I have found a solution," I told him grimly. I explained that I would sell my seven-strand pearl necklace.

My generosity startled George. "But, Marie," he cried, "that was a gift from the Emperor!"

"And those twins," I countered dryly, "are a gift from . . . Gretchen."

I wouldn't have been human if I hadn't been a bit malicious just then.

That very afternoon I went over to Schwarz & Steiner on Kärntnerstrasse. My necklace was still locked in their safe, as it had just been restrung. The amount of twenty-five thousand guilders—at that time, approximately ten thousand dollars—was immediately paid out to me. There was still a little balance left to replace the necklace with an imitation—"such as most of the aristocratic ladies are wearing nowadays," Mr. Schwarz slyly informed me. "Nobody will ever know the difference, Your Grace," Mr. Steiner added reassuringly, according me his deepest bow.

In sheepish silence George accepted the hush money and departed speedily to head off the threatening scandal.

Never before nor afterward was my husband so tractable as around Christmas, 1886. When I only hinted that I would like to spend the winter in Paris, George promptly assented. He also agreed that on the trip from Pardubitz to France we would stop off for a few days in Munich to visit my parents. I was especially anxious to do this, as I had asked our family solicitor to make inquiries about Gretchen.

It turned out that she was just "one of those girls" in the notorious Sankt-Pauli district of Hamburg, and that her actress sister was no better, although certainly "accomplished" in her way.

"What about the twins?" I asked.

The jovial old solicitor laughed. "There, Your Grace, don't tell me you ever believed that fable! Why, there simply weren't any!"

I did not know whether to laugh or to cry at this ludicrous development and ended up, merely, in thanking the man for his trouble.

When I came home that day, I remarked to my husband: "Oh, by the way, George, that old family lawyer of ours would like to see you for a minute in connection with some papers."

Unsuspecting, George called on the solicitor. His demeanor was extremely grave when he returned. He never said a word; as far as he and I were concerned, Gretchen was buried forever. And a pretty penny her "funeral" had cost me!

In the course of years I had become reconciled to George's occasional "excursions." Nevertheless, the Gretchen affair affected me considerably. Jealousy had nothing to do with it; in that case, there might have been some hope for our marriage. More than ever before, the utter futility of my marital life was brought home to me. It scarcely could be called a success, I reflected bitterly, despite our five children.

During our sojourn in Paris, in the beginning of 1887, I had arrived at the stage where I felt completely indifferent to everything . . . and then along came someone to arouse me from my spiritual lethargy. It was at the *soirée* in the residence of the Marquis d'O—— that my eyes fell upon the trim figure of a Russian army officer in spotless white uniform. He was introduced to me by Madame la Marquise as Prince Levandoff, a name which held no particular significance for me.

To my unbounded surprise, the Russian spoke up: "But we know each other, Your Grace."

I gazed at him, puzzled. Yes, his face seemed very familiar to me; still, I could not place him.

"We were married once," the Russian continued with an amused smile.

Instantly, then, I knew him; the resemblance to his sister Nadja was striking. "Why, you are Grisha!"

"And you are my long-lost little wife!"

"It seems you really know each other," observed the Marchioness laughingly.

A threesome, we repaired to a corner and the story was unraveled how Grisha, in a mock ceremony, had become my long-distance "husband" when I was a very young girl.

"But your name?" I looked at the Russian inquiringly. "It is strange to me."

The explanation was simple: Grisha had been adopted by an immensely rich bachelor uncle and, upon his death, according to Russian law, he had not only inherited the fabulous avuncular wealth, but the name and title as well. Still *en suite* his old Circassian regiment, whose uniform he wore with such inimitable swagger, Grisha had just been appointed military attaché of the Russian embassy to the Sublime Porte. In a few weeks he would be off to his new post in Constantinople, by way of the Caucasus, where he would inspect some of his property. He was in his early thirties then and still single.

"I haven't married yet, and now I know I never will," Grisha whispered into my ear, while we were at table. Tactfully the Marchioness had rearranged the seating so that I had Grisha beside me. George was at the other end, next to his old love, Buxom Barbara.

It seemed natural enough for me to call Grisha by his first name. "After all, we are married, aren't we?" he encouraged me. He was deeply touched when he noticed that I was still wearing that narrow band of Caucasian platinum which he had sent me so many years before, his name spelled inside in smallest Russian letters.

The few weeks of Grisha's furlough, before assuming his post in Constantinople, were partly spent at the Côte d'Azure and partly on Corsica. Eagerly he coaxed me to brighten his holiday with my company. George was only too willing to make the trip—the Gretchen episode was still fresh—and then, too, as a special inducement, Barbara and her husband were to join us. George thought Grisha a bore, and "this whole business of cheap familiarity between the two of you downright childish." But I was of an entirely different opinion. . . .

I am a woman of more than seventy now. It is almost half a century since those days with Grisha along the blue-canopied shores of the Mediterranean. Yet when I think back to that time, I feel every wrinkle, which life has graven into my face, vanish miraculously and once more I am that young woman, not quite thirty, neglected by her husband and grievously disappointed in love. I can well understand, today, how I became enamored with Grisha, and how I could see no wrong in surrendering to that infatuation. If doubts beset me, I ignored them in the face of George's brazen conduct with Barbara, whose husband seemed the proverbial cuckold, indispensable to every French farce.

Thoughts of my children, and not of my husband, brought me to my senses. It was they who prevented me from following Grisha to the Caucasus. He was ready to resign his office, and when he realized what kept me from him, he urged me to take my children along. I had reached a fork in the road and knew not which way to turn. My heart pulled one way, my head another. Never before had I been so hopelessly confused. Truly it was a staggering problem that confronted me.

When Grisha pressed me for a definite decision the day after our return to Paris, and just an hour before his train left for the East, I still could not make up my mind.

"I have to know 'yes' or 'no,' and I have to know it now, Marie," Grisha insisted.

I clung to my state of indecision, as if awaiting an outward sign to guide me. And then, I heard a sigh—more like a groan it sounded—and, the next moment, I was alone in the room. Poor Grisha's patience had died . . . and a hard death it had been!

Paris became intolerable, and I besought George to return to Vienna. The weeks rolled by; then, one day, I received a note from the Marquise d'O——, relaying news that had just reached her. It seemed Prince Levandoff had suffered a fatal accident upon his return to the Caucasus. "Of course, there are people who don't believe it was only an accident," the Marchioness hinted in her letter.

Only too well I knew it was no accident. . . .

I cannot clearly recall my actions that day. I only know I staggered towards the little medicine chest . . . and then it seemed an eternity before I heard the voice of our physician, as if it came from the farthest corner of the world, scolding me: "But, Your Grace, how could you ever make such a terrible mistake? Why, a little more would have finished you!"

I recuperated all too soon. I think I really came to hate my strong constitution during those days. By the time Vienna's *haute saison* arrived, I was well enough to report for duty at the *Hofburg*.

Aunt Sissy received me, seated before her dressing table, attired in a snow-white lace negligee. In her boudoir in Vienna, the Empress was surrounded by chairs and hassocks of rich brocade. The unusually wide windows were curtained with fine Brussels lace, while very heavy rugs and skins covered the floor.

It all seemed unreal to me now. Could this be the world

I had dwelt in for so many years? I had even been happy there . . . after a fashion.

Aunt Sissy glanced at me critically. "I suppose it was just nerves, Marie," she said meaningly.

"Quite so, Aunt Sissy . . . just nerves."

The Empress changed to a lighter tone, "Well, at any rate, my dear, I am very glad you are back with me once more—and there's plenty of work for you." Aunt Sissy brought out a stack of notes from her dresser. "They are all to go into that big book, Marie, and the sooner the better."

But with one thing and another, it was not before the winter 1887–88 that I found time to sit down and transcribe Aunt Sissy's notes. I was amazed to discover that the Empress, who always had shown a tendency for the occult, had fallen completely under the spell of spiritism also. I find among her writings:

When people deny the possibility of contact with departed souls, it is because they lack information. To be sure, not everybody in this terrestrial world of ours is so attuned as to be able to dwell amidst departed souls, to think with them and feel with them. Perhaps those people who can guess what to expect for dinner from savory odors wafted toward them are the happy ones; they consider themselves deeply endowed with psychic gifts on the strength of this ability. . . . So far as I am concerned, I can communicate with those who are akin to my soul, giving full play to my psychic powers. Thus it was that Heinrich Heine came to me . . . first blurred, as in a dream, so that I only surmised rather than felt his proximity. Gradually his presence became clearer to me, and now I actually converse with him. After all, that is not so astonishing as is generally assumed. Socrates, as his disciples Plato and Xenophon tell us, asserted that he was communicating with a spirit he could hear within him, and Socrates was the wisest of all the Greeks. . . .

Elucidating, the Empress goes on to say:

Many others have come to the same conclusion as Socrates, but they have not dared to tell too much about it for fear of ridicule. It is for this reason that Goethe wrote:

"The few, who thereof something really learned,
Unwisely frank, with hearts that spurned concealing,
And to the mob laid bare each thought and feeling,
Have evermore been crucified and burned."

Today, those who are really educated know more of these things. They are aware that their body is the product of a quickly and ever-changing matter, much as a river flowing by; apparently the water is the same, yet it never carries the identical drops. . . .

The ether world is invisible and immeasurable; nobody has perceived it tangibly. Still no scientist will deny its presence, because light and warmth and electricity indicate that such ether must exist.

Thus the Empress anticipated scientific discoveries nearly half a century in advance! She writes on:

So it is with the spirit we cannot see, and which, according to its own nature, molds the faces of men, depending upon how they themselves coöperate with the spirit. . . . Spirit is individual and immortal. Detached from that electrical battery which we call brain, the spirit cannot express itself in the body any longer; nevertheless, it can exert an influence on other living beings and control their brain functions, provided they have a certain suitable tendency.

I do not belong to those whose spiritual senses are closed. It is in my power to sense the thoughts and intentions of my spirit friends. Thus I see Heine. I also have seen Maximilian of Mexico; but only once, and then he was unable to communicate what he wanted to say to me. . . . Later I heard that I saw him exactly as he stood facing the deadly volley at Querétaro, in the last moment of his earthly existence.

All these pictures come to me when I am awake, somewhat in the way memories induce dream pictures during sleep. But what I see when wide awake are no dream pictures, and certainly no hallucinations, as people may say who lack the necessary understanding. All they can do is to substitute meaningless words for a very logical explanation. It gives me great satisfaction and imbues me with a wonderful peace to communicate with spirits from the Beyond. Unfortunately, there are few people who can understand this . . . and there are so many who declare everything nonsensical which they cannot grasp.

Today, in retrospect, I am not at all surprised that Aunt Sissy eventually arrived at the stage where spiritism seemed no idle theory to her, but an established fact. The pronounced superstitions which she had practised all her life grew into this inevitably. Everything that occurred in daily life held a superstitious significance for Aunt Sissy. Not only did she feel the urge to touch hunchbacks, but, with all the ceremony of performing a religious ritual, she would do obeisance to the new moon, bowing deeply, three times, to that heavenly body. When I first observed Aunt Sissy's queer behavior in Gödöllö, cold shudders pricked my spine, especially when she insisted that I follow her example. Eventually this heathenish custom became almost a habit of mine.

And then there were those pounds and pounds of odd pieces of old iron which we came across on our walks. One day, I remember returning to Gödöllö with Aunt Sissy with no less than three horseshoes and a whole pocketful of old nails. I do not know what Aunt Sissy did with all these *porte-bonheurs* which were supposed to bring good luck; in the course of years the Empress must have amassed a considerable amount of scrap iron. Then, too, she objected whenever knives and scissors were placed so that they pointed towards her—an interesting fact, considering the manner in which she met her death.

Whenever Aunt Sissy submitted to these superstitious inclinations, she wore a slightly mocking smile, so that I could never definitely decide whether she was entirely convinced by her own conduct.

When I began to transcribe her notes, the discovery that Aunt Sissy was so deeply engrossed in spiritism filled me with dismay. According to her diary, the Empress was frequently in touch with the departed soul of her "royal spiritual brother," Bavaria's ill-fated King, whose tragic fate she bemoaned in a collection of poetry and prose, entitled *A Royal Fairy Tale*. Embodied in this collection were excerpts from King Ludwig's diary, of which the Empress had a copy.

Aunt Sissy's most favored literary spirit friend was Heinrich Heine. She had always admired him greatly, but in the later 'eighties her admiration amounted to an obsession.

"Heine looks right over my shoulder when I write," she remarked one day and grew very angry when I snickered. "Of course, you, Marie, with your *Münchner Bierseele"*— Munich beer soul—"can't understand it." So bitter was she in her reproach that I never dared to express skepticism again.'

It seemed the poet impressed Aunt Sissy in her early youth, but at first superficially. She tells of it herself:

Only in the course of time, I learned to understand him, to feel with him. The more bitter my experiences, the more disappointments life brought me, the better I came to comprehend him. Today Heine looms up as the greatest, perhaps the only, philosopher. He probed humanity and came to know man at his worst. Heinrich Heine, it is for you that my soul sobs and my spirit longs. . . . Since I wedded myself to you spiritually, I think and feel as you thought and felt. . . .

Because Heine had the courage of his convictions, he was stoned by the multitudes. He groveled before nobody, not even at the foot of a throne. Frankly, he said: "I loathe the annoying vermin that nest in the cracks of old thrones!" Like Montesquieu, Heine claims mankind's characteristics to be: "Ambition allied with indolence, baseness allied with pride, the urge to enrich oneself without work, the aversion against truth, the contempt for civic duties. And all this is aggravated by the fear of princely virtues and the interest, the vicarious joy in princely vices." . . .

What cruel truth there is in these words! Yet we princes permit all that groveling and allow incense to be burned for us without even faintly surmising what may be lying in wait in the background. Isn't Heine right in his biting scorn? This

pretended worship of throne and altar is pure buffoonery, as
he so correctly called it.

With what precision Heine hits the nail on the head when
he compares these hired courtiers to circus criers, singing the
praise of a Hercules or of a giant, of a dwarf or of a savage—
all on exhibition for money! . . . Heine hoped to see the day
when people would object to being mere puppets with their
monarchs pulling the strings; when the rulers themselves
would cast aside their glittering rags designed to impress their
subjects . . . the royal purple, red as the cloak of an execu-
tioner; throw off the golden coronet drawn down over their
ears to drown out the voice of the people; lay down the golden
mace which they hold in their hands as a sham symbol of
strength and power to rule. Heine hoped the time would come
when monarchs would liberate themselves, be free as other
people, yet retain the privilege to enforce justice; do good and
make their fellow humans happier, and permit their own
hearts and minds to speak frankly. This is what Heine meant
when he coined the phrase, "the emancipation of kings."

And the others? That motley crowd of gapers, unable to
form their own opinion, lacking the courage to denounce
these fakirs' tricks? They are neither good nor bad, they are
just stupid. Cringing on their knees, their moronic eyes "in a
fine frenzy rolling," they admire those who rule by the grace
of God, never aware if one among them survives by the grace
of the Devil alone. They stare and wonder: well, why should
we care? Do we not behold, day after day, oxen and asses and
calves flaunting the selfsame stupidity? True, they have tails
to wag while human specimens have none; but they are just
as beastly stupid.

It is this category of living beings against whom Heine
raged. A noble wrath lent the biting darts of satire to his

tongue. He did not write with a pen, but with the scalpel of a
surgeon. Attempting to cure humanity, he lanced its festering
boils. Poor Heine, all his labor came to naught! He was carried to his grave misunderstood, unrecognized. Will the world
never come to understand you, Heine? You, whose songs,
despite envy, despite hatred and jealousy, are truly immortal?
Verily, you sang as the nightingale sings.

Thus writes Empress Elizabeth of Heinrich Heine, the
political philosopher. The longer she dwelt with him in her
literary life, the greater became her worship. At the beginning of the 'nineties—so my father told me—when Aunt
Sissy was in Hamburg, she went to visit Heinrich Heine's
youngest sister, Charlotte von Embden, a nonagenarian still
alive at that time. The Empress remained with the old lady
so long that the poor woman finally succumbed to a fainting spell, completely exhausted from the relentless stream
of questions with which Aunt Sissy had plied her for hours.
Later the Empress sent the old lady a coffee cup and saucer
adorned with the imperial crest.

Eventually Aunt Sissy built a monument to Heine in her
Achilleion on Corfu. How she must have jibed at Wilhelm II from the other side of the river Styx when, after he
had bought the Achilleion, years later, he immediately
ordered the Heine monument thrown out of the temple.

Elizabeth was not only interested in Heine, the poet and
political philosopher, but also in Heine, the philosopher of
religion. I read in her diary:

Absorbed by Heine's writings, I ponder long over his confession of faith. He was born a Jew and yet he was a Chris-

tian . . . to be sure, only as I interpret the word "Christian" and not in the meaning of that world-wide multifarious sect bearing the name. Heine has taught me to look upon these disliked and persecuted people in a new light. This Jew Heine had the true conception of Christ. He loved Christ not because he was a legitimate God, whose father was a God and ruled the universe for an eternity, but because he, although a Son of Heaven, was democratically minded, disliking the pomp and ceremony with which, in the course of time, human tradition had endowed him.

Elizabeth had very definite ideas on Christianity and of those who profess this faith, as her diary divulges. She writes:

What is wrong with the Christians of today? They completely lack genuine Christianity. They never think of practising it, being much too clever and worldly-wise for that. But well they know that Christianity within a state is necessary to make the subjects obey in all humility. Devil, Hell, and Eternal Perdition are preached for no other reason than to curb sin and theft and murder. Those clever ones who call themselves Christians are aware that humanity is still far from finding a moral god through enlightenment, self-discipline, and will power. Therefore, they try ever so hard to convert their neighbors to *their* Christianity. Thus they have a certain hold on a religion which, if the truth be told, they do not practise themselves because it is too taxing; moreover, it does not pay enough. Although infidels are converted and baptized day after day, all this outpouring of holy water does not help much. . . . Monopoly of a state church is just as inimical to religion as is any other monopoly to industry and commerce.

Religion will flourish only when a political equality of worship has been established—not before the "Freedom of Trade for the Gods," as it were, has been promulgated!

In another essay on Heine, the man, Elizabeth has this to say:

> People rack their brains about Heine, what he was and what he was not. When Heine, scaling the highest pinnacles of idealistic fancy, suddenly plunges into coarse reality; when, from exalted enthusiasm, he quickly changes to the depths of scathing scorn, is he not justified? He lived and loved . . . and who should blame him for that? Perhaps those hypocrites who have done the same or even worse, yet pretend to be pious and virtuous? Verily the world is despicable with all its lies and deceptions! Is anything on this earth untouchably pure? Why can't we be as God has created us? Why must everything in life be a farce, so revolting as to disgust us, even in our hour of death?

Most of Aunt Sissy's poetry is written under the influence of Heinrich Heine; especially her lighter verse is affected by the acid spirit of that Knight of Withering Sarcasm. It is in this vein that she once scribbled an amusing poem, poking fun at Katherina Schratt, that plump Viennese actress whom Elizabeth herself had chosen for her husband and elevated to the semi-official position of "companion to the Emperor."

For some reason or other, Aunt Sissy had presented Frau Schratt with a little butter churn of which the actress was inordinately proud. Like Mary and her Little Lamb, wherever Frau Schratt went, her butter churn was sure to go. Obviously the Empress had found this habit diverting, for

it inspired a poem entitled: "Consolation." I remember
chuckling over it when I copied it into the big book:

> *Your buxom angel comes anon*
>   *With roses, quite an armful;*
> *Be patient, then, my Oberon—*
>   *Excitement might be harmful!*

> *She brings along her little churn,*
>   *She'll never go without it;*
> *She likes her butter to a turn,*
>   *There're no two ways about it!*

> *Her corset is so tightly bound,*
>   *The stays are almost breaking;*
> *The while she stiffly walks around,*
>   *Her poor old ribs are aching.*

> *Imbued with aping mania,*
>   *Despite her pounds of fat,*
> *She longs to be Titania . . .*
>   *That Katherina Schratt.*

But there were times when Aunt Sissy's strain of sarcasm
yielded to tearful sentimentality. On one such occasion she
showed me a rather large silver locket containing the photograph of a little girl. "Who do you think this is?" she
asked. Before I could answer, she exclaimed: "Of course, you
couldn't know the little darling!"

Aunt Sissy was right; not until after the death of my

mother did I learn that the picture was that of the Girl of Sassetot. Only then did I realize how it had preyed on Aunt Sissy's mind that this child of hers, whom she could visit only clandestinely, was growing up away from her. And it had been just this love child that she had craved so passionately for her very own!

There were other matters, too, preying on Aunt Sissy's mind at that time. She was greatly concerned over Rudolf. Not the court alone, but the Austro-Hungarian people in general, in the course of the late 'eighties, had become aware that the Crown Prince was very unhappy with Stephanie. Time and again the Empress spoke of it, always pointing out that "the Belgians have never brought us any luck."

The Empress also worried over the many love affairs in which Rudolf was continually involved at that time, especially his affair with Mary Vetsera. So much, however, has been written about the Vetsera episode that it is needless for me to go into it in great detail again. To clear my own name, I said all I had to say decades ago.

It was in 1888 that I was reintroduced to the old Baroness Vetsera whom I first had met in Gödöllö in 1876. The Baroness and her two daughters had just arrived at the Danube capital, the Baron having recently died somewhere in the Levant. I immediately sensed an air of mystery about the Vetsera family.

Unfortunately I simply could not help becoming friendly with the Vetseras in the course of time; they were so bent upon it that nothing I could do discouraged them. Mary, hardly back from the convent where she was educated, was not only very beautiful but also extremely precocious. As I realized later, she and her mother foisted themselves upon me because Mary was madly infatuated with Crown Prince Rudolf.

Unconsciously, unwillingly, I was drawn into the most popular *cause célèbre* of that epoch which found its shocking culmination in the Meyerling tragedy. It was destined to be a tragedy not only for Cousin Rudolf, but for me as well.

Chapter Seven

SILENCE IS NOT ALWAYS GOLDEN

*U*NLIKE Lord Byron, who awoke one day to find himself famous, I awoke on the morning of January 30, 1889, to find myself the most infamous woman in all Europe. That was the Wednesday when the Vienna newspapers carried the appalling account of Crown Prince Rudolf's tragic death at his hunting lodge at Meyerling. So far, the newspapers had not learned the full details of the story; only in the most intimate court circles was it known, at the time, that together with the heir apparent, his current inamorata, Mary Vetsera, had been found slain.

Since that morning, I know how it feels to be branded a woman of doubtful reputation. To be sure, that I was to become Europe's most talked-of villainess for decades was, to a certain extent, a misfortune of my own making. I should not have kept silent then, and I certainly should not have waited almost a quarter of a century before making my first public statement. I should have spoken up immediately, frankly and freely, and so should have the authorities, for that matter, instead of permitting my name to be besmirched by stupid scandal-mongers.

During those late January days of 1889, at the Grand Hotel in Vienna, I sensed something in the air. Unfortunately I did not guess the grave import of Cousin Rudolf's indiscretion with Mary Vetsera. I had been an amused spectator to so many flirtatious interludes in high society that they actually were palling on me. Besides, hadn't Aunt Sissy taught me "to see nothing, to hear nothing, to say nothing ... especially in *affaires d'amour*"? Living up to this imperial maxim, I had kept to myself whatever information reached me. Moreover, I certainly never knew all I have been given credit for in the public press. It is perfectly true, however, that there were several aspects of the affair which I could not very well divulge years ago, as the old Emperor Francis Joseph was still alive, and Hapsburg's glory had not yet been eclipsed.

I had come to Vienna in the beginning of 1889, preparatory to spending the rest of the winter at the Riviera. My sojourn at the Kaiserstadt served two purposes: the most boresome business of having a broken tooth treated, and the far more absorbing diversion of replenishing my wardrobe for a trip south. At that time, the Rudolf–Vetsera affair was already a *fait accompli,* having begun in May, 1888, while I was away from Vienna. Probably under the irresistible spell of that romantic month, Mary Vetsera, through her maid Agnes, had succeeded in persuading Loschek, the Crown Prince's trusted man, to deliver a letter to my cousin; Loschek himself admitted as much later.

From the very moment of its inception, the affair progressed with lightning speed. If the old Baroness Vetsera did not actually connive with her daughter, then she at least lent her silent approval to the dangerous game. Mary's mother, by that time, probably had reached the conclusion that it would be impossible to maneuver Duke Miguel de Braganza into a situation where he would propose marriage to Mary.

As Count Hans Wilczek summed up the story to me years later: "The old Baroness Vetsera may have been a very shrewd woman, but that was one time when she made a bad mistake. Perhaps she was ignorant of the real nature of Mary's affair with Rudolf because then, worldly-wise as she was, she would have interfered before things had gone too far. At any rate, the old Baroness's calculations went awry if she hoped that Rudolf could be forced into a morganatic marriage—that the Crown Prince was eager to obtain a Papal annulment of his marriage with the Crown Princess was well known all over Vienna at that time—or at least be made to pay an enormous sum of money."

Vividly I recall the January afternoon when Cousin Rudolf visited me at the Grand Hotel, after sending word that he absolutely must see me on a most important matter. He came to my suite via the servants' entrance, where Jenny had been waiting for him. His brow was clouded, his whole manner disturbed. We indulged in small talk over the first cup of tea, to which he added a little cognac. When I offered Rudolf a second cup, he declined, refilling it to the very brim with cognac instead. I looked on anxiously; this seemed to bear out the rumor that the Crown Prince had taken to strong drink to steady his nerves. As a matter of fact, gossip went so far as to claim that, now and then, he took drugs to relieve the obvious tension from which he suffered.

Presently Rudolf seemed to relax; he became talkative. "Marie," he began, drumming on the table, "I am surrounded by spies."

"Why, Rudolf!"

"Yes, yes . . . I know what I'm talking about. Oh, sometimes I think life isn't worth living. It seems I am just butting my head against the petty obstinacy of others." That the Crown Prince was referring to the Emperor was perfectly plain, as he immediately added: "Mother certainly is a martyr. I most assuredly don't envy her lot."

I felt extremely uncomfortable at being made Rudolf's confidante in this way. I racked my brain to direct the conversation into more conventional channels, but my imperial cousin impatiently thrust aside these efforts at discretion.

"No, no, I came here with a purpose in mind—or rather two, Marie. You see, I simply must have my hands free. Now, more than ever before, I must be absolutely unencumbered."

I looked at him questioningly, wondering whether real importance should be attached to the whisperings that, lately, Rudolf was seriously involving himself in matters political. It appeared likely enough when Rudolf handed me that historical little steel box which I was to return to him alone or, in case of his death, deliver to the one and only person who could furnish the correct password.

I felt decidedly uneasy. However, before I could raise an objection, Rudolf continued: "And there's one thing more, Marie." He poured himself another cup of cognac, then went on to say that I must induce the old Baroness Vetsera and her daughter to spend the next few months at the Riviera.

Disliking to become entangled in my cousin's affairs, I seized upon the first excuse that came to mind. "Have you considered that the old lady might not be financially able to indulge in such extravagance, Rudolf? You know she is not overly affluent."

The Crown Prince waved away the objection; he knew all about it and intended to take care of that little matter the very next time he saw Mary. "Oh, another thing, Marie. I wish you would drop a hint to the Vetseras that I will be coming to the Riviera myself for some time. It may influence their decision to go south."

I permitted myself a short, thoughtful pause. Finally I mustered up all my courage to point out to Rudolf that although I knew—and, for that matter, everybody else knew —that he was not exactly smitten with Stephanie, nevertheless, she was the mother of his little daughter Elizabeth whom he so adored. I said all this without the slightest intention to preach, merely desiring to patch up a distasteful situation.

My cousin broke in irritably: "You are the right one to lecture me on morality, Marie! You, my own mother's go-between."

I glanced at him in quick alarm; there was nothing I could say to that accusation.

"And so far as Erzsi is concerned,"—Rudolf referred to his little daughter by her Hungarian pet name—"she certainly is a lovely child. Even now that little one knows exactly what she wants. Of course, if she were a boy . . . things

might have taken a different turn." There was an expression
of profound disappointment on his face which I readily understood. I knew that medical authorities had decided that
Stephanie could not bear him another child.

At last Rudolf left as clandestinely as he had come. I took
the little steel box he had entrusted to me and locked it
away in a trunk. The box was not very heavy, actually; yet
it seemed like a great burden in my hands. I divined that it
contained documents aiming at a *coup d'état,* with the final
abdication of the Emperor in mind.

That little steel box worried me greatly—so much, in fact,
that two or three days later I boarded the night train for
Munich to consult my father. Perhaps he could advise me
on this perilous problem. . . .

Father studied my face quizzically. "You ask me what
you should do about it, Marie? Well . . . nothing . . . at
least for the time being. Just keep your lips sealed. It never
hurts to know a few secrets . . . especially if they are the
secrets of a future Emperor."

This paternal advice did not seem altogether proper; I
would even question its authenticity today if I had to rely
upon my memory alone. But I am copying Father's very
words from my diary.

Next night I returned to Vienna, where my maid Jenny
meanwhile had remained in the same room with my trunk,
standing guard, so to speak, over the little steel box.

It was just a few days after this trip to Munich when I
was awakened by Jenny to find myself the scapegoat of the
Meyerling tragedy. Somehow the imperial secret police were

informed that Rudolf had called on me, incognito, within the last week. I had also been seen with Mary Vetsera, and so, with one thing and another, I was held responsible for that ugly blot on the pages of history.

Many were the people who came to me during those days, pretending to express their sympathy on the death of my cousin, but in reality to carry tales. Little of all I heard at that time have I been able to substantiate. One thing, however, I can confirm beyond all doubt: that it was Mary Vetsera who died with Crown Prince Rudolf was completely irrelevant; his companion in death might just as well have been Mitzi Hauser, *die fesche Probiermamsell*—that good-looking model at Jungmann's fashion *salon*. Weeks preceding the Meyerling tragedy, the Crown Prince had besought Mitzi to die together with him. Apparently Rudolf was obsessed by the fear of facing his Maker alone.

The excitement in Vienna in those days was terrific, the effects of the tragedy at the *Hofburg* indescribable. Nobody dared to inform the Emperor; it was left to Aunt Sissy to break the shocking news to the bereft father. The woman who finally emerged from the Kaiser's study, Francis Joseph leaning upon her heavily, bore scant resemblance to the Aunt Sissy I had known all my life. Under the impact of her great and sudden bereavement, the Empress seemed to have turned into stone. Only this change, brought on by the enormity of her loss, could explain why Aunt Sissy cast me aside then. I knew her to be unforgiving by nature and capable of nursing a vindictive hate. Yet I always had attributed to her a highly developed sense of justice. I was wrong, for she condemned me, unheard!

If only I had ignored her own teachings; if only I had not kept silent about the Vetsera affair and that little steel box! Had I delivered those secret documents into her hands, my life would have taken an entirely different turn at that juncture. In that case, the Meyerling tragedy would not have assumed the aspects of a love affair but of a political intrigue. It would have become evident that the heir apparent did not choose death because of disappointed love, but because he feared that he had lost a dangerous political game which he had played *va banque*.

It is no exaggeration to say that Cousin Rudolf had been driven frantic by a complication of personal and political affairs when he came to me that fateful afternoon, entrusting me with the little steel box and asking me to take the Vetseras away from Vienna. What I learned subsequently has enabled me to reconstruct the different phases of the Meyerling tragedy. I was reliably informed that, once at Meyerling, Rudolf, threatened with imminent arrest for high treason, partook of alcohol freely. Many a man in less exalted position, and with less reason, has sought to drown his troubles in drink!

While Prince Philip von Coburg, Count Hoyos, and other hunting guests, awaited Rudolf in another part of the rambling cottage, he and Mary withdrew. Mary retired and soon fell into a light slumber; suddenly she awoke to find herself alone. She jumped out of bed and peered into the adjoining room. There the Crown Prince sat, deep in thought, a revolver in his hand!

Realization of where his treacherous plans were leading him must have been tantalizing Rudolf when Mary Vetsera, clad only in a chemise—as she was found later—came upon her truant lover. Probably she upbraided him for contemplating suicide at a moment when she found herself in "an intolerable position"—her pregnancy at the time of her death is not only a matter of medical record, but also has been reaffirmed by King Ferdinand of Bulgaria, brother of Philip of Coburg. To make matters worse, Rudolf was still in love with "that young woman"—the lovely Princess K . . .—but Mary evidently was unaware that the Princess was also an expectant mother at the time.

A heated argument ensued. Rudolf, his brain inflamed by alcohol, his emotions running amuck, and finding the revolver still in his hand, raised the gun and fired. The bullet tore away Mary's cheek right beneath the temple; she toppled over and fell on the bed.

God alone knows what Rudolf thought of then, but this bloody deed—murder, whichever way one looks at it—added to his political entanglements, must have overcome him to such an extent that he turned the weapon on himself. When his valet and his princely visitors, alarmed by the shots, broke into the room, the heir to the throne of Hapsburg was dead, and so was his mistress.

This is the only way in which I can reconstruct the tragedy of Meyerling. The widespread belief that I know much more about the hunting-lodge drama probably arose from the fact that, after Rudolf's death, certain papers were found in his room; from these it became apparent that I had received sizable amounts of money from him. Of course, as long as I felt impelled to keep silent, I could not explain those "payments for my services."

Rudolf did give me money—comparatively large amounts, too. But only to turn over to Mary Vetsera, whose family had been living on their continuously shrinking principal for years and years. When Rudolf's expense vouchers were gone over with a fine-tooth comb, for possible clues, repeated entries were found with my name for amounts from five hundred to three thousand guilders. These entries and some letters which I had written to Mary, together with certain statements made by Baroness Vetsera's mother, accounted for Aunt Sissy's attitude toward me.

Meanwhile the little steel box—the *genuine one,* not the duplicate, existence of which I did not dare to reveal before —still reposed in my trunk. When entrusting the little box to me, Rudolf pointed out with a touch of glee: "I had two of these made, both absolutely identical. The other one I shall leave among my effects so they will have something to poke their noses into when the time comes."

When that time came, all "they" found in the spurious box was some innocuous notes. However, these served the purpose, since it made "them" desist from looking further. The contents of the genuine box, which I had in safe keeping, undoubtedly would have furnished the key to the whole dynastic intrigue, incidentally costing the heads of a number of people. Sensing this dénouement, I could not bring myself to break Rudolf's trust.

Looking back today, I am inclined to think I might have delivered the little steel box to Aunt Sissy if she had relented and seen me for just a few minutes. But her cruel treatment served to strengthen my stubbornness. And while I still smarted with outraged pride, there came the call for that little steel box . . . from none other than Archduke John of Tuscany.

Doubtless, under the influence of what sycophants whispered into her ear, Aunt Sissy suspected me of conspiring with Mary and the old Baroness Vetsera—a suspicion seemingly supported by the fact that I did not abandon my itinerary, but insisted upon leaving for the Riviera. My obstinacy was the very natural result of Aunt Sissy's harsh attitude toward me. When she sent Count Gyula Andrássy to me with the bitter message which banished me forever from court society, attaching an ugly stigma to my name, my common sense deserted me completely and I ignored his sound advice.

"I implore you, Your Grace," Count Andrássy had asked me with all the sincerity of an old friend, "please remain in Vienna and face the situation. After all, my dear, it's the wisest course to pursue."

"I shall go to the Riviera as I planned. And nobody can say that I am running away, either, because too many people know that I had this trip in mind for months," I told Count Andrássy. "Why, even Aunt Sissy herself knew about it. . . . Besides, Count, do you think it is right for Aunt Sissy to judge me without so much as granting me a hearing?"

An accomplished courtier and a great diplomat, the Empress's messenger made no reply save for the sad little smile playing around tightly closed lips.

Of course, I was young then and, under the stress of developments, impervious to logic. Instead of standing my ground in Vienna and fighting for my reputation, I departed for the Riviera. The consequence of that ill-chosen impulse

was that all Vienna accepted it for a fact that I had "fled."
Once again the old truth asserted itself that the absent are
always wrong for the simple reason that they cannot de-
fend themselves.

There was a single ray of light during all these dark days:
throughout the whole affair, my husband showed great understanding—something I had never expected of him. He
believed me implicitly when I assured him that there was no
guilt on my hands. But unfortunately, before the rest of the
world, there was only one man who could have cleared me
from all blame in connection with the Meyerling affair, and
that man was Archduke John of Tuscany.

While trying to make the most of my sojourn at the
Riviera, I clung to the hope that Archduke John would
appear on the scene one day, and reveal the true facts behind the Meyerling tragedy. Alas, he had meanwhile left
Austria "to die without dying."

Although Cousin Rudolf had dropped vague hints to me
of his political alliance with the Archduke, details came to
light only later.

John of Tuscany, at the time of the Meyerling tragedy,
was thirty-six years old and famous both as a military leader
and a writer. He had written books on tactics and strategy
and, as an example of his remarkable versatility, had also
furnished the libretto for a ballet and published a lengthy
treatise against spiritism. John came into especial prominence in 1887 when he aspired to the Bulgarian throne—
an ambition which subsequently made him *persona non
grata* at the *Hofburg*.

No sooner had this plan come to naught than the Archduke involved himself in a conspiracy with Cousin Rudolf. Together with the Crown Prince and two others, one a Russian and the other a Hungarian, he bent every effort to rob the Kaiser of his throne. Rudolf not only aspired to the crown of Emperor of Austria and King of Hungary, but to that of King of Bohemia as well. In this way Rudolf hoped to stabilize the perpetually tottering Dual Monarchy and pave the way to a pan-Slavic union, the selfsame aim which his successor, Francis Ferdinand, was to cherish vainly. John of Tuscany expected to become Viceroy of Tyrol, Istria, and Dalmatia, and plans were formulated to sever the Grand Duchy of Tuscany from an Italy only recently united.

The scheme carried enough dynamite to blow up all central Europe! Plans had already matured to such an extent that the immediate entourage of Emperor Francis Joseph was informed, and the arrest of the conspirators seemed imminent, provided they did not stage a successful *coup d' état* without delay. To that end, cold-blooded fixity of purpose was necessary—a trait my cousin Rudolf utterly lacked, especially at that time.

In the wake of the Meyerling affair, Archduke John was commanded to report to Emperor Francis Joseph. It is not definitely known what the two discussed behind closed doors, but from the information imparted to me in the course of years, I assume that Uncle threatened the Archduke with a speedy and severe court-martial.

John of Tuscany made it plain to the Emperor that his court-martial would mean baring the whole ugly plot, including all the details of Rudolf's political activities; moreover, the secrets of his scandalous love affairs also would have a decided bearing on dynastic questions. John probably intimated to the Kaiser what was common gossip in Vienna: that Rudolf at the first suitable moment—which doubtlessly meant after his father's enforced abdication—would have tried to induce Pope Leo XIII to grant him an annulment. He also would have established a new house law, legitimatizing any heir of his for the succession to the throne even if born out of wedlock or after his death.

To all appearances, whatever the Archduke of Tuscany revealed in his audience with Francis Joseph induced the Emperor to compromise with him. The final understanding was that John would renounce his title, keep silent in regard to the whole affair, and leave the Dual Monarchy forever.

As meanwhile the spurious steel box had been seized, further search for treasonable material was abandoned. This box, together with sundry documents bearing on the death of my cousin, among them official reports on the autopsy of Baroness Mary and a long letter her mother wrote to the Emperor some months after the tragedy, was handed over to Francis Joseph. Shortly after Aunt Sissy's death in 1898, in order to make it impossible for the documents to fall into wrong hands, the Kaiser entrusted them to Count Edward Taaffe, Minister of the Imperial Court and one-time Prime Minister of the Dual Monarchy.

Among the papers given to Count Taaffe was the correspondence between Emperor Francis Joseph and Rudolf on one side, and Pope Leo XIII on the other, regarding the annulment my cousin endeavored to obtain from the Vatican. Had these documents been placed in the Vienna court and state archives, they would have been found during the revolution in 1918. Then the real truth of the Meyerling tragedy would have been known and my good name restored to me. Unfortunately, during the winter of 1925–26, a fire destroyed Count Taaffe's Castle Ellischau and reduced the valuable library to ashes, precluding any possibility of ascertaining all the details of the Meyerling tragedy, especially since Archduke John of Tuscany had taken the genuine steel box with him on his trip to Nowhere in the summer of 1889.

Officially, John Orth, as he called himself after renouncing his royal prerogatives, was never heard from again. Unofficially, his whereabouts were known until the beginning of the war. As all the world knows, accompanied by his sweetheart, Milli Stubel, he set sail for South America on his yacht *Santa Margherita*. Nearing Rio de Janeiro, his craft went aground when a terrific storm came up. Presumably the vessel was dashed to pieces, with all hands lost.

Did all of them really perish? Did John Orth perish with them?

There is more than one reason to believe that, knowing a severe storm was approaching, John Orth, together with his crew of hand-picked men pledged to eternal silence, abandoned the vessel as a means of obliterating his tracks.

Since then many "John Orths" have been discovered here and there, all over the world, but not one proved himself the genuine former Archduke of Tuscany. For the world at large, the Meyerling tragedy had been the signal for him to pass out of the political picture forever. For me it had been the bell which tolled the end of my career as confidante to my imperial Aunt Sissy.

After that trying experience, life never again was the same for me. All too soon I discovered that I was *persona non grata* not only at the Hapsburg court, but also before the Tribunal of Fate itself.

Having once set tongues wagging, the Meyerling affair proved too choice a morsel for scandal-mongers to relinquish. Nefarious gossip in the public print and by word of mouth continued; there were even rumors that I had been "exiled" from the domain of my imperial uncle when we moved to Bavaria. Actually I desired to be near my ailing mother, and so we decided that we would stay in Munich during the winter, spending the summer in the near-by mountains. Besides, my parents had presented me with an unpretentious but comfortable country home in Rottach-on-Tegernsee which I named Villa Valerie after my oldest daughter. There we spent the greater part of the next few years, and it was from there, in 1891, that I rushed to my stricken mother. She departed for a better world while I watched at her bedside and Queen Maria—Tante Königin —held her hand. A few days later she, who had been plain Henrietta Mendel, was carried to her last rest with royal honors at the ducal crypt in Tegernsee. Most of our princely relatives attended the requiem. There were mountains of floral offerings at the funeral but none more impressive than the one bearing a broad ribbon in the imperial colors and carrying the inscription: "To my beloved sister-in-law. Francis Joseph."

Perhaps loneliness, perhaps clever schemers, drove my father into a second marriage after a short year. He incurred rather embarrassing publicity by this hasty step, but it had none of the sting of later years when his marital venture was aired in the law courts during the course of divorce proceedings. Duke Ludwig's second wife, once member of the *Corps de Ballet* of the Royal Opera in Munich, was personally a charming and modest young lady. Although she was not guilty of proverbial stepmother intrigues, the fine friendship that had bound me so closely to my father all through my life was nevertheless broken now.

Almost simultaneously, my own marriage came to an impasse. For nearly two decades I had lived, if not exactly with George, at least alongside him. Everything considered, it had been peaceful enough. However, as the years grew longer our tempers grew shorter and, finally, in 1896, our marital ways parted definitely. The divorce was the outgrowth of an originally stupid misunderstanding. No doubt, things could have been smoothed over if it had not been for the fact that, after twenty years of marital incarceration, I felt I should see how the world looked outside the walls of wedlock. And so I acquiesced when George's lawyer offered the settlement of a three-thousand-dollar annuity, a modest enough sum.

Nothing was farther from my mind than to marry again, but my father entertained different ideas on the subject. He became addicted to the theory that "it wasn't the thing to do" for me to live singly. Somewhere he discovered a very rich, decrepit lord whose poor health promised an early widowhood. However, once before my marriage bed had been made for me by somebody else; I did not propose to lie in it again unless my partner were of my own choosing.

I was weary of the label: *"that* Countess Larisch," which European society had thrust upon me. I could very well picture myself starting afresh, minus the nine-pointed coronet of earldom but plus a sufficient amount of mutual appreciation.

Life had taught me that certain things simply will not happen unless they are *made* to happen. And so, in 1897, I decided to become the wife of the Royal Bavarian Court-singer Otto Brucks. The man I chose for my second husband had been a frequent visitor to my parental home for years. My father, Duke Ludwig, like all the Wittelsbachs, loved music and, in the course of years, had gathered a number of gifted friends around him. Among these was Otto Brucks, one of the most famous Wagner interpreters of his day. When Brucks lost his wife, at about the same time my good mother died, the two widowers spent more time together than ever before. In this way I came to know him very well indeed, meeting him in my father's house a few times each week, when I accompanied him on the piano. I knew that some busybodies in Brucks's family were scheming to marry him off to a relative, very much against his own inclination; at the same time my father was urging me to accept that broken-down old lord. Small wonder, then, that the idea suggested itself to me that Otto Brucks and I should take whatever life had left us and struggle on together. I sensed that Brucks was playing with the idea, but he seemed timid about proposing to the daughter of a Royal

Highness. I therefore decided I would have to take things into my own hands.

"Listen here, *Herr Kammersänger,*" I brought matters to a head one day, "you must admit that I am a pretty good accompanist at the piano. . . . Don't you think I could do almost as well accompanying you on your way through life?"

My boldness took his breath away, and he was unable to sing one more note that night. It required the better part of a month before he summoned enough courage to call at my apartment in Munich. Even then he could not say much, but an enormous bouquet of red roses spoke for him.

I have never regretted becoming his wife and the mother of our son, Otto, Jr. Those years permitted me to enjoy, to the fullest measure, my musical talents. Because he sensed that my ducal father might find his customary visits to the opera somewhat embarrassing, now that his own son-in-law was a member of its personnel, Otto handed in his resignation as *Kammersänger* immediately after our marriage.

In the ensuing years we resided in Munich, winters; in Rottach, summers. When my husband was not giving guest performances in the more important capitals of Europe— once, for an entire season, he sang at the Covent Garden in London—he taught voice culture. Liberated from all the social obligations that formerly were mine, as niece and close companion to the Empress of Austria-Hungary, I found myself with much free time on my hands. And so I started a book which I hoped would exonerate me from the sinister part I had supposedly played in the Meyerling tragedy. Whenever I lagged in my literary labors, notices in the papers referring, in one way or another, either to "the Countess Larisch who is now the wife of the singer Otto Brucks," or to "Frau Kammersänger Otto Brucks, *ci-devant* Countess Larisch," spurred me on.

Of course I had no intention of utilizing any of Aunt 'Sissy's material which I had brought to Munich at her behest before she left for Sassetot, and which I had found among Mother's papers. Nor would I publish anything before I consulted the Empress.

During the last years Aunt Sissy had spent most of her time on Corfu or in traveling. She had visited the Orient and had been the first, among Europe's crowned heads, to inspect the ruins of Troy. When she did not sail on her private yacht *Miramar*—so-called after the castle of Maximilian of Mexico—she traveled incognito, usually under the name of Countess von Hohenembs, the thirty-eighth title of the forty-three which the Court Almanac accorded her. In the course of her travels she sought close contact with the multitudes, amused at the little indignities to which she occasionally was subjected. She liked nothing better than to be a mere globe-trotting tourist.

But regardless how far she traveled, the Empress always returned to Corfu, that island in the Ionian Sea, off the coast of Albania, which she first had visited in the 'sixties. The Greek-style château that meanwhile had been erected there, near the little village of Gasturi, consisted of one hundred and twenty-eight rooms and stables for fifty horses. This royal residence contained a truly wonderful collection of Pompeiian and Greek art.

While on Corfu, the Empress's reading was confined to

Shakespeare and Heine almost exclusively. Frequently, she slept with Heine's *Book of Songs* under her pillow. Near the château, at the foot of Mount Aja Kyriahi, in an open marble temple, stood her Heine monument. After Rudolf's death another statue was erected there, dedicated to the memory of the late Crown Prince.

Aunt Sissy was once more on her way to Corfu when a chance offered itself to consult her on the use of her material. The Empress, passing through Munich, sent word that she would see me, on the condition that I throw myself at her feet. Probably I would have done so of my own volition, but when this gesture of contrition was expressly stipulated, I refused. While I was still pondering whether I had been wise to ignore Aunt Sissy's obviously conciliatory intention, the dreadful news staggered the world that the Empress-Queen had been assassinated in Switzerland.

Her Majesty, incognito as usual, had stopped over in Geneva. It was on the 10th of September, 1898, around noon, when the Empress, accompanied by Countess Sztaray, her lady-in-waiting, left the hotel to board the steamer *Genf* for Mont de Caux. As the scheduled time of departure drew near, Countess Sztaray, as soon as they had reached the Quai du Montblanc, near the steamer landing, rushed ahead to make sure that the boat would not leave without them. That very second, a man suddenly arose from a near-by bench: Luigi Lucchini, a dangerous anarchist, who had eluded the surveillance of the Swiss authorities for an hour. He fairly flung himself at the Empress, his right hand tightly clenched. Her Majesty staggered, and passers-by rushed to her aid.

COUNTESS LARISCH
*at the time of her
marriage to Otto
Brucks, 1897.*

COUNTESS LARISCH *and her mother,*
BARONESS VON WALLERSEE, *1872.*

The ensuing commotion brought Countess Sztaray back to Aunt Sissy's side. "What is it, Your Majesty?" she inquired, bewildered.

"I don't know," came the answer in a hollow voice.

Aware that her mistress disliked nothing so much as having her incognito revealed, Countess Sztaray put off further questioning. Placing her arm around the Empress to support her, she led her aboard the steamer. As the time of departure had been exceeded, the boat left immediately.

Only then the Empress collapsed. Apparently she herself did not realize what had happened. *"Was war das?"*—What was that?—she asked the Countess. Then she lost consciousness.

When her dress was unfastened, they found a tiny blood stain over her left breast. The anarchist, using a shoemaker's awl, had pierced her heart—a heart that had beaten just as rebelliously as his own against an established order of things.

The steamer was put about and the Empress taken on a stretcher to the near-by Hôtel Beaurivage. There, a few minutes after her arrival, Aunt Sissy died . . . "by the water," as she herself had predicted years ago.

The shock threw me upon a sickbed. For months, while recuperating at Villa Valerie in Rottach, I did nothing but spend interminable hours, taking myself to task, probing every single action of mine and never arriving at any final judgment. When, at last, I roused myself sufficiently to continue my book, a messenger from Vienna arrived.

The courier of the Kaiser was a little man, a veritable Beau Brummel, who introduced himself as Director General Edward Palmer of the Royal and Imperial Dominion Bank in Vienna. He looked for all the world like a rococo statuette, except that he did not wear a peruke. His diplomacy was all that one might expect of a cavalier of Louis XV.

From the intermediary through whom I had approached Aunt Sissy some months ago, court circles had learned of my intention to publish a book to rehabilitate myself. It was this manuscript that the *Herr Bankdirektor* was eager to see, although he professed to be primarily interested in arranging a guest performance for my husband at the imperial opera in Vienna.

"What rôle would the *Herr Kammersänger* prefer?"

Naturally this was a bait my husband could not resist. "Oh, Wotan in *Die Walküre,* and Hans Sachs in *Die Meistersinger."*

"That will be perfect!" the animated rococo statuette assured us. Intently scrutinizing his patent-leather shoes, tiny enough to give even Cinderella corns, Herr Palmer came to the real point of the interview. Now that he was here . . . would there be any objection if he ran through the pages of that interesting manuscript of mine about which he had heard in Vienna?

The upshot of all this was that Otto and I decided to accept the invitation for a guest performance at the celebrated Vienna Opera because it carried with it all the earmarks of imperial favor. We told Herr Palmer that my husband felt flattered indeed; incidentally, the *Herr Bankdirektor* might care to take along my manuscript to read on the train.

Herr Palmer once more assured us that "that will be perfect!" and departed, all graciousness.

At first I had wondered why he had been entrusted with a mission apparently outside the scope of a bank director. But when he finally tripped off with mincing steps, doffing his hat again and again and bowing deeply from the waist, I knew that the Kaiser could not have chosen a cleverer courier. Besides, there had been a reason for delegating a banker, as I presently discovered: During our artistically successful visit to Vienna, where I remained in strict incognito, Herr Palmer came to see me again. He revealed that His Majesty would grant me a twenty-five-hundred-dollar annuity if I would permit the manuscript to be placed in the imperial library.

That this offer was nothing more nor less than hush money, I realized instantly. However, I felt that I could not refuse without incurring the displeasure of my imperial uncle. The Kaiser also offered me a little castle in Austria, which would be publicly announced as an imperial gift to me, in this way making it clear to the world at large that I was again *persona grata* at the *Hofburg*.

It was a tempting offer, and I would not have hesitated to accept if my friend, Count Wilczek, had not warned me. He pointed out to me that while it would be easy enough to enter that castle, it might not be such a simple matter to move out again at my own free will. The possibility that I might meet the same sad fate of other royal prisoners sent a shudder through me. Thus I declined the castle, accepting, in its stead, the equivalent of twenty-five thousand dollars.

Before we left Vienna, I visited the Crypt of the Capuchins. There, at the sarcophagus of Aunt Sissy, I did what I had refused to do while she was still alive: I sank to my knees and prayed and cried. I begged her intercession that, henceforward, the unjust curse of being Europe's notorious figure be removed from me so that I might mingle among decent society again without having it smile to my face and sneer behind my back.

With the passing years, I made use of my musical gifts more and more, assisting my husband in his artistic endeavors. I became so acclimatized to this new life—and a rich, full, satisfying life it was—that I had practically forgotten the past. Not forgotten altogether, perhaps, for my prayers at Aunt Sissy's tomb had been in vain; the newspapers continued to refer to me as *"that* former Countess Larisch." But, evidently, time had tempered the malicious persecution of the past to some degree. It had grown into a mere historical fallacy of which there are many analogous examples.

Then suddenly, one day, while we were wintering in Munich, like a wraith from the past, Count Hans Wilczek came to call on me. To all appearances his mission was as discreet as that which previously had brought the *Herr Bankdirektor* to Rottach.

When my husband rose to leave us, the Count demurred: "No, no, my dear Brucks, stay right here, because you must accompany your wife to Vienna."

"To Vienna?" we both asked in one breath.

"Yes, indeed. His Majesty wishes to see you, Countess,"

he explained, addressing me by my old title with a significance that did not escape me. "His Majesty desires information, and so you are to come to Vienna. Just for a few hours, you understand, and without creating any undue attention."

Count Wilczek glanced at me sharply, then went into further detail: "You see, His Majesty knows all . . . all! The Emperor has been told by somebody that there is an important letter written by Her Majesty somewhere. This letter was presumably addressed to your late mother. I have already consulted His Royal Highness, but Duke Ludwig insists that all your mother's papers are now in your possession."

This totally unexpected demand from the Kaiser set me trembling. "Count Wilczek," I faltered, "I know of one letter only——"

"Yes, from Sassetot, dated 1882, isn't that so?" my visitor injected.

Although I had intuitively felt that it was this letter the Kaiser wanted, I was nevertheless taken aback that Count Wilczek should be so well informed.

I hesitated, then blurted out in dismay: "His Majesty must never see that letter!"

"But I tell you, Countess, that His Majesty knows *all!*" He arose from his chair decisively: "Your husband is to bring you to Vienna on the morning train, the day after tomorrow." With those words, which were nothing short of a command, Count Wilczek left us.

I watched him go in speechless horror. I could not understand how the Kaiser had learned of that telltale letter in which Aunt Sissy had urged Mother to hasten to Vienna and assure herself that the little girl, born in Sassetot, was receiving the very best care. . . .

I felt as though I were under the influence of a powerful drug when, early in the morning of the second day, we arrived in Vienna. At the railroad station we were received by a man who, I discerned at first glance, was an imperial lackey in plain clothes. He escorted us to an unnumbered *Fiaker,* and we proceeded to a nondescript little hotel so that I could freshen up a bit. He left with the announcement that he would call for me in ample time to be at the *Hofburg* at eleven o'clock.

On the dot of half-past ten, just after I had finished making a copy of Aunt Sissy's letter for my own keeping, the carriage was in front of the hotel once more. I drove off alone—my husband was to await my return at the hotel—stopping, after a few minutes, so that Count Wilczek might join me. We reached the *Hofburg* through a little side entrance and, after taking me around innumerable corners, and what seemed to me interminable corridors through which I had never passed before, Count Wilczek piloted me into an office-like room. Upon my entrance, a man rose from behind a desk. He was Prince Rudolf Liechtenstein, who had been Aunt Sissy's "travel marshal" on her trip to Combermere Abbey in 1878.

A sudden suspicion flashed through my brain. Could he be the man who had told the Emperor about that all too revealing letter? I knew the Prince to be most meticulous in morals as well as manners. Away back at Combermere

Abbey, he had made it clear, more than once, that he thoroughly disapproved of the Empress's free ways.

My glance at him seemed to betray my thoughts, for the Prince became greatly flustered. "I hope you brought the —ah—the document along?" The fact that he avoided the word "letter" intensified my suspicion. But, after all, I reflected, what difference could it make now? . . . And so I kept silent and merely nodded.

"Very well, then. Will you please accompany me?"

Disembodied spirits must feel much the same as I felt when I followed Prince Liechtenstein. In a daze I passed through a door . . . then quickly awakened to reality when I discovered I was in the Emperor's study. A bent figure was seated behind a desk. I made my deepest genuflection.

The Kaiser looked up slowly. He seemed tired, so terribly tired. Even his voice conveyed an impression of utter weariness.

"*Setz' Dich*"—Sit down—Uncle Francis Joseph said, addressing me with the familiar "*Du.*" Then, a moment later, as if it were an afterthought, he added: "Marie."

"*Danke sehr.*" I obeyed. I meant to add "*Onkel*" but felt too choked to utter another word. More poignantly than ever, I grasped the tragedy that had dogged the monarch's life. Despite his melancholy mien, there was an air of ineffable graciousness about him.

He turned his head toward me and nodded a belated greeting. Suddenly he straightened up and gazed into my eyes intently. "Now, Marie," he said, fortifying himself with a deep breath, before embarking upon his task of questioning me.

I answered as fully as I could, but all the time one idea clung to me stubbornly: to protect the memory of my dear dead mother. "Your Majesty," I stammered, "Mother should not be held responsible for all this. She was made a confidante very much against her own wishes. . . . Certainly Mother had no choice in the matter."

"I know, I know," the Emperor interrupted. "I shall always remember your good mother as a loyal, God-fearing woman."

His words warmed my heart; I felt easier; now I could return his straightforward gaze.

And then the moment came when I was asked to relinquish the letter. Without so much as a glance at it, the Kaiser took it and pushed it under a letter weight. "And this is the only letter, Marie? The only one you have?"

"The only one I have, Your Majesty." I told the truth, for there were actually no other original letters. Of course, I still had copies of Aunt Sissy's diaries and poetry which I had taken to Munich for safe-keeping. However, the Emperor had not asked for them; obviously he did not know anything about them. Why, then, should I make an old man's heart heavier? Besides, His Majesty seemed interested only in that letter from Sassetot which gave the name of the child and identified its father.

"Thank you, Marie." The Kaiser extended his hand; I knew the audience was ended. And then I did precisely what Aunt Sissy had demanded of me: I threw myself at the Emperor's feet and kissed his hand. I felt redeemed when the Kaiser patted me on the shoulder gently. I remembered how, on my wedding day, far back in 1877 in

Gödöllö, he had sought to console me with just such a kindly gesture.

Unceremoniously I sprang to my feet and, all etiquette forgotten, I rushed from the room. I felt sure my old uncle understood that impulse.

Prince Liechtenstein awaited me outside and guided me back to his office, where I found Count Wilczek. I sank into a chair, crying my heart out, while the two courtiers tried to quiet me.

"Look here, you've got to pull yourself together. You must make that afternoon train." Count Wilczek's steady voice had its desired effect on me. In another moment I succeeded in stifling my sobs and I was on my way again.

The next morning found us back in Munich. As we stepped from the train, I remarked to my husband musingly: "I wonder why His Majesty was so intent upon obtaining that letter? He knew the facts anyway; then why bother about details now? Do you think it could be mere curiosity?"

Otto Brucks, who had spent a lifetime in the theater and was not only familiar with all the current gossip but had a very deep insight into the psychology of stage folk, smiled reflectively. "I wouldn't be the least bit surprised if some woman is behind it all."

It sounded rather plausible.

In 1906 Otto was entrusted with the combined directorship of the operas in Metz and in Luxembourg, a position involving great musical and managerial responsibilities and providing enough work for both of us. The appointment made me very happy because it gave me a long-sought opportunity to exert my artistic abilities to the utmost. My life promised to be full and rich; but, alas, the wellsprings of gossip refused to dry up. Shooting up intermittently, like the geyser I was to observe years later in Yellowstone National Park, the most fantastic tales burst forth in the public print, pillorying me as the evil spirit of the Hapsburgs. I everlastingly wrote letters to the editors, demanding retractions—a disturbing pastime in which I must indulge even today, from time to time. Now and then rumors would pile up so fast and furiously that I repeatedly wrote to Mr. Palmer, beseeching him to issue a statement to the press on my behalf. I pointed out to him that I had relinquished my manuscript with the tacit understanding that, in future, he would protect me from unwarranted attacks on my character. In his reply, the *Herr Bankdirektor* figuratively shrugged his shoulders. So sorry, but he could do nothing about it . . . and *"voilà tout"*—that was all there was to it —an expression which cropped up so often in Mr. Palmer's letters that it tried my patience to the breaking point.

Eventually, in 1912, I was forced to the conclusion that as long as the House of Hapsburg refused to battle for my good name, I must do my own fighting. I would state my case to the world—and this time the story would not be hidden away on some royal bookshelf.

I realized, of course, that I could reveal but the barest outline of the Meyerling tragedy. Not only was the old Emperor still ruling the Dual Monarchy, but too many others were alive whom I did not wish to draw into a historical episode which was becoming increasingly unsavory with

the passing of time. Then, too, at that time, my old father
—just eighty-two—was in the midst of extremely embarrassing divorce proceedings. The fact that I was still receiving
a yearly *apanage* from the House of Hapsburg did not disturb me very much, for I would simply renounce the
annuity. It seemed worth while foregoing this money if
only I could clear my name.

Preparatory to the publication of my book—which the
booming guns of the World War soon were to catapult into
oblivion—I went to London. There I accidentally ran across
a clue for which I had searched in vain for years. I was informed that a young woman, presumably the daughter of
Empress Elizabeth, had just written the story of her life.
Additional facts, which I ascertained, confirmed my belief
that this young woman could be none other than the Girl
of Sassetot. I sought to establish contact with her, but was
told that she had just left for Vienna to verify certain data
for her book. I was glad, then, that I had retained a copy
of the letter which I had been forced to surrender to the
Emperor. Doubtless my information, together with what
this young woman knew, would serve to reconstruct her
story. However, the clue was not to bring tangible results
for some time yet.

Upon my return from London I found my husband sick
abed. After a brief illness, an inscrutable Fate took him from
me. His passing marked yet another chapter in my eventful life—a life that was to assume a sterner note now. Those
years of contentment and affection I had found with Otto
Brucks could not be likened, perhaps, to the delirious pas-
sion of Tristan and Isolde; rather, they had contained the

deep understanding, the noble tranquillity of Beethoven's "Pastorale." With my husband's death, a new chord was struck that had the somber sound, the weird beat of a *danse macabre.*

In June, 1914, while visiting old friends in Baden-Baden to recuperate from the weeks of vigil at my husband's bedside, I had an experience which appears increasingly fantastic with the passing of the years. I cannot recall that I was ever troubled by nightmares; as a rule, I sleep much too soundly. Not even in the most exciting periods of my life, which followed the Meyerling tragedy and the assassination of Aunt Sissy, did my thoughts and emotions pursue me in slumber. Therefore I was astonished—nay, aghast— when, on the morning of June 28th, I awoke from an extremely disturbing dream. Aunt Sissy had appeared before me, just as of old, and I had not been at all surprised to see her. She had been dressed in a gray garment, not at all stylish, but fashioned of some soft material which accentuated her slender figure. She had worn all her beautiful pearls, a collection of world renown. Her face had been wreathed in that semi-sad, semi-ironical smile I knew so well. Handing something to me, she had said: "I want to give you a little joy, Marie."

Alas, I was never to learn what that "something" was because, at that very moment, the strands of pearls around the Empress's throat had broken, the gems pelting the floor like so many hailstones. Immediately I knelt down, gathering each jewel into my skirt. The ivory-tinted pearls suddenly had turned to blood-red corals . . . and it was then that I awoke with a start.

I was still under the spell of this terrifying nightmare, seeking to interpret its meaning, when the door was flung open. My friend burst in with the staggering news that Archduke Francis Ferdinand and his consort had been assassinated in Sarajevo. . . .

While war clouds were rapidly gathering on the European horizon, I learned that my daughter Valerie was in a most precarious condition in Lausanne. For many years she had devoted herself to medical missionary work in Africa. Now she was stricken with a grave illness, the germ of which she had contracted during her labors on the Dark Continent. However, when the first thunderbolt of the war rocked the world, I tore myself from my daughter's sickbed to return to Germany. Valerie herself knew she was beyond help. All her life she had striven to help others, and now, when death was near, she wanted nothing more than that I should serve in her place. There was work to be done at the front and, at her urging, I left to do it.

I volunteered for the Red Cross and plunged into war work. To be rushed through an emergency course of only a few weeks seemed unsatisfactory to me, and I insisted upon obtaining the most intensive training over a stretch of more than six months. After excruciating labors at field and base hospitals, in isolation barracks and at operation tables, I was finally awarded a diploma, qualifying me as supervisor. No sooner had I been accorded this office than a bloody battle ensued on the southwestern theater of war, and I was rushed by airplane to Mühlhausen in Alsace. Then and there I received my baptism of fire, for I arrived the very moment that the railroad station was showered with incendiary bombs by French fliers. Eventually I was put in charge of hospital trains, and it was in this capacity that I served to the very end of the war. In between, whenever I could snatch a short furlough, I took post-graduate courses, at the same time steadily improving my knowledge by extensive reading.

In the last year of the war, my youngest son, Otto Brucks, Jr., was called to the colors. A few months later he returned wounded and gassed. We had just been reunited in Munich when the Red Terror grasped Bavaria in its bloody claw.

Chapter Eight

ROYALTY AMONG THE REDS

$\mathcal{M}$UNICH, sanctuary of the arts and sciences, charming city of my youth, assumed an entirely new physiognomy with the signing of the Armistice. To be sure, fighting between enemy forces had ceased, but, in its place, there was internal strife and bloodshed now. Munich, often so appropriately called Athens on the Isar, fell under the sway of the Workers' and Soldiers' Council with the premiership of the Ministry vested in Kurt Eisner.

A Galician-born Jew and a social-democratic publicist, then in his early fifties, Eisner was, perhaps, a dreamer rather than a dictator. His régime received bloody support from Rudolf Egelhofer, a native Bavarian and a Catholic, who had set himself up as commandant of the city. Half-starved youths rallied to his Red flag, together with war-weary soldiers and sailors; these were augmented by criminals released from penitentiaries. The armed rebels, wearing red bands on their coat sleeves, roamed up and down Munich streets, intercepting and interrogating harmless citizens, arresting the innocent and terrorizing the help-less. Every "bourgeois" was suspected; every member of the aristocracy considered a deadly enemy.

I had returned to Munich because there no longer could be a home for me in Metz. That city, situated in Alsace, meanwhile had been occupied by the French. I had left be-hind all my belongings—not only things that money could buy. Stripped of practically everything, I arrived in Munich about the middle of November, 1918. I found lodging in a small room which I rented from a war-impoverished lady, a handsome widow in her early forties. With an old servant, Theresa, she lived in an elegant apartment house, situated in the very center of the city.

The whole world seemed upside down to me, its victims steeped in a terrible nightmare. Could it be true that Ger-many had become a republic? Was this, then, the end of a superhuman struggle against a whole world of foes? The natural reaction from years of strenuous Red Cross service now made itself felt. A frightful feeling of depression en-veloped me, a feeling that increased the farther I left the front behind me. I was still in bed—what a wonderful expe-rience to rest on a real spring and mattress, after spending years on hard narrow army cots!—when the entrance of Theresa, carrying a tray with a tempting breakfast, inter-rupted my troubled thoughts. The food itself—eggs, bacon, tea, and cake—was of secondary importance. But the amply laden platter, with its paper-thin Sèvres china, its silver knives and spoons, filled me with delight and made me realize how keenly I had missed all this. In the field hos-pitals we had to be content with broken dishes and cracked glasses; one spoon had to do service for half a dozen nurses. Moreover, we were thankful if we had anything to eat at all!

After thoroughly enjoying the luxury of breakfast in bed, I arose. My bones ached—the result of a seemingly interminable railroad trip in a coach rolling on what felt like square wheels—and I resolved to spend the day quietly. Stepping over to the window, facing the Palace of the Ministry, I saw a huge strip of material, as red as blood, fluttering from the roof.

"Good heavens," I exclaimed, "what does that mean?"

"It's the flag of the republic," answered Theresa resignedly. "You can see it everywhere, on all public buildings, and on all the palaces of the royal family."

The symbol of Germany's downfall, flying in the wind that bleak November morning, reminded me of the tragic struggle just ended. I thought of my sons. Where were they? What had become of them? Karl Larisch, an official of the prisoners' camp at Worms, would be safe enough. In case of danger, he would seek refuge in the home of his former tutor, now a preacher. But my youngest son, Otto Brucks, who had been sent to the military hospital at Munich . . . was he safe?

Theresa answered that question. "I have news for you," she said. "Your son Otto was here last night, looking for you."

"He came here . . . and you didn't call me?"

"It was late . . . he said never mind, not to disturb your sleep."

I waved my hand impatiently. "But what has happened? Why did he come?"

"A revolt broke out at the hospital when Red soldiers tried to arrest the chief physician," Theresa reported. "Some of the wounded men, who refused to recognize the republic, were shot. But it's all right, your son had the good sense to accept the new order of things. He is not strong enough yet to join the Red army, so he was assigned to office work."

"The Red army!" I exclaimed. "Do you mean to say that my own flesh and blood actually intends to join?"

"One must make the best of things," the old servant answered, shrugging her shoulders. "It's no use to fight."

Presently the door bell rang, and the next moment Otto burst into the room, in breathless agitation.

"I escaped out of the window," he panted. "Those bandits will not force me into their cursed army."

His words elated me, but a second later I was overcome with fear; I already pictured my son apprehended and shot.

"Don't worry, Mother," he reassured me, "they don't even know my name. I destroyed all my identification papers. What I need now is a suit of civilian clothes so this uniform won't give me away."

Theresa told us that her mistress had kept some of her deceased husband's clothes and might be persuaded to part with a suit. "However," she added, "you must wait . . . Madame is still asleep." It was ten o'clock then.

"But I can't lose any time," Otto urged nervously. "I may have been followed, and if they find me here, the game is up."

Theresa decided to risk her mistress's displeasure. She

fetched a suit, an overcoat, and a hat; worn and ill-fitting though they were, we considered them a veritable godsend in that hour of need.

Quickly Otto changed into them and just as quickly left, promising to keep me informed of his whereabouts. "If only I could have a piano to continue my studies," he remarked wistfully as he kissed me good-bye.

"What shall we do with this uniform?" Theresa asked after Otto's departure. "If Madame sees it, she'll be frantic." We decided to soak it with kerosene and burn it in the kitchen stove, thus removing all traces.

Soon the King's coat, which my boy had worn so proudly and in which he had fought for his country so valiantly, was reduced to a handful of ashes. . . .

After a few days of complete relaxation, I began to look about for some means of eking out a living. My money and jewelry, left in Metz, I regarded as definitely lost: to make matters worse, the allowance which Count Larisch had settled on me under our divorce agreement was losing in value in the same measure that prices advanced. There was no work for me at the military hospitals because most of them were closed now, with the wounded and convalescent scattered all over the Fatherland. To be sure, the mighty Eisner had promised to take care of them all and see that they were placed in comfortable homes in the country, but nothing had come of these plans so far. After imprisoning many of the army officers and thousands of members of the "bourgeoisie" who would not accept him as ruler, Eisner had entrenched himself at the Ministry directly across the

street from my window. From there he ruled under the
Red flag, feeding the hungry with more promises.

Hunger threatened me, too, since I was deprived of practically everything. However, luck smiled upon me eventually. I obtained a position as assistant to a young army physician who recently had married and established himself in
Munich. The doctor could pay me but a modest salary in
compensation for my services, but I did not mind and felt
more like a friend than an employee. The only drawback
was that I had to traverse the whole length of the city, twice
daily, to reach my destination, either by foot or by street car.
As hardly a day passed without bloodshed, I was always in
danger of being hit by a stray bullet.

Egelhofer, as commandant of the city, had decided that
everybody was to carry a Red passport which must be shown
on demand of Red soldiers and officials. I felt decidedly uneasy on my way to the authorities to apply for this passport, since my papers, which had to be produced for proper
identification, described me as "Baroness Wallersee, daughter of Ludwig, Duke of Wittelsbach—Bavaria." Two soldiers escorted me into the office of the Red administration,
where a beer-bloated individual, with the ruddy complexion
of a peasant, reigned supreme.

"Your papers," he growled.

I laid them before him, certain that my life was not worth
a penny at that moment. He fumbled among the documents
with thick, clumsy fingers and started to read them aloud.
They contained my record as a Red Cross nurse, listing all
the places where I had been stationed during the war. It
took him some time to study them, and when he finally

finished, he regarded me much as a lion might look upon easy prey.

"You are a Wittelsbach, eh?" he snorted.

I felt my knees weaken and, hardly conscious of what I was saying, I blurted out: "I did not choose my firm's name."

It was a silly answer, and I was afraid to look at him; never, in the midst of battle, had I been so terror-stricken as I was at that moment, knowing myself to be completely at the mercy of this brute.

He gave a shout, his heavy jowls quivering. "Your firm's name!" he laughed boisterously, holding his sides. "Well put . . . *Donnerwetter ja!*"

Changing his tone, he continued, with a touch of good humor: "I see that you have served in the war for several years. You have done your duty. I, too, was at the front and risked my life, but who, *zum Donnerwetter,* is going to thank us for it?" He stared at me, bleary-eyed. Then, thumping the desk with his huge calloused fist, he roared: "Forget your high birth . . . it won't do you any good now! You'd better hide these papers, mark my words."

I held my breath, not daring to speak or make a false move.

After a painful pause, the great man decided: "I shall make out a special pass for 'Marie Wallersee, medical assistant and nurse.' After all, you are a courageous woman and deserve consideration."

That special pass, throughout the months of terror that followed, served me well. It enabled me to go back and forth where and when I wished, day or night, even through bar-

ricaded streets when, as a rule, people were warned by a
sign: Anyone trying to pass here will be shot!

We parted as good friends, the fat fellow and I. One of
the soldiers, leading me out to the street, commented laughingly: "Well, you certainly got on all right with the old
roughneck. To be sure, he's had ten jugs of beer so far, and
by the time the office closes at five o'clock, he'll have thirty
under his belt. Then we'll have to drag him home."

Small wonder the "old roughneck" yielded to temptation, for the Red passport office was situated in one of
Munich's renowned breweries, the Malteser-Bräu.

I was overjoyed at the outcome of the dreaded visit. Our
good, simple Bavarians, I concluded, were for the most part
victims of the lure of Russian gold. They were sick of the
long, seemingly endless struggle, of living in filthy under-
ground trenches; their nerves had given out finally. Eisner
had promised them the millennium, and the people, bitterly disappointed in the old régime which had proved itself unable to avoid the horrible carnage they just had experienced, turned to him eagerly, pathetically . . . hoping
and praying that he might lead them to peace and pros-
perity at last.

King Ludwig III was a genial character; a good man
who loved his Bavarians and, in turn, had been loved by
them. However, in the face of violence, he was forced to
flee from the royal residence in the middle of the night. He
and the Queen who, at that time, was gravely ill, accompanied by their five daughters, had left the palace through
one of the rear exits. In three automobiles the party was
taken to Wildenwarth in the mountains.

Most of the other members of the Wittelsbach dynasty had fled, no one knew where. Only Prince Ludwig Ferdinand—a medical doctor and practising physician—and his family had remained, as had my own father. I believe that the Reds did not even know that Duke Ludwig, then eighty-eight years of age, was still alive, for they never molested Father.

I showed my Red passport to my employer, explaining that I had been advised to hide my old papers and become simple Marie Wallersee.

"I know this old drunkard in the Malteser-Bräu office," the physician remarked through clenched teeth. "He was owner of a tavern for many years and was known as a heavy drinker who got into brawls with his customers. If he had happened to be in ill humor, he'd just as quickly have signed your death warrant. And that uncouth beast has been given one of the most responsible positions! Well, we shall have to make the best of it and keep quiet for the time being."

Then, glancing again at my new identification card, he added: "Do you realize that this card assigns you to duty in the Red army? They may call for your services at any time, day or night, to assist their wounded in street fights!"

I nearly collapsed.

"So the beer did not deaden his senses entirely," the doctor mused. Then, noticing my consternation, he tried to console me by saying that they might not think of me, or that the old drunkard might have forgotten to enter my name in their books.

But his consolation proved to be just that and nothing

more. Hardly a week later I was called, during the night,
to give first aid to two young soldiers across the street. They
had been toying with a machine gun, ignorant of its work-
ings. The gun had gone off, injuring the two boys. Meanwhile the gun kept rattling on; not one of those Red "soldiers" knew how to stop it!

With a cloak thrown over my nightgown and in thin
slippers, I hurried out into the cold December night. Despite
my haste, I did not forget to put on my nurse's cap—badge
of my profession. I found one of the boys bleeding pro-
fusely; to all appearances, he was dying. All I could do for
him was to ease his suffering and put him to sleep by administering a morphine injection. After a while, he opened
his eyes, gave one last long sigh, and died.

The other boy was shot in the stomach. I stopped the flow
of blood and bandaged him. His comrades, fierce-looking
young bandits, stood around watching me. I felt very uncomfortable. What reckless, daring rowdies they were compared to our soldiers in the field! Yet I pitied them, believing them to be misled and tempted, after years of want, by
the high pay they received. Then, too, I knew that all these
half-grown lads had not had their fathers to watch and
to counsel them throughout the bitter years of the war's du-
ration.

At last the ambulance arrived. The doctor expressed satisfaction with my work. Then, bending low, he whispered
into my ear: "Why not let him go to the devil?"

I shook my head; I did not share his views.

When day broke, I went home, exhausted, chilled to the

bone and splattered with blood and snow. Theresa, good
old soul, had been waiting for me. Although she shuddered at my gory appearance, she undressed me and put me
to bed. After a few minutes she returned with a bowl of
camomile tea, almost big enough for a bath. She coaxed me
to drink it, and it warmed me up wonderfully. Snuggling
under the covers, I soon fell asleep and did not awake until
the sun had shone brightly for many hours.

Weeks turned into months—months of unabated terror
and endless suffering, not only in Munich but throughout
the entire Fatherland. I was still dwelling in the very midst
of things, in a neighborhood veritably studded with official
buildings. Nearly every night there was some uproar in the
street. My room was situated on the first floor front, and
now and then a stray bullet would crash through the window. My landlady had wisely retained the rear rooms for
her own use. Every night, before retiring, I placed a table
upon my trunk and further barricaded my bed with a second mattress, just in case . . . Only after having taken all
these precautions did I feel comparatively safe.

By this time the better element of Munich was thoroughly cowed, almost afraid to breathe. Nothing short of
absolute necessity could persuade them to venture into the
streets. One man alone among them, Dr. Prince Ludwig
Ferdinand, showed no fear. He and his family remained at
their palace, reserving a small apartment for themselves.
The greater part of the spacious building had been turned
over to the homeless, while a few rooms had been leased

for business purposes. The scarcity of housing was as acute in Munich as elsewhere.

The Prince, working as an assistant to a well-known physician, could be seen walking to his office daily, attired in a simple suit and wearing a mountaineer's slouch hat, adorned with a brightly colored feather. There was something about the way he strode along in his high boots, smoking his pipe unconcernedly, that forced respect even from the Reds. I used to meet my kinsman frequently. He appeared thoroughly contented, ready at all times to battle with adversity and confident of victory in the end.

The other members of the House of Wittelsbach who had fled from Munich were now living at their country estates. The dethroned King and his family had wisely chosen Wildenwarth because it bordered on the Austrian Tyrol, where they could find refuge at a moment's notice.

Crown Prince Rupprecht, who had shared every danger and horror of the war with his soldiers, now watched, with a troubled heart, the foolish antics of the fanatics in Munich where Kurt Eisner was playing at "being King." Eisner sat in the royal box at the opera and drove about in the royal automobile. He even had a "special train" in which he traveled around the country with his mistress, who called herself his second wife, while his real wife, from whom he had not been divorced, lived in dire poverty in Nuremberg.

Nevertheless I doubt that Eisner was downright bad. Probably he was just a poor deluded fool, full of romanticism and given to fantastic plans, considering himself the Messiah of Bavaria. I could not help thinking of the noble-minded King Ludwig II, who was driven to insanity, and

then kept in confinement like a wild and dangerous animal·
until death released him. Then it had been said that the
country "could not be ruled by a royal fool." Now these
same Bavarians were ruled by a fool from common stock
who brought them unspeakable sorrow and misery.

It is not my intention to discuss politics, but I feel impelled to point out a "peculiar" method of procedure—to
put it mildly—followed by these self-appointed rulers. The
prisons were opened and a number of the "gentlemen," who
had been convicted of crimes, were chosen to fill important
positions with the new "government." In order to cover up
their sometimes embarrassing antecedents, official orders
frequently were issued to destroy court records.

And, oh, the ridiculous, senseless, and childish stunts they
concocted! In the middle of the night they would drag
priests and curates out of bed and force them to ring the
bells of all the churches, simultaneously. At first the people
were terribly frightened; later they grew used to this nuisance.

People were not permitted to speak to one another on the
streets. If two people happened to meet and pause for a little
chat, they were liable to arrest for "conspiracy." Everybody
just slunk along, looking neither to the right nor to the
left; doors were kept locked securely, and when, suddenly
and without warning, shots began to fly, one did not know
where to run for shelter. More than once, on my way to or
from my place of employment, the street car would be
stopped by some incomprehensible order from one of the
"chiefs," as they called themselves. Invariably this procedure
was accompanied by shooting, and I had to throw myself

flat on the ground to escape the flying bullets. It was as bad as during the war, if not even worse.

Those were indeed miserable months for all, and the residents of Munich, in normal times a quiet, peace-loving, and good-natured people, were becoming increasingly nervous and panic-stricken. Around the middle of February, 1919, it was rumored that a detachment of regulars—White Guards, they were called—were advancing upon Munich from the north, to break the despotic Red rule. However, people were inclined to doubt these whispers, afraid to put too much faith in them.

One morning—it was February 21st and I was rather late —I hastened toward the street car and had just turned the corner when a shot fell. It was followed by another, right in front of me; almost at my feet, a man rolled in his blood. A few seconds later, another man, a little farther off, was set upon and beaten unmercifully.

I was terrified and ran back, as fast as I could, towards home. I had hardly turned the corner again when a terrific volley of shots burst forth in the very street I had just left. I reached our house as the old caretaker made ready to lock it. "Who's been killed?" I inquired.

He shrugged his shoulders. "How can anybody tell . . . nowadays?" He bolted the door. "And don't you open it," he warned me, shaking a finger at me. On several occasions I had opened the door to shelter some frightened women and children.

Old Theresa and her mistress were thoroughly alarmed over the shooting and screaming all about them. I sought to make some entries in my diary, but could not shut out from my mind the sight of those two men, one apparently dead, the other pounced upon by the Red soldiers who had beaten him cruelly with the butt ends of their guns.

Meanwhile our caretaker had gone out to learn the identity of the man. Presently he returned with the startling news that Eisner had been shot and killed by Count Anton Arco-Valley who, in turn, had been set upon by the soldiers. For the next few days I believed that the young Bavarian army lieutenant had paid, with his life, for the assassination of the Red dictator; but it turned out that he had been brought to a hospital just in time. He was tried for murder and sentenced to death. However, his punishment was commuted to life imprisonment in a fortress; later he was paroled.

I shall never forget the day of Eisner's death. The Reds raged like wild beasts, and no one dared to appear on the streets. The Reign of Terror lasted for nearly two more months. Throughout that period, it was cloaked in a deceptive calm—merely the lull before the storm. Suddenly indiscriminate arrests, in great numbers, were made in revenge for Eisner's death. It was then that I was startled by a message brought by a little boy. A friend advised me to leave my present abode at once and seek shelter elsewhere, as I was in great danger.

My landlady was beside herself with terror. "Please, leave the house at once," she screamed at me. "I won't have the Reds come up here to take you." In vain Theresa tried to calm her.

With Theresa's aid I hastily packed a valise containing only absolute necessities. My trunk was to be moved into Theresa's room, since the Reds would not be likely to suspect the old woman. As I had to take my kit of instruments —bandages and other appliances that a Red Cross nurse needs in an emergency—my bag was fairly heavy.

I did not know where to turn for shelter so late at night, but my landlady remained adamant. Again and again Theresa sought to induce her mistress to keep me at least overnight, hiding me in the cellar or under the roof, but the woman was frantic with fear. "No, no," she shrieked, "she must go, and at once!"

I did not consider arrest so dangerous. No doubt, after the arrival of the White Guards, all those who had been seized by the Reds would be released. . . . So, at least, I thought!

At last Theresa, tears in her eyes, opened the heavy outer door for me, but we did not speak. The next moment I found myself out in the street, shivering and clutching my heavy bag. The wind—it was the month of April—was still very sharp. Where could I go? To whom could I turn for shelter? I thought of several people who had been friendly enough to me, but not one of them, I was convinced, would harbor me in this desperate hour.

On the other hand, walking the streets at night would surely result in the very arrest I sought to escape. On the verge of despair, I recalled an old tried and true friend of my mother who had known me since I was six years of age. A spinster of ninety at the time, she lived with her housekeeper, who, after forty years of faithful service, was more of a friend and nurse. Fortunately they resided within a reasonable distance.

To these two old spinsters, then, I decided to go, hoping that I would not be molested on my way. The streets were deserted at that late. hour, as nobody was permitted out after ten o'clock, by order of the Red government. I had my passport and, in my nurse's uniform, the band of the Red Cross on my left arm; I could pretend, if questioned, to be hurrying to a patient's bedside.

. I almost had reached the quiet side street where my old friend lived, when my strength deserted me—something I had never experienced before. What months of arduous duty on hospital trains had not done to me, *Ersatz*—substitute food and then not even enough of it—had accomplished. Half dead and numb from the cold, I sprawled on the steps of the Main Post Office. I knew that this was the very worst resting place, since the building was filled with Reds, all the regular employees having been dismissed. However, I had reached that stage of exhaustion where I felt indifferent to anything that might happen to me.

After a little while, a Red soldier came down the steps, smoking a cigarette and whistling. Surprisingly enough, I was not too tired to be appalled by the peculiar lack of discipline in which all the Red soldiers indulged, smoking cigarettes on or off duty. I think I never saw one of them without the inevitable *Sargnagel*—coffin nail—between his lips. The Red who now approached me, apparently starting out on patrol duty, seemed extremely young.

I mustered up all my courage and, boldly looking at him, explained that I was on my way to a patient, but could not

carry my bag any further. Would he be kind enough to
help me? It was only about ten minutes' walk. I offered to
show my passport, but he laughed: "Come on, girlie,"—it
was dark and he could not see my face—"I'll take your bag.
Just tell me where you're headed for."

It struck me, then, that it might be wise to withhold my
true destination. I therefore told him that I knew the street
and the house, but that I had forgotten the number. Could
he simply carry my bag to the nearest corner?

"Very well," he agreed, and taking my bag, he walked
with me through one of Munich's main thoroughfares.

I could not help laughing inwardly. Here was I, for whom
the Reds were looking, being escorted to safety by one of
them! It was an odd situation with more than a touch of
grimness.

The lad was very cheerful and presently began to talk.
He barely had escaped from being sent to the front; the
revolution and, with it, the end of the war, had come at
precisely the right moment for him. "Oh, we are having a
fine time now," he boasted, "with plenty to eat and good
pay."

I thought of all the poor people who had to suffer that
these Reds might have "plenty to eat and good pay"—people who had been robbed of every last possession and, jobless, were facing starvation with their families. This boy
was one of thousands who, after years of deprivation, had
been hired by the Reds with the bribe of food and money!

My Red escort confided, however, that it looked as if the
good times would be over soon, for it was known that the
White Guards were on their way to Munich.

"Munich will be destroyed," was his dire prophecy, "because the Red army will build barricades and fight to the last man."

He spoke as if he were telling me something very pleasant; obviously he did not realize the horror of it all.

"What will become of you," I asked, "when the White soldiers come?"

He laughed: "I'll simply change my red band for a white one, like many another." He withdrew from his pocket a white brassard. Waxing still more confidential, he asked me: "Have you heard, girlie,"—he had not yet obtained a good look at me—"that the hostages at Luitpold College will be shot just as soon as the White soldiers enter Munich? There are ten of them so far—and they are looking for more—duchesses, countesses, and the like."

I shuddered, but I managed to inquire in a surprisingly steady voice: "Who are those prisoners, anyway?"

My escort wrinkled his brow and thought for a little while. "Well, there is some young Prince of Thurn and Taxis. They arrested him at the Park Hotel today. And then there is an artist—Professor Ernst Berger by name—and, oh, yes, a young Countess Hella von Westarp. She was employed at the Thule Society. . . . Clever how Egelhofer discovered that that society is not a charitable organization at all, but a group of royalists. Then there are a couple of White soldiers, taken prisoner at Dachau the other day—about ten of them altogether, as far as I know."

So these unfortunates had been brought to Luitpold College in Müllerstrasse where Egelhofer, bloodiest of all the

Red "chiefs," had established himself, spreading his nets to entrap helpless victims!

"Tomorrow they expect to make some more arrests," my companion continued. "I think they are on the lookout for an archbishop and some members of the royal family."

I felt a tingling sensation along my spine. I knew that the archbishop had left Munich a few days ago and sought refuge in a convent deep in the Bavarian mountains. When I heard of his departure, I concluded that he wished to escape the indignity of being forced to ring the bells of his church whenever the Reds demanded it. Now, however, I understood the true gravity of the situation.

Meanwhile we had reached the side street that was my destination. At the corner I stopped, thanking the lad for his aid and, opening my meager little purse, took out some change. "Have a glass of beer," I said, handing him the money.

He accepted the coins with a broad grin; putting down my bag, he made for the nearest tavern.

I pretended to ring the bell of a near-by house. However, no sooner had the young Red turned the corner than I grabbed my bag and hastened toward the right dwelling, which was only a few doors away. There was a light in a room on the first floor; I knew it came from the apartment of the owner. I rang his bell and, after minutes of agonizing suspense, I heard footsteps and grumbling. At last the door was opened just a crack, still secured by a heavy safety chain. A fierce voice demanded to know who had come to disturb him in the middle of the night. I gave my name and revealed my predicament in a few hasty words. As my friend had lived in the house for thirty years, the landlord knew me well. He opened the door wide and muttered bitter complaints of the terrible times.

"You will be perfectly safe here," he said as he accompanied me upstairs. He thought it advisable to ring the bell and explain to Kath'rina—my friend's nurse—that I had come to call on her mistress.

"You know," he said, "Kath'rina is a sensible woman, but the terrors of the last months have made her jumpy."

Kath'rina gave me a hearty welcome and said that I could have her room, since she slept in the bedroom of Fräulein Rosa, who could not be left alone at night. Quickly she prepared her own bed, and in fifteen minutes she had me comfortably tucked in. To my anxious question whether Fräulein Rosa would be disturbed by my sudden arrival, she answered: "Fräulein Rosa sleeps, and all the shooting and ringing of church bells cannot disturb her. You know, she is stone deaf and hears absolutely nothing. But she will be greatly pleased to see you in the morning, I'm sure." Bidding me good-night, she left me, closing the door softly.

Oh, how happy I felt in that modest little servant's room on the third floor! It had been a long, long time since I had felt so secure, so removed from harm's way. With a sigh of contentment I closed my eyes, but sleep did not come quickly. Now and then, the whip-like report of a distant shot aroused me and set me thinking of those unhappy prisoners at the Luitpold College.

What would be their ultimate fate? And what would be mine?

I awoke the next morning, after a restful sleep, with a profound feeling of security; my mother's friend, old Fräulein Rosa, was delighted to see me and to have me with her.

As she was too old to understand the precariousness of my situation, we withheld from her the real reason of my visit. Kath'rina, as far as possible, had kept her in ignorance of events. The old lady was comfortably ensconced in her armchair, a cup of coffee before her, large enough to satisfy two soldiers. She said that if I did not object to the smallness of the room where I had spent the night, she would be pleased to have me remain until October; at that time, Kath'rina's sister was expected on a visit.

Gladly, gratefully, I accepted her kind offer, for although the apartment which I had been so rudely forced to leave the day before was far more handsome, yet I felt more at home here. Moreover, the house was very quiet, being farther removed from the center of the city.

That day—it was Wednesday, April 30, 1919—was a terrible one for Munich. The White Guards were attempting to enter the city, while the Reds were determined to hold on, no matter how much blood might be spilled in the effort. They hid on the roofs of houses, and anyone who was reckless enough to venture into the street either was captured or shot down mercilessly.

I had no desire to go out, and planned to spend the day mending my uniform. Kath'rina came into my room, a market basket on her arm. "Oh, Lord," she ejaculated, "Fräulein Rosa wants vegetables for dinner and I am afraid to cross the street. Since yesterday, I have lost every ounce of courage."

I offered to go in her place. Bullets from hidden machine guns were flying thick and fast, while airplanes dropped bombs which exploded with a sickening detonation.

As I crossed the street, a man came running up behind me. When he reached within a few feet of me, there was a shot and he pitched headlong on his face. I hurried on and glimpsed two soldiers at the end of our street; at the same instant another man, turning the corner, fell, struck by a bullet.

I ran into the store, breathless. The owner, a buxom Bavarian woman, informed me: "The two men that were shot were father and son, and they were about the worst of the Red bunch."

As I recrossed the street to return home, one of the White soldiers, a sergeant, approached me and asked my name and occupation. I told him, in a few words, and he assured me that I had nothing to fear, as the Reds were fairly well subdued, a large number having been arrested. Of course, it would be best to remain indoors, as only a small detachment of the regulars had arrived so far. But a large army would be on hand next day, and then Munich would be rid of those bandits and murderers!

After jotting down my name and my nurse's registration number, he rejoined his platoon. Although a bullet might be fired at him from a roof at any moment, the man proceeded with his duty, admirably calm.

Kath'rina was anxiously awaiting me at the door, evidently relieved when she saw that I was unhurt. "Don't mention the shooting," she cautioned. "Fräulein Rosa heard nothing. I was watching from the window and was terribly worried about you."

In our neighborhood the day passed without further incident. Occasionally a shot fell, but we were accustomed to it by then; desultory shooting had no special significance any longer.

Around the very same time, in another part of the city, a terrifying scene was enacted in the court of the Luitpold College: Ten human beings—nine men and one young girl —were shot down in cold blood, at the behest of Egelhofer! He had carried out his threat to kill his hostages as soon as the White Guards entered Munich. I was to have been among those murdered so wantonly, evidently to represent the House of Wittelsbach. By that time, with General von Epp closing in on the city, the Reds had no chance any more. The wholesale slaughter of hostages was merely their inhuman way of wreaking vengeance on the innocent.

However, of all these developments, we knew very little at the time. Of course, rumors reached us throughout the day, but we had learned to distrust idle talk. I certainly paid little attention to it. I busied myself helping Kath'rina in the house, and by the time I retired to my room for the night, I was hoarse and my throat ached from shouting into Fräulein Rosa's ear.

On the following morning—I was just dressing for breakfast—Kath'rina came into my room, pale and trembling. "There is a soldier who wants to speak to you," she stammered.

The man turned out to be a member of the White Guard, wearing a white brassard with a red cross on his arm. Presumably, the sergeant who had questioned me the day before had turned in my name and address. The messenger very politely asked to be shown my passport and diploma.

Paris became intolerable, and I besought George to recross, saying as he wrote my name: "You know, we have no more counts and princes, so you are just plain Marie Wallersee-Wittelsbach now. You will report at the ambulance station at the Carls Platz. They need help there badly. I know it's a most unpleasant place just now, and it's liable to get worse. The Reds have barricaded the railroad station and the Palace of Justice, and the fools seem determined to fight to the last man. I'm sorry I must send you there, but it can't be helped."

Kath'rina, of course, had taken in every word; now she assisted me with my cap and arm band, her face full of despair, her nose red from crying, as if I were going to my certain death.

"Tell Fräulein Rosa I am invited to dinner," I told her grimly and followed the soldier. At the door he paused and said: "You had better go alone. It may not be well for you to be seen with a White Guard. Be careful to avoid crowds and throw yourself flat on the ground if there is any shooting."

I already knew all these precautions, of course, but nevertheless thanked the man for his advice.

It was not a pleasant walk under the circumstances. At the Carls Platz, where all the hounds of hell seemed to have been let loose, emergency stations had been set up under the beautiful old chestnut trees. They gave but poor shelter to the injured, the bullets tearing through the trees as though they were so much paper. Still, the wide spread of the heavy branches offered some protection. I found several nurses at work there, precisely as in the war.

Just then the regulars were trying to break in the doors of the Palace of Justice while the Reds were firing from the windows. At the railroad station, one block away, the fighting grew desperate. Never, during the entire war, had I been in the very heat of battle as on that day. Not one of the Red Cross personnel expected to leave that hell alive; yet, by some miracle, no one was killed or even injured.

Every half-hour the ambulance took the wounded to the hospital. Presently the newspaper booth near us burst into flames; an officer had commanded his troops from there, and it had been a target for the machine guns of the Reds.

"If only we could fetch that officer over there," said one of the nurses, without, however, interrupting her work of bandaging the man in her charge.

I was washing my bloody hands and, looking up, I saw the officer sink to his knees, still giving his commands in a clear, firm tone. Forgetting the danger, I rushed toward him. Passing one machine gun of the White Guard, I yelled at the men to stop firing, and they complied. The young lieutenant, a lad of barely nineteen, was lying prostrated on the ground. I picked him up, urging him to put his arms around my neck, and dragged him to shelter. He was severely but not fatally wounded. The next ambulance carried him to the hospital.

We worked without rest all through the day. Kind old Kath'rina had filled my bag with sandwiches. I never could fathom how she had accomplished this remarkable feat during those brief moments that I had conversed with the soldier. I shared my riches with my fellow nurses who were less fortunate.

At last, late in the evening, the Reds surrendered. When we finally started homeward, the lovely Carls Platz, where carefree children used to roam about and play, and romantic couples dotted the benches each night, resembled a regular battlefield. The streets were littered with the débris of battle: broken rifles, caps, sticks, and sundry articles of clothing.

Longing for the peace and quiet of my little room, I hastened home. As I neared the corner of my street, I saw several White soldiers tossing a sailor from one side of the street to the other as if he were a rubber ball. He was a tall, handsome youth, with curly golden hair. Though pale as death and apparently in great pain, he did not utter a sound. This was just one example of the intense hatred that the patriotic element of the population throughout Germany bore toward sailors, as the revolution primarily had been bred, and had broken out, in the navy at Kiel. Still, that could not excuse the brutality of the unequal fight of six against one.

"Why make a fuss and bring him to Stadelheim?" the leader of the soldiers cried. Stadelheim was the large prison where military trials took place, invariably ending in death for the accused. "Stand him up against the wall."

This poor chap was one of the many thousands who had believed every word of the Red "messiah." I was paralyzed with pity, utterly unable to move or cry out in protest. In a haze I saw the man shoved against the wall of a house.

Then a volley of shots rang out, and the victim fell, lifeless. Satisfied, at last, the "heroes" of this "glorious" deed started off, leaving the body on the sidewalk.

I reached my room, shaken as I had never been during all my years of service as a war nurse. War, after all, is regular fighting, and those who fall on the battlefield meet death in defense of an ideal. But what could one call this slaughter of brother by brother, this cold-blooded cruelty? Had the war set free all the instincts of savagery, the lust for blood and murder, inherent in human nature and merely suppressed and submerged by centuries of "civilization" and "culture"?

If that were true, at whose door should the blame rest?

Chapter Nine

AMERICAN INTERLUDE

$\mathcal{N}$o, MY Munich of old was no more!

If all the world had changed since the war, Munich had undergone a still greater transformation. It was a new life for all, but not a better one; for me, life certainly was not happier. To be sure, I was fortunate enough to have work at that time, but it lasted only until the physician who employed me accepted an academic post in Vienna. After he left, I searched in vain for a similar position. Finally I tried my hand, not unsuccessfully, at literary and film work.

On the heels of the commercial doldrums that followed the Armistice, a new spirit of enterprise had made itself felt in Germany, but it was much too hectic to last. For months I found myself vacillating between feast and famine, while the mark fell ever lower and, with it, the value of the annuity which Count Larisch had settled upon me.

Since his second marriage I had been more or less out of contact with my father. The news of his death therefore came as a surprise, despite the fact that he was a nonagenarian by that time. In his last will and testament, he left everything to the family of his divorced second wife, including my mother's jewels. However, he had set aside a villa in Munich for me, normally worth seven hundred thousand marks. In the years of inflation its value dropped to practically nothing, and even that small balance was eaten up by taxes eventually. Moreover, the upkeep of such a villa was far beyond the means of one compelled to eke out a precarious living from literary and film work.

My son, Karl Larisch, could still rely on a monthly remittance from his father. However, in the course of time, the mark—on the toboggan since the Armistice—raced headlong into wildest inflation. This became especially true after the French invaded the Ruhr in January, 1923. Moreover, Karl had just passed through a severe attack of pneumonia and, from then on, fought a losing battle with T.B. Physical defects had prevented him from serving actively in the war, but he had volunteered for service in the prison camp at Worms. Strenuous years there had weakened him beyond the possibility of recuperation. To add to my sorrow, my son Otto Brucks, who had inherited the musical gifts of his father, was unable to reënter his profession of orchestra soloist because of his war disability. Reduced circumstances finally drove him to drumming a piano, from morning to night, in a cheap picture house.

Gradually I was stripped of all means, and none of my children could come to my assistance. At that trying time friends of mine recommended me, as housekeeper, to a family they knew in Berlin. I was not unduly sensitive about accepting that sort of job. After all, I represented only one of millions of similar cases, and fortunately I was in good health. Besides, during the war and its aftermath, I had grown accustomed to a hard life.

The Berlin family was that of a rich merchant, and the position appeared the next best thing to a sanctuary when I first arrived there. But no sooner did the family discover that I was a good cook than I was cajoled into service at the kitchen range. When progressive inflation seriously infringed upon the finances of my employer, I was also made to scrub the floors, because I was good at that, too, having scrubbed many a square mile in the course of my Red Cross novitiate. Probably to keep me from boredom, during such spare time as I might find on my hands, I eventually was given the laundry also.

For years and years I had known the servant problem only from the dining-room side of the pantry door. Thus I remained completely ignorant of the fact that I was being paid only a quarter of the wages stipulated by law. Yet I was thankful to have a roof over my head and food to eat—such as it was. However, one day I found myself jobless; my employers, without giving me the prescribed notice, had left Berlin for parts unknown. As I did not even have enough money to return to Munich, I simply had to look for another place. And so I haunted Berlin employment agencies along with other servants.

By that time my appearance was decidedly shabby; moreover, my health was failing, and I showed it. Scant wonder nobody would hire me, despite all my qualifications that more than balanced these defects. When the ladies swept into the employment office, searching for likely drudges, they would nod condescendingly as I recounted my domestic accomplishments. Then they would look me over critically and terminate the painful interview with a mumbled "Thank you." It always reminded me of the proceedings of a horse market where an animal has no chance unless it is sleek-looking and boasts a full set of teeth. To be sure, the ladies never asked to see my teeth.

Desperation was right around the corner when my son Otto finally succeeded in raising enough money to take me to Munich on a third-class ticket. There Fräulein Rosa, who had sheltered me during the Red Days, took me in once more. I accepted her hospitality with alacrity, expecting to relieve the kind old lady of an additional hungry mouth within a very short time. My optimism proved unfounded, for I remained with her almost a year, all the while seeking work—a hopeless and hapless task.

Somehow, people who had known me in the days of my affluence learned of my quandary. No doubt they meant well when they sent an American newspaper man to interview me. Subsequently, one Sunday, a few months later, a fantastic story about me appeared in the United States.

One reaction to this elaborate tale was a letter from a naturopath in Florida, inviting me to join him in a business venture. With the aid of a capitalist, he was about to organize a sanitarium. On the basis of my Red Cross diploma and my war experiences, I was invited to take over the management of the institution. Eagerly I agreed to the proposition, and presently I received a prepaid ticket to New York. My spirits rose jubilantly over this sudden opportunity for a new life.

Upon my arrival in America, the naturopath and his financier were still discussing where the sanitarium should be built. The capitalist had his eye on a large country estate in New Jersey which he owned; the naturopath, on the other hand, wanted the sanitarium to be erected on his property in Florida.

The naturopath—whom I shall call Mr. Fleming—and the capitalist frittered away a whole year trying to decide on the location of the sanitarium. During that twelvemonth I found myself completely helpless in America, and when Mr. Fleming proposed marriage to me, I had no alternative but to accept; otherwise, the American government would deport me upon the expiration of my visitor's permit. Moreover, as an employed superintendent of the sanitarium, I would have to pass an examination for a registered nurse, whereas, as the wife of the owner, this would be superfluous.

Eventually, in 1926, the financier died of a stroke—perhaps the negotiations had been too exciting for him—and my husband *de convenance* found it necessary to drive down to Florida to look after his interests. We made the trip in a little car, and its repeated breakdowns afforded me an excellent chance to see a great deal of the Eastern seaboard states. Any surprises they held for me were topped by a far greater surprise when we arrived in Florida. There, in a little village near the Indian River flats, I discovered that Mr. Fleming's much-talked-of residence was a very simple bungalow indeed. What I had pictured as a block house, imbued with the romantic spirit of *Uncle Tom's Cabin,* of Leatherstocking, and of Chingachgook, turned out to be nothing more than a modest dwelling, surrounded by great tracts of land.

Our stay there was terminated by the tornado of 1926, and like thousands of others we trekked back north, spending the next years in New York, with an occasional side trip to Chicago. While Mr. Fleming feverishly sought to revive the sanitarium project, I found something akin to peace in Hoboken, New Jersey; there I had very modest lodgings, on the top floor of a third-rate sailors' boarding house.

Perhaps, after all my other adventures, my life needed that final nautical note. Any inbred fastidiousness, however, had been overcome long since; by then a roof was a roof. If it were no longer the roof of a castle that sheltered me—well, then it was a sailors' lodging house, and better than none at all!

COUNTESS LARISCH *during her American years.*

COUNTESS LARISCH *and her second husband,* OTTO BRUCKS.

Chapter Ten

THE CIRCLE CLOSES

AROUND the time we left Florida, news of the recent death of Her Majesty, Queen Maria of Naples and the Two Sicilies, reached me through Duchess Karl Theodor of Bavaria, lady-in-waiting to my late aunt. From then on, it became increasingly difficult for me to stem the backwash of the dynastic world from surging to my very door. Since the end of the war. I had been out of touch with crowned heads and their lesser satellites. However, once in Hoboken —not exactly the place where one might be expected to keep the *Almanac de Gotha* within easy reach—I ran across traces of royal and imperial love children, time and again. It seemed almost as if the whole of the United States were overrun by the illegitimate offspring of one reigning house or another. There is a German legend which refers to such love children as "Cuckoo Eggs," so-called because of Mother Cuckoo's singularly odd habit of dropping her eggs into strange nests for hatching.

While living in the States, I either met or heard of a num-

ber of assorted characters, each of whom claimed to belong
to a reigning royal house. Most of them were just impostors,
of course; a few very clever, to be sure. On the other hand,
I also discovered honest-to-goodness wild shoots from the
most illustrious European family trees. Among these were
illegitimate scions of a German emperor and of a king of
Spain.

With so many living evidences of royal romance about
me, I was not especially surprised when the imperial Hapsburgs, as well as another ruling house, were added to this
picturesque group of expatriated descendants. I received a
letter from an A. E. F. veteran in the Middle West one day;
it was signed "James Cleveland Longstreet." The information it contained pointed to the possibility that he might be
none other than the posthumous son of my late cousin Crown
Prince Rudolf and the Princess K . . .—"that young
woman," as Emperor Francis Joseph had once referred to
her in my presence. When he sent me his picture, I was
struck by the extraordinary resemblance to my cousin
Rudolf.

To be sure, I had an inkling of the existence of "a missing heir." A few years after the Meyerling tragedy, my old
friend, Count Wilczek, had told me about a lost putative
Hapsburg offspring. At that time there were whisperings
that a little boy had been brought to the *Hofburg,* presumably an American-born son of Cousin Rudolf. Hearsay
had it that Emperor Francis Joseph had been informed that
"that young woman" had borne Rudolf a son and that the
boy, following his mother's death, was being raised in an
American orphanage. However, the baby boy brought to the

Hofburg proved to be a changeling, a substitution having been effected probably for political reasons and in order to obliterate all traces of the genuine "heir." No sooner had the Emperor learned of the fraud than he solicited the assistance of General James Longstreet, known to history by the sobriquet of "General Lee's war horse." This famous Confederate soldier had officially represented the United States Government at the marriage of Rudolf and Stephanie and, later, had remained friendly with the Crown Prince. General Longstreet instituted a search which lasted more than a decade. His investigation was on the point of yielding tangible results when he died in 1904. Once again, all traces of the "lost heir" faded into complete oblivion.

I practically had forgotten the whole story—just one of many astonishing recitals I had heard during my lifetime—when I received that letter from James Cleveland Longstreet. Then every word that Count Hans Wilczek had told me of the Crown Prince's romance came back to me. Despite their marked difference in age, Wilczek and Rudolf were very good friends. Although their friendship wilted somewhat after Rudolf's marriage, the Count, who considered the Crown Prince highly intelligent albeit weak, remained in touch with him.

According to what Count Wilczek told me, Rudolf was especially unhappy, just before the Meyerling tragedy, over the fact that he could never hope for a male heir. It was this that preyed on his mind when he again met "that young woman." She was the second of two lovely daughters born to Princess K . . ., a member of a famous noble family who had been veritably snatched from a convent by a European ruler when she was barely fifteen years old. For decades the affair furnished an inexhaustible source of gossip in court circles, enhanced by the fact that, shortly after the death of his first wife, the monarch, to the amazement of the world, made his mistress of many years his morganatic consort. Long before her status had been accorded this semblance of equality, the convent-bred princess had borne the ruler three children, a son and two daughters; the younger girl was destined to become Cousin Rudolf's inamorata—capturing his fancy for a longer period than had any other woman.

. When the marriage question of the heir apparent to the Dual Monarchy was under consideration at court, Rudolf implored his imperial father to consent to a match with the young Princess, despite the fact that she was not of equal birth. If Francis Joseph had only agreed, it is possible that the World War might have been averted. Political jealousies between that country and Austria might then have been eliminated. However, for dynastic reasons, the Hapsburgs, as well as the other house, objected. When, all through his married life, Rudolf sought to obtain a papal annulment, it was in the hope that it might yet be possible for him to marry Princes K . . .

In the fall, 1888, in despair over personal and political problems, Rudolf returned to the young Princess for surcease from his troubles, meeting her, incognito, in Switzerland. Then, in January, 1889, the Meyerling tragedy occurred; to a certain extent it may have been brought on by the fact that, by that time, Rudolf knew that his passionate intermezzo with his lady love would bear results. The young Princess meanwhile had been disowned by her family; only her older sister communicated with her secretly and provided for her.

Immediately after the Meyerling tragedy, the young Princess, in greatest secrecy, and accompanied only by her old amah, departed for America. There is reason to assume that she embarked upon this trip upon the advice of an American general. The latter had been minister plenipotentiary to the court of the European ruler for many years and, in the course of that time, had become exceedingly friendly with the monarch. In fact, the American general was intimately informed about all the family affairs of the ruling house and even after his return to the United States, he remained in constant correspondence with the European court.

A few months after her arrival in the United States, a boy was born to the young Princess, somewhere in a city along the Eastern seaboard. Soon thereafter the young mother and child and the old nurse embarked on a trip to the West coast, but they never reached there. The Princess's health, always very delicate and grievously overtaxed at that time, broke down completely. The old nurse, loyal and true, but handicapped by the sluggish brain of an aging peasant, left the Princess somewhere in the Middle West and returned to Europe to secure funds and beg the forgiveness of the Princess's family.

In the course of the ensuing months the young Princess, desperately awaiting help that never came from the other side, lost her grip on life rapidly. She died in the charity ward of a hospital, around the same time that a baby boy was committed to a foundling home and later to the Roman

Catholic St. Joseph's Orphanage in St. Louis, Missouri, to grow up as James Cleveland. Incidentally, when James Cleveland left the orphanage, he added "Longstreet" to his cognomen and, until the World War, was known as James Cleveland Longstreet, the name under which he first wrote to me.

The foundling home has since been torn down to make room for a public school. Most of the sisters who brought up the waifs have long since died, and records are no longer available; all James Cleveland will vouchsafe about his identity is the fact that he was placed in the orphanage in November, 1890, when scarcely more than a year old.

According to my information, there is no doubt that the nurse reached Europe; thereafter all traces of her vanished. It is not unlikely that she "disappeared" in order to save her own and the Austrian court from possible embarrassment. At any rate, the old amah had succeeded in establishing contact with the older sister of the Princess, informing her of the birth of Rudolf's child. Without delay she set out to ascertain the whereabouts of the former Archduke John of Tuscany. She knew that John Orth not only had been the Crown Prince's most trusted fellow conspirator, but had also known of Rudolf's infatuation for her younger sister. It was her intention to appeal to him for assistance in legitimatizing her little nephew.

The Austrian court, at practically all times, knew very well where to find the "vanished" ex-Archduke. Nevertheless, the older Princess K . . . had considerable difficulty in locating John Orth, as the secret of his whereabouts was guarded carefully. As far as outsiders were concerned, the former Archduke had covered up his tracks with consummate forethought.

Count Hans Wilczek had been as intimate with John of Tuscany as he had been with Crown Prince Rudolf. He had frequently met the ex-Archduke in Pola, then the home port of the Austro-Hungarian navy. On account of his arctic travels, Wilczek was greatly interested in maritime matters and extremely well informed in all things nautical. In his opinion the "shipwreck" near Rio de Janeiro was the clever strategy that one might expect from such an experienced army leader as the Tuscanian. The ex-Archduke had thought of everything, even carrying several sets of ship's papers so that nobody would suspect his craft of being the *Santa Margherita*. Originally he had mustered an Austrian crew, but dismissed it as soon as the *Santa Margherita* made the next port. The exiled Archduke then took recourse to any number of clever tricks to disguise the appearance of his vessel, succeeding so well that nobody recognized the craft. Count Wilczek knew many additional details, obtained from a navy officer he once had met in the *entourage* of the ex-Archduke.

The *Santa Margherita,* her name changed, sailed the seven seas and weathered many a severe storm in the course of months. It was during a hurricane that John Orth, at the risk of his own life, rescued a young Oriental sailor named Bechir, a dark, slim fellow of melancholy mien and haughty bearing. Orth had noticed the young quartermaster on several occasions as he went about his chores, for he was totally unlike the other seafaring men.

Following the rescue, Bechir, his enigmatic eyes fixed on

John Orth, bowed and said: "Thou hast saved my life, O master. Permit me to watch over thee, and perhaps I may save thy life one day!" With this he turned away and set to work as if nothing had happened.

Some weeks later John Orth again changed his crew, still intent upon erasing all traces, and again sailed forth with a third set of ship's papers. Of all the crew, Bechir was the only one he retained, and the yacht was now called *Ignota* —The Unknown. John Orth steered up the Yangtse-kiang and ultimately settled on the slope of the Tangla Mountains, dwelling there peacefully with Milli Stubel, now his wife, and Bechir, his body servant.

It was there, according to Count Wilczek's story, that an Austrian railroad engineer, having lost his way in the wilderness while engaged in surveying work for the new Lantshow–Shanghai line, caught a glimpse of the ex-Archduke. He recognized him instantly, for he had served under him in the Austrian army.

Celebrating his safe return with more drinks than he could carry, in one of the numerous saloons of Shanghai, the engineer forgot his word of honor to his erstwhile commander and babbled of his discovery.

One of the detectives employed by Princess K . . .'s older sister, ever on the alert for gossip of this kind, subsequently heard of it. Promptly he hired a couple of horses and men and set out for the Tangla Mountains. Simulating sickness, he succeeded in being taken in by John Orth. Convinced that he had discovered the long-sought ex-Archduke, he immediately dispatched an explicit report to the older

Princess, promising to follow as soon as possible. But he never arrived.

It is said that he died "quite suddenly" after dispatching his letter by a special native runner. Details of his "sudden" death are not available and, in any case, are inconsequential as far as this story is concerned. As for the Austrian railroad engineer, he committed suicide in a moment of bitter remorse for having betrayed his erstwhile commander.

Although the detective failed to report personally to the Princess, she received his message and immediately sought an audience with the Emperor. She divulged the story of Rudolf's little son in far-away America together with her plan to enlist the ex-Archduke's aid to legitimatize the boy. Francis Joseph yielded to her pleas finally, assuring the Princess that John Orth could return, provided he would testify to the identity of Crown Prince Rudolf's only male issue. The ex-Archduke would be permitted to reside in his castle near Gmunden Lake, in strict retirement and without his old title and prerogatives.

From my own knowledge of my uncle and from what Count Wilczek intimated to me, I am certain that the Princess, in her frantic efforts, obtained the Emperor's permission to communicate with John Orth only on condition that she keep his whereabouts secret. Since she was free to go, in any case, the Emperor could only use his authority to demand secrecy.

Overjoyed, the Princess made ready to go to the Far East, accompanied by her secretary, a resourceful and daring Hungarian who later fell at the head of his regiment during the Great War.

Reaching China and the slopes of the Tangla Mountains, she soon confirmed the fact that, a few years before, an Italian, Giovanni Orterro, and his young wife had settled there. Immediately the Princess, together with her secretary, hired the very best horses they could find in the neighborhood, reconnoitered carefully and, after observing Giovanni Orterro's estate through a spyglass for many days, from a near-by pagoda, noticed him taking a stroll in his park.

At breakneck speed she galloped down the dirt road, took the high hedge with one jump, and faced the ex-Archduke. "Your Imperial Highness, heaven be thanked that I have found you!"

There was a momentary change in John Orth's face . . . then complete blankness.

But nothing could stop the Princess now. "I bring the forgiveness of the Emperor," she continued in German. "I am the Princess K . . ., the sister of Crown Prince Rudolf's love! I beg of you, come back to Austria and help to legitimatize Rudolf's son!"

The man known as Giovanni Orterro shook his head. "I am sorry, madam," he said in Italian, with a polite little bow, "it is my misfortune not to understand the language in which you address me."

The Princess jumped from her mount. She rushed over to him, seized his hand, and in halting Italian implored him to return with her and testify to the identity of Rudolf's son. But John Orth clung to his new rôle. Just as eager as the Archduke of Tuscany once had been to wear the royal purple, so Giovanni Orterro now preferred the simple ways of a commoner.

Finally the frantic Princess reminded him of his old mother. "Don't you remember her any more? She clings to her rosary, praying to hear from her lost son. May I not bring her a word of cheer?"

Giovanni Orterro's face hardened. "My mother is dead!" he exclaimed icily.

Only then did the Princess desist; there was nothing else to do. She knew that John of Tuscany had adored his mother, and if he disowned her now rather than return to Austria, her efforts were futile.

The ex-Archduke sensed her surrender to the inevitable. "I assure you, I am Giovanni Orterro. I must ask you to accept this statement," he added, glancing significantly, almost threateningly, at the Princess's secretary.

For the first time, the latter joined in their conversation. "Princess," he said, "doubtless you must be mistaken."

It was this secretary who told Count Wilczek the whole story; he admitted that the expressive glance of the ex-Archduke had made him prevail upon the Princess to abandon her desperate attempt.

From another source Count Wilczek learned the sequence to this tale. On the morning after his meeting with the Princess, Giovanni Orterro informed his wife and Bechir: "We have been robbed of our peace. We must leave this place as soon as possible. Bechir, I leave everything to you. Prepare ship and crew so that we may renew our wanderings once more."

A few days later Giovanni Orterro's home was deserted. A typical Chinese junk called *Nirvana* left Shanghai. John Orth, standing on deck, was watching the coast disappear when Bechir approached him in his quiet, dignified manner.

"Thou need no longer be homeless, my master," he said. "Follow me to my country, and thou shalt dwell in contentment."

"And where is that, Bechir?" the ex-Archduke asked.

"Away over yonder," the man replied, pointing toward the northwest. "Persia is my native land."

In answer to the surprise in Orth's eyes, Bechir explained: "I am Prince Bechir, Shah Muzaffar-ed-Din's nephew! Like thee, I have been exiled from my country for political reasons. For the last three years I have yearned to return, as I have meanwhile been forgiven. But I would not leave thee, O master! I knew the day would dawn when I might offer thee the hospitality of my native land."

And so John Orth steered up the Gulf of Persia and settled in the world-renowned Rose Valley of Cashmir, where he was still residing when Count Wilczek told me the story. The count secured my promise not to repeat his disclosures while he was alive, but his demise in 1920 removed the seal from my lips. More and more, in recent years, the secret archives of central Europe have been thrown open; one of these days this story is bound to come to light, and so I feel that I may speak freely now.

In telling me all this, Count Wilczek explained that he had a premonition he would never see me again. He thought I was entitled to know the truth—as much as ever could be known! I never did see Count Wilczek after that, for the Great War broke upon a startled world, and dynastic questions faded in the presence of far greater international issues.

But I could not resist writing a letter to the secretary of

the Princess, in command of a regiment of cavalry in the Carpathian Mountains. The letter was returned to me with the laconic annotation: *"Empfänger im Felde gefallen"*— Addressee killed in action. I had no time to explore any further into the mysteries of the case, as Red Cross service claimed my whole attention.

Having succeeded, in the course of long months, in locating John Orth, although the Tuscanian would not admit his identity, the older Princess K . . . would not relinquish her efforts to legitimatize Rudolf's son. For some time she remained unaware that, meanwhile, her sister had died and the little boy had been placed in a foundlings' home. Once more the disconsolate sister sought an audience with the Emperor, but this time it was refused her. She was unable to ascertain whether His Majesty was disappointed because she had failed in her mission, or whether court intrigues were at work against her. At last she desisted in her efforts, having lost track of the old amah, as well as of her sister and little nephew. Apparently there was no possibility to ascertain the whereabouts of either; certainly she did not dream that, meanwhile, in a St. Louis orphanage, a boy was growing up under the name of James Cleveland.

I have made inquiries into the possible origin of this name and have been informed that it is the custom, in many foundling homes throughout the United States, to name a child after some fragment of identification that is found on him. In the present case it seems logical to conclude that the swaddling clothes of the baby bore the label of a Cleveland store. Christian names, such as James, are usually chosen from an alphabetical list. That James Cleveland was committed to a Roman Catholic orphanage—Catholicism being the house religion of the Hapsburgs—is easily accounted for, if we assume that the child wore a rosary. This may be taken for granted, inasmuch as the young Princess was Catholic herself, although of the Greek persuasion of that faith.

James Cleveland, when fourteen years of age, came under the tutelage of Judge James C. Gillespy, of Columbia, Missouri, a staunch Mid-Westerner of pioneer stock, who encouraged the boy to become a good American citizen. According to James, Judge Gillespy was well informed of his antecedents. He remained the boy's trusted counselor until he passed away a few years ago. The judge believed that it would be wiser for James to remain in America, avoiding everything that would savor of pandering to the royalty or nobility of Europe. Eventually James went to the state of Washington, where he obtained employment in a clerical civil service position; later, he went to Washington, D. C.

On the basis of my own knowledge, and aided by such information as James himself volunteered, I have tried to reconstruct the whole life course of Cousin Rudolf's son. To some extent I was assisted by an old friend of mine, a former chamberlain of my imperial uncle. This man lives in what used to be the gatekeeper's quarters of his own castle in Tyrol, the castle itself having gone the way of all inflated values. Hardly known to anybody outside of Austria, the one-time chamberlain was mentioned by James Cleveland in his first letter to me, the name serving as a password.

The fighting blood James Cleveland might have inherited from his forbears stirred in him mightily, in 1916, when trouble with Mexico threatened. He offered to undertake the raising of a brigade of troops, in case of possible war with Mexico, but as serious difficulties were averted, nothing came of it. When America plunged into the World War a year later, and before the draft law had been promulgated, James Cleveland once more attempted to organize a volunteer detachment. Perhaps he wished to impress the Austrians with the fact that a Hapsburg offspring was drilling a body of troops to fight them. In connection with his plan, James consulted Provost Marshal General Enoch H. Crowder and also Senator William J. Stone, then chairman of the Committee of Foreign Relations and political brother-in-arms of his "snowy-haired friend," Judge Gillespy. Both convinced him that it would be far wiser to enter the service in a quiet, unobtrusive manner. As the draft law, meanwhile, had been enacted and Congress had decided that there would be no volunteer units, James abandoned his idea. Registered on the roster of the Port Townsend, Washington, Draft Board as James Cleveland Longstreet Hapsburg, he joined the A. E. F. and spent nineteen months in the headquarters detachment of the Engineering Corps, most of the time suffering from influenza which eventually developed into pneumonia.

Returning from the war with very weak lungs, James made three attempts to gain a seat in the House of Representatives or the Senate, each time meeting defeat by a very small margin. In the course of these years, James had the Hapsburg part of his name legally eliminated, calling him-

self James Cleveland Longstreet, the cognomen by. which
he went until he married recently. Then, by another court
proceeding, he had his original surname—Cleveland—restored, so that he is now officially known as Longstreet
Cleveland.

Meanwhile Judge Gillespy, a man of eighty-five, had died
and James roamed the country from the Atlantic to the
Pacific, finally returning to Missouri. Putative scion of two
families who were lords of all they surveyed, he felt the
inherent urge at least to be a country squire in his own right.
Thus, Providence, Boone County, Missouri, a former settlement and steamboat town on which nature long ago had
played the treacherous trick of cutting a new course for the
river a mile away, leaving the little village high and dry,
became "Journey's End" for James. The tract he acquired,
and still owns, comprises about a half-hundred acres with a
little knoll almost in the center of it upon which "Emperor
James"—as somebody once dubbed him—hopes to erect his
new home one day. At present he dwells in an old rambling
house of pre-Civil-War days and desires nothing so much as
to live his own life in his own way.

It is from there that he corresponds with me, affectionately calling me "Aunt Marie Louise" in his frequent and
long letters. How typically Rudolfian these letters are; how
they remind me of those voluble missives that my unfortunate cousin Rudolf sent me in the late 'eighties in Vienna!
And how much he resembles the late Crown Prince of the
Dual Monarchy!

When, in July, 1933, Longstreet Cleveland married, he

and his bride signed a prenuptial contract in which they agreed to discourage all attempts by representatives of "any of the royal houses of Europe, and especially of the House of Hapsburg and the House of Romanoff," to obtain custody of any child born of their union. This unusual document serves to emphasize the fact that Longstreet Cleveland renounces all such claims which he conceivably might make as the putative offspring of that unconventional union between my cousin Rudolf and his beloved Princess. In fact, Cleveland is very anxious to have it clearly understood that at no time in his life has he made the claim that he is the rightful heir to the crown of Hapsburg. In any case, he never could become heir, since Hapsburgian house laws, which have never been revoked, unequivocally stipulate that neither a morganatic nor an illegitimate offspring can be considered eligible for the crown of Hapsburg.

Cleveland's views on his possible claims were contained in a letter which I received from him as far back as November, 1926. At that time he wrote:

I am an American citizen! As such I have done my bit in the war, and as such I have run time and again for the Senate and the House of Representatives. . . . I am content to go on my way as a plain, unimportant personage, with no other antecedents or background than a Roman Catholic orphanage. Prince or pauper blood—whichever may flow in my veins—I will strive to live my life as best I can under the circumstances. . . . I think it best in my case, even though I should be related to the princes and kings of the earth, to claim nothing, but to go on and live in the future as I have in the past, confining my life to the "short and simple annals of the poor," doing all the good I can in my humble way and as little harm as possible. . . .

Longstreet Cleveland's appearance in the royal picture recalled all that my old friend, Count Hans Wilczek, had told me of Crown Prince Rudolf's romance with the young Princess K. . . . In its wake, other vague shadows crowded into my ken, reminding me of Goethe's dedication to Faust:

Again ye come, ye hovering Forms! I find ye,
As early to my clouded sight ye shone!

Around this time I made a short visit to the Orange Blossom State and, while there, received a letter from Tampa, signed "Rose." She who had been my guardian angel in Paris as the Viscountess d'Avary, née Duchess de Monglyon, was now running a little stationery store in that Florida city. One day she came to visit me. What had Fate wrought of my beautiful, elegant Rose of yore! I did not recognize her at all, but she knew me at first sight because my hair was still arranged *à l'impératrice*. Correctly enough, Aunt Sissy used to refer to the hairdress which she popularized, if not actually invented, as our *lettre de cachet*.

A few years before the war Rose had left her husband. After her only son had been killed on the field of battle, she was practically alone in the world, and so she had gone in search of a long-lost stepbrother. On her prolonged journey through the Western Hemisphere, she eventually discovered him in Cuba and brought him to Florida. There the two had set up a little stationery store.

No sooner had she established herself than she wrote to
Paris, asking her former sweetheart, a French count of oldest lineage, to join her. The letter was returned with the
laconic information: "Addressee deceased."

Here was yet another royal romance and, like nearly all
the others, it ended sadly. I heard from Rose just once more
while I was living in Hoboken. With that inimitable generosity of hers, she invited me to share such little comfort
as she enjoyed. I was on the point of accepting, but before
the necessary arrangements could be made, Fate interfered
again. Dear Rose had joined the endless procession to the
Great Beyond.

The greatest surprise of all was still in store for me. Since
I had happened upon the first clue of the whereabouts of
the Girl of Sassetot in London, I had never given up hope
of finding her. And one day, my hopes were realized. I discovered her in America, the mother of Elissa Landi of film
fame. Together we could reassemble the entire story of her
life. Where my knowledge ended, she took up the thread of
the tale. In her daughter, Aunt Sissy's grandchild, I perceived the reincarnation of all the fine traits and rare gifts
which graced the late Empress of Austria-Hungary.

More and more, "hovering forms" drew about me. The
day dawned when I came from Hoboken to see enacted, on
the stage of the Theatre Guild in New York City, the sad
fate of my uncle Emperor Maximilian I of Mexico. As if
transported back into the past, there I saw moving, before
my very eyes, startling replicas of those whom I had known
so well in life. It came to me, then, more poignantly than
ever before, that I had run the gauntlet of life's tragic ex-

periences. Had I not lost position, good name and fortune, my husband, and—final blow—all but two of children: my first-born and my last-born? Francis Joseph von Larisch, world-famous oceanographer, leads the cloistered life af a learned savant in Tegernsee, Bavaria, while Otto Brucks, Jr., is still struggling to throw off the after-effects of the war.

Back in my native Bavaria again, dwelling in the shadow of the very convent where I was born, I have time for much reflection. From my pilgrimage through life, I have gleaned one great truth: There is no such thing as real evil in any human being! We are often misled; we frequently run afoul of our goal. But we all strive upward, though sometimes we take a roundabout route, lured, perhaps, by a false lodestar.

In Aunt Sissy, whose joys and disappointments I knew so well, I had a truly memorable example. The rôle which Fate assigned to her in history's great drama has been interpreted often but seldom sympathetically. She has been severely criticized because she was little understood. There was never a girl with a sunnier disposition than the young Princess Elizabeth of Bavaria. My mother once read a letter to me written by Aunt Sissy's governess Fräulein von Tenzl, in which Elizabeth was called "Sunny Girl."

Then, one day, Sunny Girl found herself—mayhap through her own making—in the stifling atmosphere of the imperial court in Vienna. It was not the young Emperor who actually ruled there, but the old cold-hearted Archduchess Sophie whose purpose in life seemed to be to subdue the young Empress and teach her *mores*. Bitterness filled

Elizabeth's heart; she tried to break her shackles. If Elizabeth had been indolent by nature, she would have submitted to life finally. But her nimble mind would not permit that; she fought on, a rebel against traditions, a kin in spirit to the anarchist who killed her because he did not understand her.

What Elizabeth had romantically pictured as a life of Sundays unfolded into years and years of dreary weekdays. True, her imperial husband was tolerant enough, but he was by no means an exciting or even interesting companion on life's highway. He was painstakingly correct, deeply imbued with an appreciation of his responsibilities. These characteristics were insufficient "to clear out the way, lift up every stumbling-block," as Aunt Sissy's writings show only too well. The chief trouble was that husband and wife lived in entirely different worlds.

"The Emperor is duty personified," Aunt Sissy said to me one day. "Aside from that . . ." She shrugged her shoulders. There was a hopeless expression on her face which I shall never forget to my dying day.

My writings can never fully express what is in my heart. Perhaps others could paint Empress Elizabeth's life in glowing colors, as "the Golgotha of a Woman." But there are few who can probe the depths of Elizabeth's despair or understand, through compassion like Parsifal, the sting of the thorns strewn in her path to Calvary. Practically all through her lifetime, after the heavy gates of the *Hofburg* had closed behind her, she yearned for Nirvana. She herself once discovered the *leitmotif* of her life in a poem by Friedrich Beck

from which she had quoted the first line to me the night
before she left for Sassetot:

> *To be prepared as for the final journey,*
> *Day after day, without a thought of fear;*
> *That is the only way the Great Attorney*
> *Will smile upon you . . . and be ever near.*
>
> *Whatever you may long for, you can't hold it;*
> *Eternally you try to master Fate;*
> *And if you finally succeed to mold it,*
> *You soon discover, it is all too late.*
>
> *However, if you shun good luck and glamour*
> *Fate's bloom will flower richly and not rot;*
> *But mark, if unavailing proves your clamour,*
> *Accept it quietly . . . as just your lot!*

THE END